Women and Resistance in Contemporary Bengali Cinema

Historically, Indian cinema has positioned women at the intersection of tradition and a more evolving culture, portraying contradictory attitudes that affect women's roles in public and private spheres.

Examining the work of three directors from West Bengal, this book addresses the juxtaposition of tradition and culture regarding women in Bengali cinema. It argues the antithesis of women's roles, particularly in terms of ideas of resistance, revolution, change, and autonomy, by suggesting they convey resistance to hegemonic structures, encouraging a re-envisioning of women's positions within the familial-social matrix. Along with presenting a perception of culture as dynamic and evolving, the book discusses how some directors show that with this rupturing of the traditionally prohibitive, and a notion of unmaking and making in women, a traditional inclination is exposed to align women with ideas of absence, substitution, and disposability. The author goes on to show how selected auteurs in contemporary Bengali cinema break with certain traditional representations of women, gesturing towards a culture that is more liberating for women.

Presenting the first full-length study of women's changing roles over the last 20 years of Bengali cinema, this book will be a useful contribution for students and scholars of South Asian Culture, Film Studies and Gender Studies.

Srimati Mukherjee is Professor of English at Temple University in Philadelphia, USA.

Routledge Contemporary South Asia Series

1 **Pakistan**
Social and cultural transformations
in a Muslim nation
Mohammad A. Qadeer

2 **Labor, Democratization and
Development in India and
Pakistan**
Christopher Candland

3 **China–India Relations**
Contemporary dynamics
Amardeep Athwal

4 **Madrasas in South Asia**
Teaching terror?
Jamal Malik

5 **Labor, Globalization and the
State**
Workers, women and migrants
confront neoliberalism
*Edited by Debdas Banerjee and
Michael Goldfield*

6 **Indian Literature and Popular
Cinema**
Recasting classics
Edited by Heidi R.M. Pauwels

7 **Islamist Militancy in
Bangladesh**
A complex web
Ali Riaz

8 **Regionalism in South Asia**
Negotiating cooperation,
institutional structures
Kishore C. Dash

9 **Federalism, Nationalism and
Development**
India and the Punjab economy
Pritam Singh

10 **Human Development and
Social Power**
Perspectives from South Asia
Ananya Mukherjee Reed

11 **The South Asian Diaspora**
Transnational networks and
changing identities
*Edited by Rajesh Rai and
Peter Reeves*

12 **Pakistan–Japan Relations**
Continuity and change in
economic relations and security
interests
Ahmad Rashid Malik

13 **Himalayan Frontiers of
India**
Historical, geo-political and
strategic perspectives
K. Warikoo

14 **India's Open-Economy Policy**
Globalism, rivalry, continuity
Jalal Alamgir

15 **The Separatist Conflict in Sri Lanka**
Terrorism, ethnicity, political economy
Asoka Bandarage

16 **India's Energy Security**
Edited by Ligia Noronha and Anant Sudarshan

17 **Globalization and the Middle Classes in India**
The social and cultural impact of neoliberal reforms
Ruchira Ganguly-Scrase and Timothy J. Scrase

18 **Water Policy Processes in India**
Discourses of power and resistance
Vandana Asthana

19 **Minority Governments in India**
The puzzle of elusive majorities
Csaba Nikolenyi

20 **The Maoist Insurgency in Nepal**
Revolution in the twenty-first century
Edited by Mahendra Lawoti and Anup K. Pahari

21 **Global Capital and Peripheral Labour**
The history and political economy of plantation workers in India
K. Ravi Raman

22 **Maoism in India**
Reincarnation of ultra-left wing extremism in the twenty-first century
Bidyut Chakrabarty and Rajat Kujur

23 **Economic and Human Development in Contemporary India**
Cronyism and fragility
Debdas Banerjee

24 **Culture and the Environment in the Himalaya**
Arjun Guneratne

25 **The Rise of Ethnic Politics in Nepal**
Democracy in the margins
Susan I. Hangen

26 **The Multiplex in India**
A cultural economy of urban leisure
Adrian Athique and Douglas Hill

27 **Tsunami Recovery in Sri Lanka**
Ethnic and regional dimensions
Dennis B. McGilvray and Michele R. Gamburd

28 **Development, Democracy and the State**
Critiquing the Kerala model of development
K. Ravi Raman

29 **Mohajir Militancy in Pakistan**
Violence and transformation in the Karachi conflict
Nichola Khan

30 **Nationbuilding, Gender and War Crimes in South Asia**
Bina D'Costa

31 **The State in India after Liberalization**
Interdisciplinary perspectives
Edited by Akhil Gupta and K. Sivaramakrishnan

32 **National Identities in Pakistan**
The 1971 war in contemporary Pakistani fiction
Cara Cilano

33 **Political Islam and Governance in Bangladesh**
Edited by Ali Riaz and C. Christine Fair

34 **Bengali Cinema**
"An other nation"
Sharmistha Gooptu

35 **NGOs in India**
The challenges of women's empowerment and accountability
Patrick Kilby

36 **The Labour Movement in the Global South**
Trade unions in Sri Lanka
S. Janaka Biyanwila

37 **Building Bangalore**
Architecture and urban transformation in India's Silicon Valley
John C. Stallmeyer

38 **Conflict and Peacebuilding in Sri Lanka**
Caught in the peace trap?
Edited by Jonathan Goodhand, Jonathan Spencer and Benedict Korf

39 **Microcredit and Women's Empowerment**
A case study of Bangladesh
Amunui Faraizi, Jim McAllister and Taskinur Rahman

40 **South Asia in the New World Order**
The role of regional cooperation
Shahid Javed Burki

41 **Explaining Pakistan's Foreign Policy**
Escaping India
Aparna Pande

42 **Development-induced Displacement, Rehabilitation and Resettlement in India**
Current issues and challenges
Edited by Sakarama Somayaji and Smrithi Talwar

43 **The Politics of Belonging in India**
Becoming Adivasi
Edited by Daniel J. Rycroft and Sangeeta Dasgupta

44 **Re-Orientalism and South Asian Identity Politics**
The oriental Other within
Edited by Lisa Lau and Ana Cristina Mendes

45 **Islamic Revival in Nepal**
Religion and a new nation
Megan Adamson Sijapati

46 **Education and Inequality in India**
A classroom view
Manabi Majumdar and Jos Mooij

47 **The Culturalization of Caste in India**
Identity and inequality in a multicultural age
Balmurli Natrajan

48 **Corporate Social Responsibility in India**
Bidyut Chakrabarty

49 **Pakistan's Stability Paradox**
Domestic, regional and international dimensions
Edited by Ashutosh Misra and Michael E. Clarke

50 **Transforming Urban Water Supplies in India**
The role of reform and partnerships in globalization
Govind Gopakumar

51 **South Asian Security**
Twenty-first century discourse
Sagarika Dutt and Alok Bansal

52 **Non-discrimination and Equality in India**
Contesting boundaries of social justice
Vidhu Verma

53 **Being Middle-class in India**
A way of life
Henrike Donner

54 **Kashmir's Right to Secede**
A critical examination of contemporary theories of secession
Matthew J. Webb

55 **Bollywood Travels**
Culture, diaspora and border crossings in popular Hindi cinema
Rajinder Dudrah

56 **Nation, Territory, and Globalization in Pakistan**
Traversing the margins
Chad Haines

57 **The Politics of Ethnicity in Pakistan**
The Baloch, Sindhi and Mohajir ethnic movements
Farhan Hanif Siddiqi

58 **Nationalism and Ethnic Conflict**
Identities and mobilization after 1990
Edited by Mahendra Lawoti and Susan Hangen

59 **Islam and Higher Education**
Concepts, challenges and opportunities
Marodsilton Muborakshoeva

60 **Religious Freedom in India**
Sovereignty and (anti) conversion
Goldie Osuri

61 **Everyday Ethnicity in Sri Lanka**
Up-country Tamil identity politics
Daniel Bass

62 **Ritual and Recovery in Post-Conflict Sri Lanka**
Eloquent bodies
Jane Derges

63 **Bollywood and Globalisation**
The global power of popular Hindi cinema
Edited by David J. Schaefer and Kavita Karan

64 **Regional Economic Integration in South Asia**
Trapped in conflict?
Amita Batra

65 **Architecture and Nationalism in Sri Lanka**
The trouser under the cloth
Anoma Pieris

66 **Civil Society and Democratization in India**
Institutions, ideologies and interests
Sarbeswar Sahoo

67 **Contemporary Pakistani Fiction in English**
Idea, nation, state
Cara N. Cilano

68 **Transitional Justice in South Asia**
A study of Afghanistan and Nepal
Tazreena Sajjad

69 **Displacement and Resettlement in India**
The human cost of development
Hari Mohan Mathur

70 **Water, Democracy and Neoliberalism in India**
The power to reform
Vicky Walters

71 **Capitalist Development in India's Informal Economy**
Elisabetta Basile

72 **Nation, Constitutionalism and Buddhism in Sri Lanka**
Roshan de Silva Wijeyeratne

73 **Counterinsurgency, Democracy, and the Politics of Identity in India**
From warfare to welfare?
Mona Bhan

74 **Enterprise Culture in Neoliberal India**
Studies in youth, class, work and media
Edited by Nandini Gooptu

75 **The Politics of Economic Restructuring in India**
Economic governance and state spatial rescaling
Loraine Kennedy

76 **The Other in South Asian Religion, Literature and Film**
Perspectives on Otherism and Otherness
Edited by Diana Dimitrova

77 **Being Bengali**
At home and in the world
Edited by Mridula Nath Chakraborty

78 **The Political Economy of Ethnic Conflict in Sri Lanka**
Nikolaos Biziouras

79 **Indian Arranged Marriages**
A social psychological perspective
Tulika Jaiswal

80 **Writing the City in British Asian Diasporas**
Edited by Seán McLoughlin, William Gould, Ananya Jahanara Kabir and Emma Tomalin

81 **Post-9/11 Espionage Fiction in the US and Pakistan**
Spies and "terrorists"
Cara Cilano

82 **Left Radicalism in India**
Bidyut Chakrabarty

83 **"Nation-State" and Minority Rights in India**
Comparative perspectives on Muslim and Sikh identities
Tanweer Fazal

84 **Pakistan's Nuclear Policy**
A minimum credible deterrence
Zafar Khan

85 **Imagining Muslims in South Asia and the Diaspora**
Secularism, religion, representations
Claire Chambers and Caroline Herbert

86 **Indian Foreign Policy in Transition**
Relations with South Asia
Arijit Mazumdar

87 **Corporate Social Responsibility and Development in Pakistan**
Nadeem Malik

88 **Indian Capitalism in Development**
Barbara Harriss-White and Judith Heyer

89 **Bangladesh Cinema and National Identity**
In search of the modern?
Zakir Hossain Raju

90 **Suicide in Sri Lanka**
The anthropology of an epidemic
Tom Widger

91 **Epigraphy and Islamic Culture**
Inscriptions of the early Muslim rulers of Bengal (1205–1494)
Mohammad Yusuf Siddiq

92 **Reshaping City Governance**
London, Mumbai, Kolkata, Hyderabad
Nirmala Rao

93 **The Indian Partition in Literature and Films**
History, politics, and aesthetics
Rini Bhattacharya Mehta and Debali Mookerjea-Leonard

94 **Development, Poverty and Power in Pakistan**
The impact of state and donor interventions on farmers
Syed Mohammad Ali

95 **Ethnic Subnationalist Insurgencies in South Asia**
Identities, interests and challenges to state authority
Edited by Jugdep S. Chima

96 **International Migration and Development in South Asia**
Edited by Md Mizanur Rahman and Tan Tai Yong

97 **Twenty-First Century Bollywood**
Ajay Gehlawat

98 **Political Economy of Development in India**
Indigeneity in transition in the state of Kerala
Darley Kjosavik and Nadarajah Shanmugaratnam

99 **State and Nation-Building in Pakistan**
Beyond Islam and security
Edited by Roger D. Long, Gurharpal Singh, Yunas Samad, and Ian Talbot

100 **Subaltern Movements in India**
Gendered geographies of struggle against neoliberal development
Manisha Desai

101 **Islamic Banking in Pakistan**
Shariah-compliant finance and the quest to make Pakistan more Islamic
Feisal Khan

102 **The Bengal Diaspora**
Rethinking Muslim migration
Claire Alexander, Joya Chatterji, and Annu Jalais

103 **Mobilizing Religion and Gender in India**
The role of activism
Nandini Deo

104 **Social Movements and the Indian Diaspora**
Movindri Reddy

105 **Identity Politics and Elections in Malaysia and Indonesia**
Ethnic engineering in Borneo
Karolina Prasad

106 **Religion and Modernity in the Himalaya**
Edited by Megan Adamson Sijapati and Jessica Vantine Birkenholtz

107 **Devotional Islam in Contemporary South Asia**
Shrines, journeys and wanderers
Edited by Michel Boivin and Rémy Delage

108 **Women and Resistance in Contemporary Bengali Cinema**
A freedom incomplete
Srimati Mukherjee

109 **Islamic NGOs in Bangladesh**
Development, piety and neoliberal governmentality
Mohammad Musfequs Salehin

Women and Resistance in Contemporary Bengali Cinema
A freedom incomplete

Srimati Mukherjee

LONDON AND NEW YORK

First published 2016
by Routledge

2 Park Square, Milton Park, Abingdon, Oxfordshire OX14 4RN
711 Third Avenue, New York, NY 10017

Routledge is an imprint of the Taylor & Francis Group, an informa business

First issued in paperback 2018

Copyright © 2016 Srimati Mukherjee

The right of Srimati Mukherjee to be identified as author of this work has
been asserted by her in accordance with sections 77 and 78 of the
Copyright, Designs and Patents Act 1988.

All rights reserved. No part of this book may be reprinted or reproduced or
utilised in any form or by any electronic, mechanical, or other means, now
known or hereafter invented, including photocopying and recording, or in any
information storage or retrieval system, without permission in writing from the
publishers.

Notice:
Product or corporate names may be trademarks or registered trademarks, and
are used only for identification and explanation without intent to infringe.

British Library Cataloguing-in-Publication Data
A catalogue record for this book is available from the British Library

Library of Congress Cataloging-in-Publication Data
Mukherjee, Srimati.
Women and resistance in contemporary Bengali cinema : a freedom
incomplete / Srimati Mukherjee.
  pages cm. – (Routledge contemporary South Asia series ; 108)
  Includes bibliographical references and index.
  ISBN 978-1-138-12095-2 (hardback) – ISBN 978-1-315-65139-2
  (ebook) 1. Women in motion pictures. 2. Feminism and motion pictures.
  3. Motion pictures–India–West Bengal–History and criticism. I. Title.
  PN1995.9.W6M819 2016
  791.43'65220954–dc23   2015031155

ISBN: 978-1-138-12095-2 (hbk)
ISBN: 978-1-138-61578-6 (pbk)

Typeset in Times New Roman
by Wearset Ltd, Boldon, Tyne and Wear

This book is dedicated to my mother, Debjani Mukherjee, and to my daughter, Mini Mukherjee Racker

Contents

Acknowledgments		XV
Introduction		1

PART I
Representations of disjuncture: antithetical responses to
resistance in public and private spheres — 35

1 Feminism in a Kolkata context: assault, appeasement, and
assertion in *Dahan* — 37

2 The impossibility of incestuous love: woman's captivity
and national liberation in *Utsab* — 55

3 Impermanence in *Dekha*: the fragility of the present and
the passing of a "traditional" perspective — 72

PART II
Narratives of waste and rupturing the prohibitive — 89

4 Woman as alienated commodity and surplus goods in
Bariwali — 91

5 *Chokher Bali*: a historico-cultural *translation* of Tagore — 110

xiv *Contents*

PART III
From transactional commodities to subjects in meaningful exchange 131

6 *Mondo Meyer Upakhyan*: a reading of rebellion within broken social systems 133

Index 151

Acknowledgments

I would like to thank the College of Liberal Arts at Temple University for a Research Incentive Fund Award in 2007 and a CLARA, a second research award in 2009. These helped me travel to India to begin work on this book.

I am also grateful to my colleagues Professor Susan Wells, former director of the first-year writing program at Temple, and Professor Shannon Miller, then chair of the English department, for my research and study leave during the academic year 2009–10. I was able to use this time to further work on my book. Loving thanks to my long-time friend and colleague Steven Newman of Temple for reading my work, for his unfailing support and democratic vision, and for giving me the opportunity to teach my first course on international film when he was director of undergraduate studies. Thanks are also due to Terry Halbert, who as director of general education at Temple enthusiastically approved my course proposal "Women in Bengali Film." A number of ideas in this book have their origin in that proposal.

I am deeply grateful to the three acclaimed Bengali directors Rituparno Ghosh, Buddhadeb Dasgupta, and Goutam Ghose for agreeing to be interviewed by me in Kolkata in the period 2007–09. Although Rituparno Ghosh's unexpected death in 2013 is an irreparable loss, many of my arguments in the book were deepened and enhanced because of extended conversations with him. Buddhadeb Dasgupta addressed questions I raised at length as well, solidifying my understanding of his films and elaborating on his views on women's issues. Goutam Ghose was warm and engaging, answering questions comprehensively and helping me to situate his films within a broader socio-political context in India.

I would like to thank Madhuchhanda Karlekar, Rajashri Dasgupta, and Soma Marik for making time to talk with me in Kolkata in 2009. As long-time activists for women's rights, they helped me understand better the contemporary scene in Kolkata as regards women's issues, particularly in relation to sexual violation and social class.

To Natalie Foster, editor at Routledge, I extend thanks for passing my manuscript on, in the initial stage, to Dorothea Schaefter, senior editor of Asian studies. Dorothea's help and encouragement at every stage of the evaluation and review process have been invaluable to me. I cannot thank her enough for her

xvi *Acknowledgments*

guidance and kindness. I am grateful as well to Jillian Morrison, associate editor of Asian studies, for her help. I would like to thank Sophie Iddamalgoda, editorial assistant of Asian studies at Routledge. Sophie's remarkable generosity and efficiency have guided me every day through the final stages of completing and submitting this manuscript. Thanks are due to my copyeditor, Philippa Mulberry, and to Hannah Riley and Phillippa Clubbs for their help with proofs. I would also like to express my gratitude to the two anonymous readers at Routledge for valuable commentary, which has helped me expand and deepen my arguments in the book.

Thanks are due to Chuck Kleinhans, Julia Lesage, and John Hess, co-editors of *Jump Cut: A Review of Contemporary Media*, for allowing me to use "*Chokher Bali*: A Historico-Cultural *Translation* of Tagore," which appeared in *Jump Cut* 54 in 2012, in expanded form as Chapter 5 of this book. I would also like to thank Deborah East of Taylor and Francis and *Quarterly Review of Film and Video* (*QRFV*) for giving me permission to use two articles I previously published in the journal. The first appeared in *QRFV* 22.3 (online, available at: www.tandfonline.com/doi/full/10.1080/10509200490474302): "Feminism in a Calcutta Context: Assault, Appeasement, and Assertion in Rituparno Ghosh's *Dahan*." The second appeared in *QRFV* 29.5, online, available at: www.tandfonline.com/doi/full/10.1080/10509201003719274: "The Impossibility of Incestuous Love: Woman's Captivity and National Liberation in Rituparno Ghosh's *Utsab*." These articles have been expanded into Chapters 1 and 2 respectively of this book.

To friends Cecelia Luongo, Anthony Fonseca, Melissa Goldsmith, Bansari Mitra, Helen Mallon, Mary Carruth, Nikhil Sarkar, Joysree Sarkar, and Sumitra Chatterjee, I extend thanks for continuing conversations about Bengali film and culture and their faith in my work. I am grateful as always to my ex-husband, David Racker, for taking care of several chores that leave me time to do my research and writing. Thanks are also in order to my sister Susmita Banerjee, for clarifying the significance of some aspects of the Bengali wedding ceremony, and to my sister Srilata Mukherjee, for gifts of CDs with films by Satyajit Ray and Ritwik Ghatak, the viewing/re-viewing of which helped me elaborate on some of my claims.

My father Sudhiranjan Mukherjee's commitment to and love of writing, intellectual vigor, and unparalleled affection remain motivating forces daily for me even 25 years after his passing away. This book is dedicated with love and gratitude to my mother, Debjani Mukherjee, and my daughter, Mini Mukherjee Racker. When I mentioned to my mother, a few years ago, that I had not produced a book yet, she responded casually, "Bōi ekta likhé phelō" ("Just get a book written.") I followed her advice, and it worked. My daughter Mini, then in her early teens, had the difficult task of listening to sections of chapters I wrote. She frequently responded with "It's a good book, Mama. It has difficult words." Her day-to-day support, unfailing optimism, and regular question "Got some work done on your book?" helped me bring this project to completion.

Introduction

In his significant text *Religion of Man* (1931), Rabindranath Tagore makes a categorical distinction between a form of tradition and, what I understand as, the evolving nature of culture. He argues that tradition sometimes upholds the static, dead, or moribund aspects of a nation, while the future signals towards the dynamic; it evokes possibilities of accommodating change. Tagore's vision of the future is marked by flexibility and an inherent openness. He observes:

> We Indians have had the sad experience in our own part of the world how timid orthodoxy, its irrational repressions and its accumulation of dead centuries, dwarfs man through its idolatry of the past. Seated rigid in the centre of stagnation, it firmly ties the human spirit to the revolving wheels of habit till faintness overwhelms her.... This mechanical spirit of tradition is essentially materialistic, it is blindly pious but not spiritual, obsessed by phantoms of unreason that haunt feeble minds in the ghastly disguise of religion.
>
> $(86)^1$

> The continuous future is the domain of our millennium, which is with us more truly than what we see in or (*sic*) history in fragments of the present.
>
> $(87)^2$

In his addressing of the "continuous future," Tagore, in my view, affirms his faith in a culture that does not unquestioningly adhere to tradition but looks to regenerate the mind and spirit through a sustained receptivity to change. With this distinction in mind, in my study, *Women and Resistance in Contemporary Bengali Cinema: A Freedom Incomplete*, I examine the work of three directors from West Bengal—Rituparno Ghosh, Buddhadeb Dasgupta, and Goutam Ghose—to address the juxtaposition of tradition and culture in selected films from their oeuvres.

While it is true that in Indian cinema historically, women have at times been located at the intersection of tradition and a more evolving "culture," I approach and engage this juxtaposition by focusing on four primary areas for discussion integral to this study. I argue that the films of these directors often reveal an

2 Introduction

antithesis or, more specifically, paradox, that is, the representation of a disjuncture between the public and private spheres, particularly as this applies to ideas of resistance and revolution. The study illustrates how such contradictory attitudes affect women as portrayed in this cinema. Next, I locate an attempt in the films of these directors to rupture the traditionally prohibitive, and a simultaneous effort to validate "alternate" lives, narratives, and desire within the social structure. Further, my study examines the foregrounding of notions of unmaking and making in women at the same time as these films expose a traditional inclination to align women with ideas of absence, substitution, and disposability. And last, following from this third point, I argue that a number of these films portray women as active agents in processes of meaningful "exchange" rather than transactional commodities. Thus, by analyzing these four areas of directorial focus, I show how selected auteurs in contemporary Bengali cinema break with certain traditional representations of women and gesture towards spaces that are more akin to Tagore's understanding of a "continuous future" and, in my reading, a culture that is more liberating for women.

Further, this book is an analysis of women's changing roles in late twentieth- and early twenty-first-century Bengali cinema. Early books on Indian film, such as Ashis Nandy's 1998 edited collection *The Secret Politics of Our Desires: Innocence, Culpability and Indian Popular Cinema*, point to substantial connections between cinema and politics.[3] Approximately a decade later, Ashish Rajadhyaksha's 2009 *Indian Cinema in the Time of Celluloid: From Bollywood to the Emergency* addresses "cinema's dissemination of contestatory forms of state identity," the author considering it an "effective instrument of political use" (194).[4] Yet, such significant studies can clearly be complemented by a full-length work on the representation of women in Indian cinema, particularly as such representation connects with rapidly changing politico-cultural perceptions.

In *The Cinematic Imagination: Indian Popular Films as Social History* (2003), Jyotika Virdi devotes selected chapters to representation of women in Hindi films, addressing crucial issues such as how the figure of the woman has been appropriated in the nationalist discourse; the hyper-visibility of the female body; and the absence of the theme of "desire" in cinematic portrayals of women.[5] This book takes up a number of these issues, but with an exclusive focus on representations of women in Bengali cinema at the turn of, and through the first decade of, the twenty-first century, and shows how contemporary auteurs of this cinema portray women in markedly different ways than those addressed above. Alka Kurian's recently published *Narratives of Gendered Dissent in South Asian Cinemas* focuses on the female narratival perspective but addresses non-Bengali films.[6]

Yves Thoraval's generally comprehensive *The Cinemas of India* (2000), with selected sections on Bengali cinema, mentions in one section the rendering of women as "sacred" or the "desexing" of love in Indian/Bengali film as also the prevalence of an "enduring Manichean theme in the treatment of women on the screen—goddess or vamp?" (Thoraval 31)[7] More recently, in his *Mourning the Nation: Indian Cinema in the Wake of Partition* (2009), Bhaskar Sarkar addresses changing representations of women in the films of Satyajit Ray and Ritwik Ghatak in the 1960s, as Bengali women began to enter the workforce in significant numbers.[8] Yet, this in-depth and engaging study by Sarkar is about the impact of the 1947 Partition on Indian cinema across regions, as Thoraval's book is a study of different cinemas in India. Moreover, although they are valuable contributions to the criticism on Indian cinema, these studies do not address Bengali feature films of the twenty-first century. As stated earlier, my study focuses on late twentieth- and a number of early twenty-first-century Bengali films, illustrating how representations of women coincide with a changing cultural terrain.

Sharmistha Gooptu's very recent *Bengali Cinema: "An Other Nation"* draws our attention to the progressive empowering of the female figure in 1950s Bengali cinema, specifically as this process played out in the screen presence of actress Suchitra Sen. Towards the very end of her book, Gooptu notes briefly that work of directors such as Aparna Sen and Rituparno Ghosh in the 1980s and 1990s "raised some very pertinent questions about gender and sexuality, marriage and motherhood which fragmented Bengali middle-class complacencies" (181).[9] The scope of Gooptu's very interesting book is such, however, that she stops at this point. My study continues the discussion of the empowerment of the female figure and addresses extensively not just gender, but notions of rupture, cultural re-conceptualization, and the re-shaping of audience expectations in and through Bengali cinema of the late 1990s and the twenty-first century.

Why Rituparno Ghosh, Goutam Ghose, and Buddhadeb Dasgupta?

The temporal arc of this project is approximately 1995 to 2010. Although selected directors, notably Aparna Sen, have done considerable work with women's issues in Bengali cinema in the above-mentioned period, I choose to focus largely on the films of Rituparno Ghosh, Goutam Ghose, and Buddhadeb Dasgupta because several of their films reiteratively address the themes I explore in this study, namely disjuncture between attitudes in, or towards, the private and public spheres; women rupturing the traditionally prohibited; processes of unmaking and making in women; and women portraying agency and being mobilized by these directors to show meaningful exchanges.

In Part I of this study, I address at length how two of these directors expose double standards in characters' attitudes to the public and private domains, as these attitudes relate to women and resistance or revolution. Even as these films were made at the turn of the twenty-first century, the directors span decades and depict both urban metropolitan and more rural settings to locate such attitudes. Thus, as audiences, we are witness to such disjuncture in multiple settings and in time periods as different as the early 1970s and late 1980s in Bengal. What this group of directors alerts us to is that while women's resistance and autonomy continue to be manifest, traditional dichotomous attitudes to private and public domains within the cultural fabric show no significant shifts.

4 Introduction

These three directors also consistently represent women rupturing the prohibitive and in processes of unmaking the "traditionally" expected and "making" or asserting the value of the culturally "new." As mentioned above, I focus in my study on films they made in the period between 1995 and 2010, yet what is unique about them is their interest in depicting these two issues in a sustained way through their careers. Earlier films by Goutam Ghose and Buddhadeb Dasgupta, for instance, capture these processes in impactful ways. Ghose's 1982 *Dakhal* (*The Occupation*), set in the context of post-Independence India as land reform legislation was being passed in Bengal, has as protagonist Andi, who struggles fearlessly against the possible occupation of her land by the local landlord. In this his first Bengali feature film, Ghose brings us Andi, a woman who has left the *Kagmara* gypsy tribe to settle down with a farmer and who, when the film opens, is also a widow and mother of two. Ghose situates the forces of rupture and unmaking in this gypsy/peasant subaltern woman, showing how such women were slowly participating and intervening in systems of justice.[10]

That Andi does not think in conventional ways is clear to the spectator when in response to her dead husband's friend's questions "Are you not afraid to stay alone? On this shore, a woman without a man?" she replies, "I know what men are. I have a son and daughter. I have myself. I am not afraid of anyone."[11] Ghose depicts the rupturing of traditional expectations even more explicitly in the sequences set in a rudimentary rural courtroom. When the local landlord and his henchman, a tax-collector, try to appropriate her land since new laws prevented any landowner from having more than 25 acres, Andi takes advantage of the post-Independence political-legal context to appeal this. In the resultant courtroom sequence, she is overwhelmingly surrounded by men—the judge himself and corrupt men such as the tax-collector who in order to dispossess her, accuses her of being a gypsy whore not married to her dead partner, who cultivated the land, and with no claim to it. Framed within an unfamiliar judicial and masculinist setting, Andi does not hesitate to grab her attacker and challenge him, firm in her belief that she has claim to the land having lived with her partner for many years and borne his children. Further, she does the same to the man who is set up to declare that he "visits" her regularly. In both instances, the camera focuses on Andi's physical and verbal aggression, as also her "victims," as Ghose highlights her rupturing and unmaking of normative expectations of gendered behavior.

Buddhadeb Dasgupta's 1994 *Charachar* (*Shelter of the Wings*), a film released prior to the period I cover in this study, focuses on Loka, the bird-seller who is too tender-hearted and enamored of his birds to sell them and lets them escape. Yet, Dasgupta's treatment is objective and non-sentimental enough to reveal the economic and marital repercussions of such love for Loka's wife, Sari. In a scene in bed with Loka, Sari voices her sense of emptiness clearly, saying that she has forgotten the grief of their dead son, but no other child came. Loka has his birds, but she has nothing, absolutely nothing. Sari's subsequent departure with her lover, Notōbor, is unusual in itself, but her extended explanation of the reasons for this to Loka, in one of the last sequences of *Charachar*,

Introduction 5

foregrounds Dasgupta's interest in portraying women in processes of rupture and unmaking.

In this sequence, Sari makes it clear to her husband that although her lover has fulfilled her material needs and provided her security, she did not leave Loka because of economic dearth, which, ironically, is the only thing he gave her. Dasgupta constructs the scene in which Sari gives her reasons for leaving Loka with both husband and wife in the frame, but the husband's face remains in shadow, and all the dialogue belongs to the wife. "Why do you want to take me back to you?" asks Sari.

> Do you love me? Perhaps you do. But you love your birds a thousand times more. I cannot reach you across them. They have entered in between you and me a long time ago. That man [her lover] wants just me.[12]

When Loka asks Sari if she is happy, she responds that if the fulfillment of material needs makes one happy she is, but she does not really know what happiness is. Following her words, Loka himself asks Sari to return to her lover, who Dasgupta shows as dimly outlined in the background and whose face is also cast in shadow.

In a film largely about an emotional hero who is still haunted by vivid memories of his lost son, Dasgupta introduces notions of rupturing the traditionally prohibitive and the unmaking of conventional expectations, through his characters, by shifting easily to the woman's space and mind. What Dasgupta emphasizes in one of the final sequences of the film then is the woman's sense of self; her understanding of the value of being desired by her partner and desired without other things intervening in a disruptive way. Even if she is unclear about the meaning of happiness, she follows Loka's advice and returns to the lover who desires her for herself. That Loka himself, who has been advised within the hegemonic, patriarchal construct of his society to "guard" his home and woman,[13] encourages Sari to go with her lover adds a nuance to the themes of rupture and unmaking, solidifying their impact for the audience.

In my 2007 interview of him in Kolkata, Dasgupta mentioned to me that Sari's needs are different from Loka's and she could not have made herself in his image, as what he wanted her to be. Further, according to Dasgupta, Sari's role helps raise in the minds of the audience the question "What is happiness?" I will add that, although this is a universal question that has arisen across time, Dasgupta's film poses it from the perspective of the woman who has ruptured the confines of a domesticity meaningless to her and "made" her choice based on her individual needs. Films such as *Dakhal* and *Charachar*, by Ghose and Dasgupta respectively, demonstrate forcefully how themes of rupture and unmaking/ making as they relate to women are persistent in their oeuvres.

As my focus group, I argue that these three directors—Rituparno Ghosh, Goutam Ghose, and Buddhadeb Dasgupta—have also shown sustained interest in portraying women as empowered agents who enact meaningful exchanges. In this study, I mostly address how these directors represent women as rejecting

6 Introduction

their position as objects to be exchanged between men or exploited in trans-actions conducted by them. While it is true that other directors of contemporary Bengali cinema, such as Aniruddha Roy Chowdhury and Srijit Mukherjee, have explored this theme in thought-provoking ways in individual films,[14] Ghosh, Ghose, and Dasgupta have shown a long-term investment in portraying it. As my preceding discussion may have made clear, the undercurrents of this theme are evident in the actions and dialogue of the female protagonists in both *Dakhal* and *Charachar*.

In *Dakhal*, Andi forcefully protests a masculinist conspiracy to deprive her of her land, and following her physical and verbal attack of the culprits, leaves the courtroom challenging them to try and dispossess her. The shocked surprise writ large on the faces of both the judge and the tax-collector—Ghose using medium and close-up shots to show this—indicates her undoing of their perception of her as a rural, vulnerable, passive "object" to be exploited or helped through a male-dominated legal system. While Andi undermines such a perception through her agency and vocalizing of anger, Sari in Dasgupta's *Charachar* additionally shows a movement towards meaningful exchange as she leaves her empty marriage to go with her lover[15] and subsequently explains to Loka why she has done so.

In *Shubho Muharat* (*The First Shoot*, 2003), Rituparno Ghosh mobilizes cinema to show women's agency and meaningful exchange, not just for women, but between women, in a refreshingly novel way. In my interview of him on September 28, 2009, Ghosh underscored the fact that although he learnt the cin-ematization of the detective story from Satyajit Ray's *Sonar Kella* (*The Golden Fortress*, 1974), his own *Shubho Muharat* offered a revision of this genre. I address this further in the extended section on unmaking and making in this introductory chapter. For now, it is sufficient to say that this film presents a non-judgmental female detective, and in the final scenes a bond emerges between her and the "criminal," also a woman. The detective is a middle-aged widow, *Ranga Pishi*—literally translatable as "Crimson Aunt," whose journalist niece is doing a cover-story on the first film produced by the famous actress Padmini Chowd-hury. Two members of the cast and crew of this film are murdered in quick suc-cession. Yet when *Ranga Pishi*, with ultimate help from the culprit, unravels the fact that the murders are chain reactions spurred by a mother's unresolvable grief following the unnecessary death of her son, she lets the murderer go without consequence. She says to the "criminal" that she will not tell anyone anything and to have no fears in this regard. At the end of the film, the "killer" writes a lengthy letter urging her never to give up her detective work.

Although at first glance, such exchange may seem sentimental, according to Ghosh, he wanted to portray here a detective who "was not the police"; who did not resort to any form of violence; and who could forgive.[16] Ghosh in *Shubho Muharat* introduces not only an astute female detective, an older, middle-class Bengali woman engaged daily in various domestic chores, but also the notion of an exchange between two women, an exchange based on mutual understanding, support, and forgiveness in which no man or male-dominated punitive system, such as the police force, intervenes. While Andi, in Goutam Ghose's early film

Dakhal, rejects a patriarchal legal system in which women can be grossly misused, the two principal female characters in Rituparno Ghosh's *Shubho Muharat*, made over two decades later, choose to work outside such systems, enacting their own form of exchange. Such films, made several years apart, together with Dasgupta's *Charachar* show how these directors have striven to depict women characters who reject their own exploitation in masculinist systems and choose forms of exchange more beneficial or meaningful to them.

Disjuncture between responses to resistance in public and private spheres

Several of the films under discussion in this study reveal a hiatus between the public and private domains, particularly as regards ideas of resistance, revolution, change, and autonomy. I address this hiatus with a special focus on how it affects the predicament of women within the private/domestic sphere. Here, I use the terms "private sphere" and "domestic sphere" interchangeably and do not mean the private sphere of business and industry. Of relevance is Jürgen Habermas' distinction as he speaks of the second half of the eighteenth century in Europe: "The sphere of the market we call 'private'; the sphere of the family, as the core of the private sphere, we call the 'intimate sphere'" (55).[17] I am thinking of the family as the "core" or "essence" of the private sphere. To go back to my previous point on the condition of women, in an essay entitled "The Law of Suffering," written in the context of India's nationalist struggle, Mahatma Gandhi says,

> We must refuse to wait for the wrong to be righted till the wrongdoer has been roused to a sense of his inequity. We must not, for fear of ourselves or others having to suffer, remain participators in it. But we must combat the wrong by ceasing to assist the wrongdoer directly or indirectly.
>
> (115)[18]

Some 68 years after India's freedom movement ended with the gaining of the country's political independence, it seems crucial to assess how such ideas as Gandhi's have been or could be carried over into the private sphere and whether they have or have not affected the lives of individual citizens "trapped" in non-normative situations. As I mention above, my specific focus is the predicament of women.

As Gandhi notes, resistance to and rising up against injustice or oppression almost inevitably entails suffering. This remains true even if we shift focus from the realm of public political activity, with its discrete histories of selflessness and martyrdom, to the domestic sphere. Yet, what is striking is that a number of the films addressed in my study reveal that while acts of resistance and revolt against political or class-based domination are acclaimed and, in some cases, even idealized, such resistance against traditional and entrenched structures and systems that work to oppress women is often subject to censure.

8   *Introduction*

I will argue and illustrate in this study that some of the films under discussion posit that while many Bengali families and individuals have shown a marked commitment to the nationalist cause, prior to Independence, and Leftist revolutionary movements to eradicate class-based oppression in the late 1960s and early 1970s,[19] such passion for liberation and change has not, necessarily, been extended to a re-conceptualization of women's roles.[20] A divide between the public and private domains is also evident when women's success in helping female victims of injustice is highlighted by the press, but, in some cases, resented by members of the victim's family. Within the body of films under analysis in this work, such gaps between public and private become manifest when the directors focus on women involved in incestuous romances who take uncalled for "retribution" from family; present-day working mothers who choose to leave the confines of abusive marriages; and women who intervene when another woman is being assaulted.

Thus, Rituparno Ghosh's film *Utsab* (*Festival*, 2000) dramatizes the polarity in the responses to national and individual situations that cry out for change and liberation by depicting the mother, Bhagabati, as a paradoxical figure. She commends and idealizes the father's commitment to the nationalist cause prior to Independence, while she is complicit, some decades later, in confining her daughter, Parul, who is involved in an incestuous romance with her cousin. I address in Chapter 2 Parul's reaction to this captivity and her ultimate movement towards "self-assertion."

Similarly, in *Dekha* (*Seeing*, 2001), Goutam Ghose suggests the existence of a gap in the ways in which his male protagonist, Sashibhushan, views resistance and revolution in the national or political realm and in the lives of the individual women around him. While Sashi is paralyzed by the thought that Communism, as a revolutionary force, might disappear from the country, and the film represents him as generally committed to ideas of resistance, his response to women (and mothers) who leave oppressive marriages and carve out careers for themselves is hopelessly archaic.

A different kind of chasm between public and private becomes apparent in a film such as Rituparno Ghosh's *Dahan* (*Crossfire*, 1997) in which a female schoolteacher's intervention in the incident of another woman's assault is acclaimed by the press, but her later attempts to contact the victim and work with her towards gaining a just verdict are resented and spurned by the victim's family. Ghosh here illustrates how a familial sense of "honor" within the domestic realm precipitates a movement towards silence and denial, even as the incident is publicized in the media.

What I am arguing here is that through representing such a disjuncture and through the foregrounding of paradoxical figures, Ghosh and Ghose compel us to consider those aspects of tradition that restrict individuals to prescribed ways of seeing and that prevent us from noting what is crumbling around us and what needs to be re-conceptualized. At times, adherence to these aspects unfortunately makes individuals "participators," to use Gandhi's word, in what is wrong and oppressive. As a counter-thrust to such aporia, a number of contemporary

Bengali directors present women in roles that clearly convey resistance to hegemonic structures and that encourage a re-envisioning of women's positions within the familial-social matrix. I read such representations also as a movement in late twentieth- and early twenty-first-century Bengali cinema towards seeing (or wanting to see) culture as a changing, accommodating, dynamic force that enables the progressive empowerment of women.

Rupturing the prohibitive

I believe that in line with such a perception of culture, selected directors of Bengali cinema show also a rupturing, a shattering of the traditionally prohibitive. In many cases, it seems as if such rupturing helps directors center the importance of erotic pleasure in women's lives. Within the traditional Bengali, and, in fact, Indian family, women's erotic pleasure is not generally addressed, and the trope of motherhood predominates in definitions of the "ideal" woman. An excerpt from Mahasweta Devi's story "Breast-Giver" will help illustrate this:

> Such is the power of the Indian soil that all women turn into mothers here and all men remain immersed in the spirit of holy childhood. Each man the Holy Child and each woman the Divine Mother. Even those who deny this and wish to slap *current posters* to the effect of the "*eternal she*"—"Mona Lisa"—"La passionaria"—"Simone de Beauvoir," et cetera, over the old ones and look at women that way are, after all, Indian cubs. It is notable that the educated Babus desire all this from women outside the home. When they cross the threshold they want the Divine Mother in the words and conduct of the revolutionary ladies.
>
> $(226)^{21}$

Further, more recently, in explaining the concept of "*bhalo meye*" ("good girl") in an essay on women with "locomotor disabilities" (58) in West Bengal, Nandini Ghosh notes:

> Culturally, the concept [of *bhalo meye*] is a repository of all the aspirations and idealizations of the Bengali patriarchal structures that project women into an exalted status as mother, comparing her to the goddess and nation, while constraining and subjugating her in the private domain and relegating her to a secondary status within the home and in society.
>
> $(59)^{22}$

It is needless to say that mainstream Bengali, and Indian, cinema continues to perpetuate such "exalted" depictions of motherhood. "In the image of the mother, order and progress mingle to form one of the most compelling myths of colonial Bengal. The refraction of this may be found in popular fiction and cinema even today" (Bagchi, "Representing" 66).[23] I will not dwell on this point here since it is outside the purview of my analysis. In more than one film

10 *Introduction*

addressed in this study, the directors undercut such idealizations of motherhood and bring us portrayals of women's lives that are far more realistic because of their complexity. Such representations with a focus on multi-dimensionality include mothers who are ready to give over their daughters as "pleasure-inducing" commodities to ensure future survival for both themselves and their daughters and mothers, who as single parents and careerists still understand and affirm the value of erotic pleasure in their lives. In Chapter 6, I take up again the discussion of a mother, as she is represented in Buddhadeb Dasgupta's 2002 film *Mondo Meyer Upakhyan* (*A Tale of a Naughty Girl*), who largely understands her daughter as a commodity. For the purposes of this section of my Introduction however, a brief mention of the mother Sarama, in Goutam Ghose's *Dekha*, is in order. At one point in his film, Ghose presents Sarama, a single working mother, as deliberately seeking out erotic pleasure from her lover when she could be assisting her young son with homework or providing him company. The de-prioritizing of such "maternal time" and the cinematic foregrounding instead of a time of sheer pleasure for the mother are elements that help situate *Dekha* on an axis with other contemporary Bengali films that question and undo traditional expectations.

Other than the idealization of woman as mother, critics of Indian cinema have persistently addressed de-eroticized representations of women and the need to eliminate or underplay desire in the depiction of female characters. As mentioned earlier, Yves Thoraval, for instance, notes the frequent portrayal of women as "sacred" and the "de-sexing" of love in Indian and Bengali cinema. Thoraval traces a tendency, that she believes started with the classic film *Devdas* (1935), to represent women in a "Manichean" way—either as "goddess" or "vamp" (31).[24]

Similarly, in her discussion of Hindi films such as *Gumrah* (*Deception*, 1963) and *Sangam* (*Confluence*, 1964), Jyotika Virdi observes that "[t]he constant refrain is that heterosexual love demands 'sacrifice'—conveying the need to obfuscate desire, to belie the intrinsically narcissistic logic of monogamy which lays claim to the desire to be exclusively desired" (129–30). Virdi continues that love-centered plots often call for "selflessness," the other side of which is "repressing the individual, obliterating the self in favor of some higher goal—nurturing motherless children as in *Gumrah*" (130). Virdi's discussion of the Hindi version of *Sahib Bibi aur Ghulam* (*The Lord, His Wife, and Slave*, 1962), set in Kolkata at the turn of the twentieth century, and more specifically her addressing of the character of Chhoti Bahu (youngest daughter-in-law) is also relevant here. She notes that "the entire plot involving Chhoti Bahu—is about the need to desire and be desired, a theme traditionally absent from filmic and cultural representations of women" (Virdi 134).[25]

Towards the end of her essay "French Feminism in an International Frame," Gayatri Chakravorty Spivak observes:

> One cannot write off what may be called a uterine social organization (the arrangement of the world in terms of the reproduction of future generations,

where the uterus is the chief agent and means of production) *in favor of* a clitoral. The uterine social organization should, rather, be "situated" through the understanding that it has so far been established by excluding a clitoral social organization.... Investigation of the effacement of the clitoris—where clitoridectomy is a metonym for women's definition as "legal object as subject of reproduction"—would persistently seek to de-normalize uterine social organization.

(152)[26]

If we can generally equate "a clitoral social organization" with a move in which one affirms the legitimacy of women's erotic pleasure, then such a move is evident in a number of the films under discussion here. The directors are invested in going beyond socio-conceptual constructs that project women in unidimensional ways and are not hesitant to address the significance of the erotic in women's lives.

However, I also see such representations of rupture of the traditionally prohibitive as deliberate attempts to bring to Bengali audiences, and global audiences of Bengali cinema, explorations of lives and desire that could be classified as "non-normative" and "different." Again, the mobilizing of such narratives through film suggests to me a directorial engagement in presenting culture as something that should be broadly inclusive and receptive to "alternative" truths. In other words, what some of these films seem to convey is that unlike tradition, culture cannot just be a single or dominant narrative or way of envisioning the world; it cannot be and is not a system espoused by some and always intact and in place. Rather, I argue that these directors present culture as a terrain, more specifically a conceptual terrain that is sliding, shifting, and indefinitely open to accommodating multiple points of view and "unexpected" manifestations of desire. Such rupturing of the traditionally prohibitive is suggested in Goutam Ghose's *Antarjali Jatra* (*The Voyage Beyond*, 1987), a film not addressed at length in my study, and Rituparno Ghosh's *Chokher Bali: A Passion Play* (2003, Indian title in English *Sand in the Eye*).

Goutam Ghose's *Antarjali Jatra*, set contextually in 1829, the year *Sati*—the burning of a Hindu widow on her husband's funeral pyre—was outlawed in India, teases out the tension between a dying tradition and ways of seeing that are more resistant. Ghose locates the major force of resistance in the body of Baiju, the Chandala—the untouchable man in the Hindu caste structure—whose job is to burn dead bodies on the bank of the Ganges. When a young girl is married to a decrepit and dying man at this cremation ground by consent of a priest, an astrologer, and her father, with the clear possibility that she may soon be burned along with her dead husband,[27] it is the Chandala who screams against this and declares he will not be complicit by building *that* funeral pyre.

The "mechanical spirit" of tradition that Tagore censures in *Religion of Man*, that tradition that is "blindly pious but not spiritual, obsessed by phantoms of unreason that haunt feeble minds in the ghastly disguise of religion" (86), is concretized by Ghose in the body of the dying husband. The Chandala's wild,

12   *Introduction*

frenzied movements around this static body and premature shouting of *bolo hori, hori bol*, the words chanted as bearers bring dead bodies to the burning site for their last rites, situate him as the demolisher of this form of tradition. Not any less forceful is his picking up of the body and carrying it to the water to drown even before it is dead.

Ghose complicates the tension between tradition and what Tagore calls a "continuous future" (87), the evolving face of culture through his representation of the young, Brahmin wife, coming from the highest caste of Hindu society.[28] Even as she stabs the Chandala from behind with a piece of driftwood when he attempts to drown her husband, soon after, she crawls over and clings to him, claiming she has lost everything and is casteless. In this and in her playful flirtation with him later in the film, Ghose foregrounds a woman's acts of transgression that rupture the prohibitive, both as regards sexuality and an inviolable caste structure.[29] Yet, in this film, no less important is the fact that such transgression is also the effect of a fear and vulnerability induced in the girl by a "tradition" that has her face imminent death.

In *Chokher Bali*, Rituparno Ghosh takes liberties with Tagore's 1901–02 novel of the same name (the novel was first published serially) to foreground a young, educated Bengali widow, Binodini's rebellious attempts to affirm the value of erotic pleasure in her life. While Binodini's socio-political environment in the early twentieth century is rife with ideas of resistance and revolutionary acts against the British, and she herself, as the film later shows, is active in thinking through the injustices of British rule, her own efforts to work against unjust stipulations against Hindu widows are met with surprise or censure in a tradition-bound domestic realm in which only austerity should mark her existence. In Chapter 5, I draw on Walter Benjamin's essay "The Work of Art in the Age of Its Technological Reproducibility" and focus specifically on Benjamin's notions of the "shattering of tradition" (22) and the "destructive cathartic side" of film (22) to discuss how even as Ghosh presents Binodini as sharply aware of the innumerable restrictive stipulations of orthodox Hinduism, he re-activates her as ready and able to destroy the "immobility" of the "mark" that is her widowhood. In bringing us a version of *Chokher Bali* that is largely constructed from the widow's perspective, Ghosh offers a heterodox and "alternative" cultural narrative vis-à-vis the prescriptive traditional narrative of orthodox Hinduism.

Unmaking and making in women

Yet, it is not only through rupturing and defying the forbidden that women characters in the body of films under analysis here differentiate themselves from the normative. What we also see are sustained representations of women in processes of unmaking and making.[30] Such deconstruction and re-making is not always about shattering the prohibitive. In his 2009 interview with me, Rituparno Ghosh observed that what we are given at birth is a "template" by which to live. In contrast, the desire for independence and individualization is a "magic feeling" that comes and goes. According to Ghosh, "human instinct," in fact "the magic is to break the template," and each individual "breaks and re-makes it in her/his own way."

In this study, discussion of such impulses of unmaking and making in women characters runs through several of the chapters, although I have not devoted a specific chapter or section to this subject. Earlier in my Introduction, I addressed this theme briefly, and before I provide some quick examples from the films themselves, it is important to note that representation of these processes in women in Bengali film of the late twentieth and early twenty-first century also discloses a parallel unmaking and making in the mindscapes of these directors. In choosing to cinematize these endeavors of women who have largely been accorded secondary status in a patriarchal culture, the makers of these films break traditional "templates" themselves, opening the way for a re-conceptualization of given or expected roles. The fact that a number of these women characters suffer a double disempowerment as, say, victims of abuse, prostitutes, or widows, and still engage in such unmaking and making renders such directorial choices even more significant.

In *Twilight of the Idols*, Friedrich Nietzsche says of the unusually talented person,

> All innovators of the spirit have at some point had that pale and fatalistic sign of the Chandala on their foreheads: *not* because they were seen this way, but rather because they themselves felt a terrible gap separating them from everything conventional and honourable.
>
> (219–20)[31]

In speaking of how the innovator must take on, even if temporarily, the "symptoms" of the Chandala, the "mongrel man" or outcast in Indian society, Nietzsche underscores the significance of borrowings that facilitate crossovers into non-normative spaces occupied by underprivileged subjects.

As I have argued, in contemporary Bengali cinema, selected directors reiteratively show a facility in effecting such crossings. While it is true that these crossovers are not always into spaces that could be categorized as "non-normative," overall, they speak of a consistent identification with the under-privileged. Further, to use Nietzsche's words, they help us move beyond that which "already *is*," that which "has stopped *becoming*" (220).[32] Thus, by often choosing to cinematize the non-customary and by representing female characters in processes of unmaking and making, these directors veer away from the static, from the unchanging and point us towards unexpected possibilities in women.

It is necessary to clarify here whether I address unmaking and making both in the lives and art of these directors. Contrary opinions to mine no doubt exist, but I believe Rituparno Ghosh has made it amply clear through the actions of his own life how the unmaking and making of one's assigned sexual identity is possible.[33] Not only did he appear dressed as a woman at various public events and media interviews in India, but in a series of editorials for the magazine *Rōbbar*

14   *Introduction*

(*Sunday*), he also spoke about gayness and transsexuality.[34] In these pieces, he writes about the struggles of being sexually non-normative in a largely essentialist culture. Further, he draws on Michael Jackson's gradual change of appearance from masculine to more feminine, and points out that Western spectators or media did not reject this. Ghosh addresses fearlessly his own difficulties and brings in examples such as Jackson to argue that unmaking and making of sexual identity is and should be possible.[35]

Ghosh's acts, reflections, and last writings are no doubt revolutionary in the context of Indian cinema. I can think of no other director of Bengali or, for that matter, Indian feature films who has by gesture or words made such explicit statements about his or her sexuality. Yet, while it is impossible to completely separate an artist's life actions from his films, this study focuses on how such processes of unmaking and making are manifest in the cinematic work of the three directors covered rather than in their personal lives. Even as my particular focus is the predicament and responses of women as represented in this body of films, some broad comments about these directors' attitudes to notions of unmaking and making in Indian cinema itself are also in order.

In my interview of him on August 20, 2007 in Kolkata, Goutam Ghose spoke about his moving beyond the urban metropolis to areas where aboriginals live. He was born in the city,[36] but made a deliberate and sustained effort to research agrarian populations and other indigenous communities, his persistent question to himself being "what is this country?" He traveled widely and met these people who lived outside of cities. More specifically, Sushil Jana,[37] for instance, provided him information about then Mudnapore district in West Bengal, where gypsies and farmers at times live together.[38] Ghose mentioned that a film based on these real characters in this context had not been made in Bengal before. His *Dakhal* with a focus on a gypsy/peasant woman's resistance and rebellion within such a milieu helps us understand the "wisdom and strength of a parallel system" in the nation, even though the female protagonist is not very literate.[39] Ghose emphasized that unless we know these people, we do not know all of our own history, "India's multi-layered society."[40]

While individual films about resistance and endurance in rural contexts have been made by directors in Bengal, Goutam Ghose presents an entire body of work in this regard. As a Bengali director, he works also as a historical anthropologist, and he "makes" a substantial addition to the canon of Indian cinema by reiteratively alerting us to the lives and potential of communities beyond the limits of the city.

In a recent interview for the *Daily Star*, Buddhadeb Dasgupta observes that the biggest "problem" for Bengali cinema is that it does not have a "brand."[41] He continues, "Whatever branding is there is individual name-based; like Satyajit Ray, and to some extent Ritwik Ghatak" (Dasgupta).[42] Although Dasgupta does not elaborate on what exactly he means by "brand," we can assume that he is encouraging us to move beyond a mere "deification" of certain directors to associating late twentieth- and early twenty-first-century Bengali cinema with a set of identifiable features.[43] In the same section of the interview, he says that a

Bengali film should draw on "raw materials from here." As an example, he mentions his film *Bagh Bahadur*, noting that one "cannot find this 'tiger-dance' in any other part of the world" (Dasgupta).[44]

In the following section of this interview, Dasgupta says that "films can actually take a lot more from poetry."[45] Gautaman Bhaskaran, who covered the Dubai International Film Festival for the *Hindustan Times* in 2012, notes that "Dasgupta has made 13 shorts out of 13 of Tagore's poems, carefully choosing those that helped him win the Nobel Prize for Literature."[46] Bhaskaran adds, "The Festival screened four segments out of the 13 ... and titled them as *Quartet 1*. These were pure cinema, marked by a beautiful economy of words, and visualized with brilliant imagination." Yet, he is shocked to see a number of people in the audience, made up mostly of Bengalis, walk out halfway through the film.[47]

Such observations, both from Dasgupta himself and Bhaskaran, point to impulses of unmaking and making; a desire to see changes in the way certain directors and the Bengali cinema-going public conceptualize film. More specifically, Dasgupta urges a movement towards basing films on things globally identifiable as from Bengal and also encourages a radical innovativeness as when he uses Tagore's poetry to create a series of short films. Although such gestures, as the latter, may be rejected by a body of spectators, they pave the way for change in audience expectations. In fact, basing films on poetry can become a feature distinctly associated with Bengali cinema in the future because of this sort of endeavor or "making" as also a meditated unmaking of spectator expectations by a director such as Dasgupta.

Towards the end of Chapter 5 in this study, I address Rituparno Ghosh's unmaking and making of audience expectations in Bengal as he "re-makes" a classic text of Bengali literature—Tagore's novel *Chokher Bali*—into a film in 2003, over a hundred years after the text's publication. Both Dasgupta and Ghosh work adroitly across genres to re-make audience expectations about Bengali cinema. While Dasgupta cinematizes poetry in a bold move, Ghosh deploys cinema to show how "classic" cultural texts can and should be re-read within changing historical contexts.

But while these directors work across genres to influence and change audience expectations, unmaking and making is also interestingly evident within a sub-genre of Bengali film. In my 2009 interview of Ghosh, he spoke at length about the sub-genre of the detective film; his indebtedness to Satyajit Ray in this connection; as also his "departure" from Ray. Ghosh noted that Ray's *Sonar Kella* foregrounds distinctions between the "unalloyed good" and "unalloyed bad."[48] Further, the detective Feluda, who provides the intellectual force of the film, his cousin and assistant Topshe, who represents the curiosity of the child, and their traveling companion and writer Lalmohanbabu, who provokes humor, are all male. It is as if this detective work is a "superior game where it is best for women not to enter."[49]

As I address earlier in this Introduction, in Ghosh's re-working of the detective film genre in *Shubho Muharat*, the detective who eventually unravels the

16 *Introduction*

mystery is a middle-aged Bengali widow and towards the end of the narrative, she lets the murderer go free. Ghosh spoke of this film as his attempt "to read sleuth and 'criminal' over again" and "re-define" notions of culpability and justice as filtered through the "instinct" of the detective.[50] The fact that he situates two women at the center of this sort of unmaking and making of a sub-genre in Bengali cinema helps substantiate my claim on women's key role in illustrating a shifting and evolving cultural terrain.[51]

As I return to my discussion of how women are represented in such processes by these three directors, it is necessary to reiterate that I focus on unmaking and making as a phenomenon that is shown to occur within individual women across different historical periods, and in urban centers as well as rural areas. What I address here is more of a personal impetus that propels these female characters in Bengali cinema to question long-established "traditional" constructs; to re-conceptualize their roles temporarily; or in a few cases, have the courage to break away from stifling situations and entirely re-define themselves. Undoubtedly, many of the constraints they act against are in place because of socio-cultural factors or economic issues, as I will elaborate in the various chapters of this book. However, my focus is not on a specific historical period that necessitated such acts in women.

I do not, however, want to ignore periods in the history of Bengali cinema when directors have represented such unmaking and making in women characters as a response to political issues and broader socio-economic pressures. Bhaskar Sarkar's comprehensive study of the effects of the 1947 Partition on Indian cinema shows, for instance, how such forces affected the lives of Bengali women and, as a result, their depiction in cinema.

Sarkar refers to the 1950s and notes that "the sheer economic necessities of a post-Partition Bengal with its destitute refugee families forced many women to take on jobs" (147–8). As regards filmic representation, he continues:

> The melodramas of the 1950s and 1960s recognized women as a productive force of economic growth and simultaneously reiterated women's role as homemakers. The fundamental operation they carried out was that of bringing the categories of patriarchy, capitalism, and the modern nation-state into a new alignment, thus recasting existing gender hierarchies in rational-functionalist terms that were more acceptable in a modernizing society.
>
> (148)[52]

Sarkar draws on Satyajit Ray's *Mahanagar* (*The Big City*, 1963) to address the female protagonist's conflicted sense of self as she balances her commitments to work and home with the new job that she takes on.[53] In relation to my discussion here, the point is Ray's representation of a woman's unmaking and making, but in the face of economic pressures.

Similarly, Sharmistha Gooptu addresses the effects of the post-Partition period in Bengal and on Bengali cinema as well. Gooptu notes that the "new text of the 1950s Bengali film was emblematic of a generation which had been through the experience of political upheaval and rapid social transition" (108). She mentions, among other things, "uprooting," "loss of families," "resettling," "loss of male authority within families," and "the changing position of women," which even if not experienced personally "marked the psychic world of the 1950s generation" (Gooptu 108–9).[54] Gooptu theorizes that the immensely popular romantic comedies that featured the two top stars of Bengali cinema at this time—Uttam Kumar and Suchitra Sen—foregrounded a world that helped audiences move beyond this sense of rupture and loss. She suggests that central to this foregrounding was the "emergence of the romantic couple" and the significantly empowered "figure of the woman who absorbs the crisis of masculinity without overtly posing a threat to the male order—a perfect balance of permanence and change" (Gooptu 109).[55]

Gooptu's discussion of the screen persona of Suchitra Sen and the roles she played is also interesting in this connection. She observes that in the "most emblematic films of the genre, the Suchitra Sen figure emerges as a controlling presence—almost a surrogate mother figure to the male protagonist—displaying an uninhibited openness in initiating the romantic process and an enormous resilience towards sustaining romantic love" (Gooptu 108).[56] Gooptu points out that Sen often played the medical professional, combining in her roles aspects of nurture, typically associated with the female, with "feminine spaces" that signified beyond the familial. Sen's screen portrayals bring us an "agency" that cannot "be contained within the conventional paradigm of femininity" (Gooptu 108).[57]

Gooptu addresses the solidification of power in the figure of the female protagonist, but chiefly in a decade following considerable political and cultural turmoil in Bengal. Thus, as she argues, we see in 1950s Bengali cinema an unprecedented and dynamic female presence in the screen persona of Suchitra Sen, but this "making" on the part of directors seems to be a concerted gesture of affirmation in the face of the Bengali peoples' recently suffered losses and deep levels of uncertainty.

In contrast to such "making" of women figures as a response to socio-political events in a particular historical period, my study locates and discusses examples of these processes in women, as represented by select directors in contemporary Bengali cinema, but across historical periods. These periods include, among others, early twentieth-century colonial Bengal, rural Bengal in the late 1960s, and urban Bengal close to the century's end.

Such unmaking and making is suggested by Rituparno Ghosh in his presentation of both the mother and the daughter, Parul, in *Utsab*. The mother's impassioned identification with her husband as freedom fighter, involved in India's anti-colonial struggle, situates her temporarily for some spectators outside of her given social role as nurturer. Similarly, towards the end of the film, Parul seems to momentarily cast off the fetters of her unhappy arranged marriage and re-identify romantically with her cousin/lover from the past. However, such shifts remain temporary and merely conceptual within the diegetic material of the film. Such a tendency towards "making" is also evidenced in Ghosh's representation of Binodini, the widow, in his *Chokher Bali*, not only in her receptivity to

18 *Introduction*

physical passion, but in her ultimate prioritizing of female friendship and solidarity over heterosexual romantic passion within the frame of a markedly patriarchal social system in early twentieth-century Bengal. Yet, this too figures only as a promise and possibility at the close of *Chokher Bali*. I address these processes, as mobilized in *Utsab* and *Chokher Bali*, in greater detail in Chapters 2 and 5 respectively.

Within the films under analysis in my study, it is in Buddhadeb Dasgupta's *Mondo Meyer Upakhyan* that we see this notion of unmaking and making clearly concretized in action. The daughter, Lati's intransigence in the face of fierce maternal opposition and her final daring escape from the space of the brothel where she has grown up are also her repudiation of a social arrangement in which women are pleasure-giving commodities in transactions generally concluded between men. This process of "unmaking," this relinquishing of the familiar by a young girl in rural West Bengal in the late 1960s is made possible by her keen interest in education. Lati's faith in education undergirds her belief, as her actions exemplify, that her identity cannot be pre-determined by her past, by a life she is born into. Rather, the beginning of her journey towards the end of Dasgupta's film is the breaking of the "template" that she has been given and a movement to re-make her identity through the subjective understanding that learning brings her.

What Gilles Deleuze says about the "crystal-image" in his discussion of "a new breed of signs, *opsigns* and *sonsigns*" in neo-realistic Western cinema is relevant to an analysis of these processes of unmaking and making in current Bengali cinema (6).[58] Deleuze argues that the "purely optical situations" of neo-realistic cinema "are fundamentally distinct from the sensory-motor situations of the action image in the old realism" (2), in that they are "no longer ... induced by an action, any more than ... extended into one" (6). The "opsign" is thus "the actual image cut off from its motor extension: it then form[s] large circuits, and enter[s] into communication with what could appear as recollection-images, dream-images, and world-images" (Deleuze 69). But "the opsign finds its true genetic element when the actual optical image crystallizes with *its own* virtual image, on the small internal circuit" (Deleuze 69). This is what Deleuze defines as the "crystal-image." "The crystal-image is, then, the point of indiscernibility of the two distinct images, the actual and the virtual" (Deleuze 82).[59]

More applicable to my discussion of processes of unmaking and making are Deleuze's observations on how time and "over-conforming roles" are contained within the crystal and what force manages to burst forth:

> From the indiscernibility of the actual and the virtual, a new distinction must emerge, like a new reality which was not pre-existent. Everything that has happened falls back into the crystal and stays there: this is all the frozen, fixed, finished-with and over-conforming roles that the characters have tried in turn, dead roles or roles of death.... And yet the trying out of roles is indispensable. It is indispensable so that the other tendency, that of presents which pass and are replaced, emerges from the scene and launches itself

towards a future, creates this future as a bursting forth of life.... Then the real will be created; at the same time as it escapes the eternal referral back of the actual and the virtual, the present and the past.

$$(88)^{60}$$

While characters such as Parul in *Utsab* and Binodini in *Chokher Bali* are represented as attempting to cast off such "roles of death," "over-conforming roles" that accord them neither possibility of pleasure nor change, these films end before we are able to see, if indeed, their "presents ... are replaced" and a radically different future is created for them. Dasgupta's *Mondo Meyer Upakhyan*, however, brings us the imminence of such a future as Lati leaves behind the "crystal"/brothel, a space that encapsulates her present and past, and is shown, in one of the last shots of the film, boarding a moving train to travel to Kolkata for better educational opportunities.

What is particularly significant about such films by Rituparno Ghosh and Buddhadeb Dasgupta is that not only do they provide non-normative and alternative cultural narratives about Bengali women, but they also exemplify changing and multiple perspectives within the characters of these narratives themselves. In other words, such directors of Bengali cinema do more than give us extended stories about characters who are non-normative or who inhabit the social fringe. For instance, precisely when we begin to think that a woman involved in an "incestuous" romance has been co-opted by tradition and settled into an arranged marriage, she is shown to be drawn to the magic of that romance again. Similarly, just as we begin to think that a prostitute is complicit in her objectification and exchange in a system controlled by men, we are given a sub-plot tracing incipient erotic attraction and the possibility of lesbianism amongst a group of prostitutes within the same brothel. The latter is seen in Dasgupta's *Mondo Meyer Upakhyan*. Reiteratively then, these films destabilize notions even of the alternative or non-normative, undercut one perception of a prostitute for example, allowing the subjects of these narratives to consistently surprise us through processes of unmaking and making.

Disposability and substitutability of woman—call for change

Yet, these directors do not fail to underscore a tendency within Bengali tradition to, at times, view women as disposable or, at least, substitutable. As he discussed with me the role of the young widow in his film *Chokher Bali* in the 2009 interview, Rituparno Ghosh observed that "an accident could not determine an individual's existence." In addressing depictions of strength and vulnerability in cinema, he further noted that women, as portrayed "normatively in art and literature," became "regular vehicles in expressing vulnerability." Earlier in this Introduction, I speak of dynamism in Ghosh's depiction of Binodini in *Chokher Bali*, a feature deployed no doubt to counteract the more traditionally typical representations of the widow in Bengali cinema as static and oftentimes vulnerable. Yet, this story of her dynamism is accompanied ceaselessly by another text

20   *Introduction*

in the film itself, the text of what Binodini would be in its absence—a figure not to be desired and easily relegated to the social fringe.[61]

Ghosh examines this "traditionally" determined disposability of woman in an earlier film, *Bariwali* (*The Lady of the House*) made in 1999, although the film focuses not on a widow, but on a woman whose groom does not show up on the wedding night. In Chapter 4 of this study, I discuss how Ghosh dramatizes the themes of waste and disposability in this film. Its protagonist, Banalata, despite some effort, is not as successful as Binodini in moving out of socially prescribed spaces. I argue, however, that we could read *Bariwali* as a film that shows both the power and limits of cinema as regards working against the waste of human potential. In other words, Ghosh's representation of the central character and her failure, even as it draws us into the diegesis, is instrumental in moving us beyond the diegetic material to consider our own role in addressing such traditional relegation. In this regard, Ghosh's use of a film within a film in *Bariwali* is remarkable for signaling where, as cinema audiences, our responsibility starts for effecting social change.

Other than disposability, another issue that troubles these contemporary Bengali directors is woman as substitutable. Clearly for them, this is an area of vulnerability that is a consequence of certain "traditional" perceptions of women as temporary pleasure-givers. Rituparno Ghosh's 2006 film *Dosar* (*Emotional Companion*), for instance, begins with a wide shot of a woman, with her back to the camera, singing a song by Rabindranath Tagore, *Aaj Jemon Kore Gaiche Aakash, Temni Kore Gao Go* (*Sing Today like the Sky Is Singing*).[62] In sum, the remainder of this song by Tagore that she sings translates "Gaze today as the sky is gazing/As the wind, stirring among the leaves, makes the forest weep,/Weep so in the midst of my heart and make (me) weep." A few sequences later, this woman is killed in a car crash, and we learn shortly after, that she was involved in an illicit relationship with the hero of the film, Kaushik. The balcony in which she was singing the opening song adjoined the hotel room she occupied with her lover, who, although injured, manages to survive the car crash.

In a number of unconnected scenes subsequently in the film, Ghosh brings us back to this hotel room. In the first of these, male "housekeepers" efficiently remove and change sheets and pillowcases. The insertion of such a scene, not of any relevance to the narrative proper, establishes the concept of sterilizing the room after the departure of the "other" woman who has already been wiped out in an "accident." It prepares us for the motif of progressive "cleansing" in that other space, the hero's legitimate home, so that he can slowly rebuild his marriage free of the taint of such illicitness. The second scene, set in the hotel, has a young, honeymooning couple arrive in this room, and an even later scene shows the husband beginning to make love to his wife. Ghosh offers us here the visibility of love-making within marriage to evoke the specter of a love-making we are never allowed to see in *Dosar*.

With a stroke of irony, and in true Wordsworthian vein where the dead beloved is "[r]olled round in earth's diurnal course,/[w]ith rocks, and stones, and trees" (113),[63] Ghosh renders the opening song a prophecy of the singer's own fate: that is, she is forever disembodied for her lover who even on his hospital bed is obsessed about finding out how she fared in the accident. This bodiless "other" woman perhaps remains for him in the song and gaze of the sky and makes him weep as the rustling wind makes the forest weep. What I wish to emphasize here is the strategic accretion of scenes that focus on absence, cleansing/sterilization, and substitution,[64] Ghosh thereby signaling, albeit not without sarcasm, that what is traditionally unacceptable can only be indicated through substitutes and needs to be efficiently discarded.

For me as a viewer, what continues to rankle as the hero, through the process of convalescence, settles back into a romantic relationship with his wife is the relative ease with which he moves between women, seeming to find deep pleasure, if not happiness, with either. The thought that hangs heavy although unspoken within the frame of the last shot in the film, a scene in which the hero and his wife lie closely in bed, is that the wife has been as expediently substituted as the dead woman. Other than the adroit insertion of sequences set in the hotel room that suggest this easy substitutability of bodies, Ghosh's last shot in *Dosar* has the wife sit up and away from her husband in bed, reciting a poem about lips meeting which she read on the screen of the cell phone of the dead woman,[65] a poem shared earlier, no doubt, by the latter and the hero. At the close of this 2006 film, Ghosh places the wife in a position that contrasts that of woman as object of (illicit) attraction/pleasure with which the film opens. It is not so much here a question of what is legitimate and what is not, but a categorical presentation of woman as one who reads and understands the text of her own substitution.

From transactional commodities to agents of meaningful exchange

Three major issues stand out when contemplating the representation of women as transactional commodities in recent Bengali cinema. The first factor and one that is surprising is that men who are intelligent, educated, and oftentimes personally invested in producing art are shown to be culpable in this area. Directors juxtapose these men's artistic inclinations, their innovativeness, and progressiveness with their complicity in such transactions.

In Srijit Mukherjee's 2010 *Autograph*, the break-up of the romantic relationship between a young, ambitious, and thoughtful film director, Subhobroto and his girlfriend and female lead, Srinandita, happens when he succumbs to the possible lucrativeness of such a transaction. Subhobroto releases to a television channel a tape that his girlfriend inadvertently kept running when super-star and the hero of his film, Arun Chatterjee, confessed his transgressions and emotional vulnerability to her. Despite the fact that he promises her that he would keep the tape to himself, Subhobroto compromises not just his hero, Arun, but his girlfriend whom the tape captures offering solace and compassion to Arun in an intimate way. The promotional value of such a tape immediately before his film's release and the possibility of commercial gain propel Subhobroto into this

22   *Introduction*

act, through which Srinandita's individual and genuine emotion is reduced to a form of titillating advertisement to be lapped up by the masses.

While such a transaction using woman as one of its objects to increase a film's allure and accelerate sales is situated in contemporary times in *Autograph*, Rituparno Ghosh's *Abohomaan* (*The Eternal*, 2009) transports us to the second half of the nineteenth century to show the historical span of such processes. In this film, the noted Bengali intellectual, playwright, and actor Girish Chandra Ghosh (1844–1912) is depicted as attempting to use his mentee and star actress, the well-known Nōtee Binodini to consolidate gains in their world of theater. *Abohomaan* brings us a multi-layered representation of the commoditization of woman. Historically, the actress Binodini's biographical details alert us to the fact that she engaged in prostitution as a means of survival. In Ghosh's film, Binodini's mentor Girish Ghosh encourages her to favor a Marwari client[66] over a Bengali one who "keeps" her financially from month to month and to whom she feels more attached. The former client, however, committed to build a theater in Binodini's name, and Girish Ghosh indicates Binodini should mobilize deception to benefit her extended family—the theater troupe. I must point out here that Binodini's dialogue in this sequence categorically underlines woman's transactional "value." She tells Girish Ghosh that the client will build the theater "not *for me* but *in exchange for me*."[67]

As director, Rituparno Ghosh uses in this section of the film a wonderfully constructed deep-focus shot in which Girish Ghosh and Binodini converse in the foreground; the middle space is devoid of activity; and our gaze eventually carried to the background where female figures dance incessantly. This visual depth and layering in the scene accentuates the multi-leveled transaction of woman suggested in the conversation between Girish Ghosh and Binodini. The pleasure a "patron" gets from a woman's body given to prostitution translates into gain not so much personally for her[68] as for the theater company. Her reduction to a "commodity without emotion" is also clear as Girish Ghosh suggests supplanting one "patron" with another.[69]

The second issue is that while such commodification and conceptualization of women as items of exchange automatically imply a negation of women's emotion, current directors of Bengali cinema reiteratively foreground such emotion, coming from women, even as they dramatize exploitation. The many recent cinematic instances of contrasting transactions involving women with the expression of their forceful emotion prepares the way for the spectator to begin to think of them reacting against such exploitation and ultimately moving to more meaningful exchange(s).

Depiction of resistance through such emotional expression, although resistance in varying degrees, is evident in the characters of both Srinandita and Binodini in the two films I address above. In order to elaborate on this point, I move now to a brief discussion of (arranged) marriage represented by some contemporary Bengali film directors as a system that reduces women to transactional commodities and sometimes stands in the way of more meaningful exchange. In Chapter 2, I draw on Gayle Rubin and Gayatri Chakravorty Spivak to elaborate

Introduction 23

on this notion of transaction of women, a process that has historically strengthened patriarchy while attenuating possibilities in women as subjects. In the chapter, I focus specifically on arranged marriage as such a form of transaction in Rituparno Ghosh's *Utsab*.

In this regard, perhaps one of the most hard-hitting scenes in contemporary Bengali film in which the equating of woman with an object is concretized for the spectator is one in Aniruddha Roy Chowdhury's *Anuranan* (*Resonance*, 2006), in which Amit, a husband, abandons his wife, Preeti, on the middle of a Kolkata highway and drives away. The camera zooms out, and the shot, which gives us a long view of the solitary Preeti and her purse, is deliberately structured to collapse the distinction between the woman and the only object she carries, underscoring that if we adopted Amit's perspective, there is not much of a difference between the two "commodities." Preeti's "mistake," when she needed a break from the mundaneness of her life, was to visit overnight and out-of-town Rahul, a business colleague and friend of the couple, who is also married.[70] Several scenes towards the close of *Anuranan* dramatize Bengali society's censure of such a hetero-social encounter in the absence of the spouse, with people and the press immediately jumping to the conclusion that Rahul and Preeti were having an affair. What is more relevant to my discussion here is that Amit's complete insensitivity to his wife's physical and emotional needs, evident to the viewer in earlier sequences of *Anuranan*, chiefly because of his absorption in making money and business profits, transforms here to a brutal objectification and abandoning. When the wife who is no more than a commodity to help meet his social needs makes a subjective decision, she is no longer "useful" in his conceptualization of what marriage is. Roy Chowdhury's shot that I discuss above thus works in multiple ways to highlight the commodification and rejection of an "object" when "it" no longer offers use value. As mentioned above, in the face of such attitudes, a number of contemporary Bengali directors position forceful expression of emotion coming from women.

The last factor, and one that I consider the most unfortunate, is that women are shown to also be participators in such transactions involving women. My discussion of this third factor in contemporary Bengali cinema is limited in this study to the representation of prostitution and how in this area women enable such transactions of women, but primarily for purposes of survival. In Chapter 6, I discuss this issue more extensively, drawing on Buddhadeb Dasgupta's film *Mondo Meyer Upakhyan* for substantiation. I show in the chapter that if a "traditional" conceptualization of women as commodities for exchange has spawned a system as deeply entrenched as prostitution, a system in which even mothers are ready to trade their daughters for benefits, then Dasgupta leads us to consider multiple sites and agents within culture that help subvert such transactions.

Here I must return, even if briefly, to my point on women's expression of emotion. What is also noteworthy in recent Bengali cinema is that such emotion is often shown to be exchanged *between women*. In my discussion of Ghosh's *Utsab* in Chapter 2, I address Gayle Rubin's point that woman becomes a "conduit" in her "exchange" *between men*.[71] If this is the case, and patriarchal

24   *Introduction*

social systems and at times marriage are a form of tradition that has perpetuated such exchange, then exchange of emotion between women is a feature used by contemporary cinema directors to signify the evolving dynamics of culture.

In my interview with director Buddhadeb Dasgupta in 2007, in a discussion of his film *Mondo Meyer Upakhyan*, Dasgupta spoke of the motif of the journey and how the film captures women's need to locate to a "different planet"[72] where they will not need men. Dasgupta was addressing broadly women's resistance against masculinist social systems. In Chapter 6 of this study, I show how in relation to the theme of the journey, America's moonlanding in 1969 figures metaphorically in his film. However, other than dramatizing (women's) resistance against male-dominated social structures on many levels, the film portrays such resistance specifically in a few sequences of emotional exchange between women. I do a more detailed discussion of these sequences in Chapter 6. Focused on three female prostitutes, these sections of *Mondo Meyer* bring us dialogue such as "We will be each other's partners."[73] The shots in which the women lovingly caress one another's body parts foreground a level of caring and desire that easily suggests incipient lesbianism.[74]

I am arguing here that although exchange of emotion between women obviously does not always carry an erotic charge, such a charge is explicitly used by some Bengali directors to show the force of resistance against the commodification of women by men. Thus, even though the commoditization of women is a subject that has been extensively addressed in theoretical and critical studies, it was necessary for me to discuss it briefly in this section of my Introduction to show in what ways contemporary directors of Bengali cinema not only represent such a process but also the cultural forces that work against it.

As I note in the immediately preceding paragraphs, one such force is the unrestrained expression of emotion *by* women, as seen in recent films such as *Autograph* and *Abohomaan*, and another is an exchange of emotion *between* women with such emotion occasionally carrying an erotic or romantic charge. Although in a culture such as Bengal's, which has normatively been heterosexual, it is difficult and challenging to cinematize and bring to majority audiences such a charge, the fact that in the last two decades more than one director has done it demonstrates that they are committed to representing cultural dimensions that reflect change.

The question may arise as to how this expression of emotion by and between women is different from emotion expressed in the genre of melodrama. Any consideration of the characterizing features of melodrama reveals that these are exaggerated emotions; typecast characters such as embodying good or evil with these presented as undiluted categories; and oftentimes the representation of conflict between such stereotyped characters. In the chapter "'Bengali' Cinema: Its Making and Unmaking" in the *Routledge Handbook of Indian Cinemas*, Sharmistha Gooptu addresses melodrama in Bengali cinema. She notes the economic downturn of the Bengali film industry in the late 1970s and also how in the "late 1970s and early 1980s, Bengali cinema lost out on a sizeable proportion of its audience with the proliferation of television sets in middle-class homes"

Introduction   25

(Gooptu 44). She further observes that in the 1980s, the majority of audiences for mainstream Bengali cinema were no longer the middle-class but rural people and the urban proletariat. She notes also "a departure from social realism into the realm of folk and fantasy" (Gooptu 46). As an example, Gooptu discusses the 1991 mega-hit *Beder Meye Jyotsna* (*Jyotsna, the Snake Charmer's Daughter*), which "drew heavily on the cult of snake worship prevalent in rural Bengal and the related folk culture, and was severely criticized for being like the *jatra* or indigenous theatrical performance popular in both rural West Bengal and Bangladesh" (46). What is particularly relevant to my argument in Gooptu's discussion is her comment that "For many in the industry it was a non-film, generally considered Bengali cinema's lowest ebb for its theatricality and high melodrama" (46).[75] In my reading, the 2008 Bengali film *Mon Amour: Shesher Kobita Revisited* is clearly melodramatic in its use of heightened emotion, in particular the needlessly excessive crying on the part of its female lead. Interestingly enough, this film with its early shots of Kolkata and upper middle-class urban characters is targeted towards a city audience.[76]

In his essay "From Cultural Backwardness to the Age of Imitation: An Essay on Film History," M. Madhava Prasad discusses the prevalence of the "melodramatic plot" in Indian cinema through the twentieth century. He notes that thus for this cinema, realism "became a state-supported aesthetic venture" (Prasad 13). He makes the point that

> A general culture of realism, however, implied not just a sociological or ethnographic documentation of the interior or a psychological portrayal of middle-class subjectivities but a concrete sense of the contemporary, the here and now, a registration of the reconstitution of social life by clock time. The time of melodrama was the time of generations.
>
> (Prasad 13)[77]

When I address the representation of emotion by and between women on the part of the directors covered by my study, I am talking of something very different from melodrama. Melodrama by portraying women in exaggerated emotional states and keeping them in stipulated roles, as good or evil, often in cliques or conflicts against one another perpetuates their depiction as one-dimensional and vulnerable because they are divided. The emotion expressed by Srinandita, in Srijit Mukherjee's *Autograph*, and Nōtee Binodini, in Rituparno Ghosh's *Abohomaan*, is not melodramatic but a protest against their objectification by patriarchal men. By verbalizing this emotion as protest, they are also shown to defy any compartmentalization of them as "essentially feminine" and therefore "passive." Unlike in melodrama, they are depicted as breaking out of confining categories, and their rejection of traditional expectations aligns them with "clock time."

In Buddhadeb Dasgupta's *Mondo Meyer Upakhyan*, the exchange of emotion and homo-erotic bonding between female prostitutes is a signifier of solidarity and empowerment rather than division. To use the words of Prasad,

26 *Introduction*

this emotion between women in *Mondo Meyer* also brings us a "reconstitution of social life by clock time"; it indicates that the patriarchal commodification of women via the system of prostitution is resented by many women who participate in it of necessity. They can break out of it if they choose to. Dasgupta here shows not the "generational" "time of melodrama" but the imperatives of the "here and now" (Prasad 13). A similar focus on "contemporary" needs of women is evident in Aniruddha Roy Chowdhury's *Anuranan*. Far from being melodramatic, the exchange of emotion between women, represented by the director, suggests that the protagonists stand poised to break free of categories in which "traditional" social censure would confine them and to explore other possibilities.

In this connection, it seems fitting to conclude this segment of my Introduction by returning to Roy Chowdhury's *Anuranan* and its final sequence. As a result of abandonment by her husband and severe social censure, Preeti attempts to commit suicide. She survives and is visited in the hospital by Nandita, her friend and the woman whose husband she met out-of-town. She lies on the hospital bed with bandaged wrists and admits to Nandita that she attempted to fly like a bird (i.e., to seek liberation) but failed. Nandita tells her to fly with her heart, with all her life. As Nandita breaks down in tears (one possible reason could be the death of her husband), Preeti reaches her hand out to console her. Yet, the deep bond between the two women here seems to go beyond one particular issue, i.e., the death of Nandita's husband.

Roy Chowdhury complicates this sequence by introducing on the soundtrack Tagore's song "Aha tōmar shongé praner khela/Priyō amar ōgō priyō" ("In this game of the heart with you/Beloved, oh my beloved"),[78] rendered by the noted male singer Ustad Rashid Khan. Although the still figure of the now dead husband is superimposed on the shots of the hospital room as the song unravels, and the lyrics could point to this loss,[79] the fact that Roy Chowdhury offers this song in the voice of a male singer rather than a female one, suggests more than it signifying just the wife's lament for her husband. Roy Chowdhury's strategic undercutting of more traditional audience expectations, effected through his choice of the gender of the singer in this last sequence, prepares us for a corresponding movement away from "normative" gender relations as well.

In my reading, this deeply romantic song by Tagore, a song that in the view of some could also be seen to carry an erotic charge, may very well be used by Roy Chowdhury to suggest Nandita's loss if Preeti's attempted suicide had indeed become a reality. Thus, the translated lines of the song—"Will you, in this way,/only enchant me and disappear?"—then take on a different valence, carrying the audience back in time to the growing friendship between these two women and putting into words what they cannot quite verbalize. I want to say here that in the face of the brutal objectification that Preeti and other women have taken historically, the possibilities of the "romantic" mobilized by some directors of contemporary Bengali cinema, in their depictions of exchange of emotion between women, do not, necessarily, indicate a forthcoming romantic

Introduction 27

relationship per se between the characters concerned. While this is one potential scenario, as in the sequence suggesting lesbianism in Dasgupta's *Mondo Meyer Upakhyan*, the "romantic" also comes richly laden with the force of that which is still unknown but possible between women.[80] In this way, as in Roy Chowdhury's *Anuranan* where the ambiance of Tagore's song in the voice of a male singer in a sequence of emotional exchange between two women continues to unexpectedly resonate for us at the film's end, the "romantic" prepares the ground for more meaningful exchange between women, beyond their commodification, even though we sometimes do not know exactly what the nature of that exchange will be.

I have discussed in the preceding paragraphs the main themes and objectives of this book. Structurally, the book is divided into three sections, and as I mention earlier, the theme of women's unmaking and making as it manifests itself in different ways in recent Bengali cinema is addressed in all three sections of this study.

Part I of this book focuses on the disjuncture between responses to resistance that occurs in the public sphere and resistance from women in the private sphere. I draw on two films to show this dichotomy: Chapter 2 is on Rituparno Ghosh's *Utsab* and Chapter 3 on Goutam Ghose's *Dekha*. Chapter 1 in this section, on the former director's *Dahan*, engages the subject of disjuncture from a different angle, discussing contrasting responses to women's resistance from agents in the public and private spheres.

Part II addresses notions of waste and disposability as these relate to women. Chapter 4 on Rituparno Ghosh's *Bariwali* focuses primarily on these issues. This second section of the book also illustrates how contemporary directors of Bengali cinema mobilize possibilities of "rupture" within their films. In Chapter 5, on Ghosh's *Chokher Bali*, I consider at length such possibilities. Finally, Part II also addresses audience responsibility; how literary texts are "re-made" in contemporary Bengali cinema; and how such re-making aims to reshape audience expectations and effect a shift from certain traditional forms of conceptualizing to ones that show a dynamism within the culture.

Part III is on women's movement from being transactional commodities historically in many situations to engaging in meaningful exchanges as subjects. In Chapter 6 on Buddhadeb Dasgupta's *Mondo Meyer Upakhyan*, I elaborate on this final theme of the book.

Notes

1 In *Rabindranath Tagore Omnibus II.* New Delhi: Rupa, 2003. 1–175.
2 Ibid.
3 See Ashis Nandy ed. *The Secret Politics of Our Desires: Innocence, Culpability and Indian Popular Cinema.* London: Zed, 1998.
4 See Ashish Rajadhyaksha, *Indian Cinema in the Time of Celluloid: From Bollywood to the Emergency.* Bloomington: Indiana UP, 2009.
5 See Jyotika Virdi, *The Cinematic Imagination: Indian Popular Films as Social History.* New Brunswick: Rutgers UP, 2003.

28 Introduction

6 See Alka Kurian, *Narratives of Gendered Dissent in South Asian Cinemas.* New York: Routledge, 2012.

7 See Yves Thoraval, *The Cinemas of India.* New Delhi: Macmillan India, 2000.

8 See Bhaskar Sarkar, *Mourning the Nation: Indian Cinema in the Wake of Partition.* Durham: Duke UP, 2009.

9 See Sharmistha Gooptu, *Bengali Cinema: "An Other Nation."* London: Routledge, 2011.

10 Ghose underscored this point on such subaltern women's progressive involvement when I interviewed him on August 20, 2007.

11 Translation mine.

12 Translation mine.

13 We see this earlier in the film.

14 I discuss their films in more detail a bit further on in my Introduction.

15 When Loka attempts to strangle Notōbor towards the end of *Charachar* hoping to reclaim his wife, Sari tells her husband to stop and that she will go with him. As revealed in my interview of him, in Dasgupta's opinion, Sari's decision, however, has "no force," and she does ultimately leave with Notōbor.

16 Ghosh mentioned these issues in my interview of him.

17 In *The Structural Transformation of the Public Sphere: An Inquiry into a Category of Bourgeois Society.* Trans. Thomas Burger with the Assistance of Frederick Lawrence. Cambridge: MIT, 1989.

18 In *Non-Violent Resistance (Satyagraha).* New York: Schocken, 1961. 112–15.

19 For a detailed discussion of radical left-wing movements in West Bengal in the late 1960s and early 1970s, see Sumanta Banerjee, *India's Simmering Revolution: The Naxalite Uprising.* London: Zed, 1980. See Marcus F. Franda, *Radical Politics in West Bengal.* Cambridge, MA: MIT, 1971. Of particular relevance is chapter 6. See also Samar Sen, Debabrata Panda, and Ashish Lahiri eds. *Naxalbari and After: A Frontier Anthology.* Vols. I and II. Calcutta: Kathashilpa, 1978. See Srila Roy, "The Everyday Life of the Revolution: Gender, Violence, and Memory." *South Asia Research* 27 (July 2007): 187–204 for a discussion of "gendered" perceptions even within the Naxalite movement. Roy notes, for example,

> The irony, of course, is that within the radical redefinition of marriage in the movement, the labels of "wife" and "widow" were largely rendered redundant. Yet, as "wives" and "widows," women were made to perform symbolic and actual roles that effectively renewed middle-class codes and expectations of femininity in the political domain.
>
> (192)

20 Postcolonial critics, such as Partha Chatterjee, have addressed how during the period of India's nationalist struggle, Indian women were equated with an inner sanctum of "purity" as opposed to the foreign colonial influence. In "Representing Nationalism: Ideology of Motherhood in Colonial Bengal," Jasodhara Bagchi discusses how, in the late nineteenth and early twentieth century, Bengali nationalists appropriated the ideology of motherhood into the anti-colonial rhetoric. In the concluding sections of her essay, Bagchi comments negatively on this practice:

> By extolling an ideology that apparently rested on a show of the empowering of women, it was ultimately a way of reinforcing a social philosophy of deprivation for women.... The internalisation of this so- called ideal that nationalism put up for women simply reinforced the traditional notion that the fruition of women's lives lay in producing heroic sons.... Bengali mothers had to contend with the unspoken call to renounce any other form of self-fulfilment. Child-bearing and nurturing became the only social justification of women's lives.
>
> (70)

See *Economic and Political Weekly* October 20–29, 1990: WS 65–71.

Introduction 29

In another essay, "Socialising the Girl Child in Colonial Bengal," Bagchi notes of nineteenth- and early twentieth-century Bengal:

> As I have argued elsewhere, the familial mode with a distinct accent on maternal nurturance marks the predominant culture of Bengal.... It is within the family that the girl child finds her natural habitat.... Her mental universe is constructed as one long preparation to be a good wife and a good mother.
>
> (2214)

See *Economic and Political Weekly* October 9, 1993: 2214–19.

While this particular note and the previous one, Note 19, mention critical works that show how revolutionary/radical political movements in Bengal relegated women to positions of deprivation or accorded them subordinate status in many cases, my study will address two films, *Utsab* and *Dekha*, to illustrate how such impulses continue decades after such movements are over.

21 See Gayatri Chakravorty Spivak, *In Other Worlds: Essays in Cultural Politics.* New York: Routledge, 1988. 222–40.

22 Ghosh, "Embodied Experiences: Being Female and Disabled." *Economic and Political Weekly* April 24, 2010, Review of Women's Studies sec.: 58–63.

23 Bagchi, "Representing Nationalism."

24 See Thoraval, *The Cinemas of India.*

25 See Virdi, *The Cinematic Imagination.* Virdi also has a strong argument on how the figure of the woman was appropriated in nationalist discourse "to mobilize against imperialism" (86) and in the post-Independence period, "by majority and minority communities as a sign of community identity," ultimately affecting "legal reform discourse, which sacrificed women's rights as equal subjects" (86). See pages 85–6.

26 Spivak, "French Feminism in an International Frame." In *In Other Worlds: Essays in Cultural Politics.* New York: Routledge, 1988. 134–53. In this regard, Jasodhara Bagchi also notes in "Representing Nationalism," "Women's exclusive confinement to reproductive function and the attendant emphasis on nurturance have rendered the domain of motherhood specially vulnerable to patriarchal control" (65).

27 The most obvious reasons for the marriage are first, the father will be able to be free of the "burden" of an unmarried daughter, and second, if she were to follow her husband in death voluntarily, the site would be consecrated.

28 Of course, any broad understanding of Hindu culture should make it clear that this does not necessarily mean that she or her father is economically privileged.

29 Rajeswari Sundar Rajan undertakes a more extended discussion of the girl Jashobati's sexuality and subjectivity in the film. See Rajeswari Sunder Rajan, *Real and Imagined Women: Gender, Culture and Postcolonialism.* London: Routledge, 1993. See especially pages 52–3.

30 Without being quite aware of it, embedded in my mind must have been Gayatri Chakravorty Spivak's essay title "Unmaking and Making in *To The Lighthouse.*" See *In Other Worlds: Essays in Cultural Politics.* New York: Routledge, 1988. 30–45.

31 Friedrich Nietzsche, *The Anti-Christ, Ecce Homo, Twilight of the Idols, and Other Writings.* Eds. Aaron Ridley and Judith Norman. Trans. Judith Norman. Cambridge Texts in the History of Philosophy. Cambridge: CUP, 2005.

32 Ibid.

33 Ghosh passed away on May 30, 2013. In my opinion, it is evident that he was transsexual.

34 See Rituparno Ghosh, "First Person." *Prōtidin-Robbar* June 9, 2013: 6–17. This issue, in which a number of his editorials appear, was published after his death and dedicated entirely to his life and art. Especially relevant are editorials numbered 5 and 10.

35 His film *Chitrangada* (*The Crowning Wish*, 2012), released one year before his death, addresses these issues more extensively.

36 Ghose was born in Kolkata in 1950.

30   *Introduction*

37 Jana is the author of the story on which Ghose's film *Dakhal* is based.

38 Midnapore district was divided into *Purba Medinipur* (East Midnapore) and *Paschim Medinipur* (West Midnapore) on January 1, 2002.

39 These were Ghose's words in my interview of him.

40 It is important to add here that Ghose's first feature film, *Maa Bhoomi* (*Our Land*, 1979) in Telegu, focuses on a rural peasant group and its rebellion in Hyderabad State. His *Paar* (*The Crossing*, 1984), in Hindi, is about a laborer, who rises up against exploitation, and his wife in rural Bihar. His Bengali *Padma Nadir Majhi* (*The Boatman of the River Padma*, 1993) is set in the rural delta of the Padma River in what is now Bangladesh.

41 See Buddhadeb Dasgupta, "Cinema Has a Language of Its Own." Interview by Fahmin Ferdous. *Daily Star* June 27, 2014: Entertainment. Online, available at: www.thedaily star.net/entertainment/cinema-has-a-language-of-its-own-buddhadeb-dasgupta-30548.

42 Ibid.

43 What immediately comes to mind is the association of New Wave with French cinema and Neorealism with Italian cinema for example.

44 See "Cinema Has a Language of Its Own."

45 Ibid.

46 See "Buddhadeb Dasgupta's *Quartet 1* Is Sheer Poetry." *Hindustan Times* December 12, 2012: Entertainment-regional. Online, available at: www.hindustantimes.com/entertainment/regional/buddhadeb-dasgupta-s-quartet-1-is-sheer-poetry/article1–971765.aspx.

47 Ibid. Bhaskaran gives us *Troyodoshi* as the Bengali title of *Quartet 1*.

48 There are at least three references in the film to "*dushtu lōk*," "a bad man."

49 This was Ghosh's comment when I interviewed him.

50 In quotations are Ghosh's exact words from the interview.

51 In the history of Bengali film, the protagonist in the detective sub-genre has almost always been male. Other than the Satyajit Ray films with Feluda in the lead, we have as many examples films with the male detective Byomkesh Bakshi. See, for instance, *Chiriakhana* (*The Zoo*, 1967), *Byomkesh Bakshi* (2010), *Abar Byomkesh* (2012), and Ghosh's own *Satyanweshi* (2013). For a more detailed discussion of Ghosh's detective films, see Madhuja Mukherjee, "En-gendering the Detective: Of Love, Longing and Feminine Follies." *South Asian History and Culture* Latest articles (ahead of print). Online, available at: www.tandfonline.com/doi/full/10.1080/19472498.2014.9 99441#.VNf7ifnF-So. See also Ghosh's comments on the male and female detective as quoted in Somdatta Mandal, "Of 'Women' and 'Relationships' in Contemporary Bengali Cinema: Rituparno Ghosh's Oeuvre." *Asian Cinema* (USA) Fall/Winter 2002: 85–104. Online, available at: https://sites.google.com/site/mandalsomdatta/publications. Ghosh focused on the woman's "intuition," "innate common sense," "native intelligence," "power of observation," noting that these seemed "to be a more interesting way of tackling crime" (Mandal 13).

52 See Sarkar, *Mourning the Nation.*

53 Ibid.

54 See Gooptu, *Bengali Cinema.*

55 Ibid.

56 Ibid.

57 Ibid.

58 In *Cinema 2: The Time-Image*. Trans. Hugh Tomlinson and Robert Galeta. Minneapolis: U of Minnesota P, 1989.

59 Ibid.

60 Ibid.

61 This is clear when we observe the portrayal of other widows in *Chokher Bali.*

62 Translation mine.

Introduction   31

63 William Wordsworth, "A Slumber Did My Spirit Seal." In *The Complete Poetical Works of Wordsworth*. Cambridge Edition of the Poets. Ed. Andrew J. George. Boston: Houghton Mifflin, 1904. 113.

64 We are witness to a different kind of substitution when the husband of the dead woman brings home a prostitute and engages in violent sex with her, possibly to alleviate his own pain and frustration.

65 After the car accident, this phone happened to be with her husband's belongings, which she picked up from the police station.

66 The Marwaris are originally from north-western India, but some settled permanently in Bengal. They are known for their business acumen.

67 Translation and italics mine.

68 According to Binodini's *My Story*, this patron was Gurmukh Rai. The Star Theatre, as this theatre came to be called, was inaugurated on July 21, 1883. See Binodini Dasi, *My Story and My Life as an Actress*. Ed. and trans. Rimli Bhattacharya. New Delhi: Kali for Women, 1998. See especially the chapter "On Matters Relating to the Star Theatre."

69 Although she is engaged in the trade of prostitution, Binodini's feelings for the Bengali client that Girish Ghosh refers to are made clear in the film. In *Abohomaan*, the Girish Ghosh–Binodini episodes are a part of a film within the film that is directed by Aniket, the male lead of Ghosh's film. The role of Binodini is played by Shikha/Srimati, the female lead of *Abohomaan*. Aniket becomes romantically involved with Srimati, and later she feels used or played with when he seems detached from her. The commodification of woman thus works on yet another level here.

70 Because of a possible cardiac condition, Rahul dies on the night of Preeti's visit.

71 Gayle Rubin, "The Traffic in Women: Notes on the 'Political Economy' of Sex." In *Toward an Anthropology of Women*. Ed. Rayna R. Reiter. New York: Monthly Review P, 1975. 157–210.

72 Dasgupta's original words were "*ōnyō grōhé.*"

73 Translation mine.

74 Dasgupta spoke of lesbianism too and mentioned that in this instance, it stems from hatred against men who have used these women's bodies as commodities again and again.

75 Gooptu specifies that this film was an "Indo-Bangladeshi joint venture" (46). See "'Bengali' Cinema: Its Making and Unmaking." In *Routledge Handbook of Indian Cinemas*. Eds. K. Moti Gokulsing and Wimal Dissanayake. London: Routledge, 2013. 37–50.

76 Sharmistha Gooptu notes that from the second half of the 1980s, Bengali "middle" cinema—including films made by Aparna Sen and Rituparno Ghosh—drew middle-class audiences back into movie theaters (48). See "'Bengali' Cinema: Its Making and Unmaking."

77 In *Routledge Handbook of Indian Cinemas*. Eds. K. Moti Gokulsing and Wimal Dissanayake. London: Routledge, 2013. 7–18.

78 Translation mine.

79 The lines in the song—"Kebōl tumi ki gō emni bhabé/rangiyé mōré paliyé jabé"—translate "Will you, in this way,/only enchant me and disappear?"

80 I am trying to trace a movement here from the reduction and one-dimensionality implicit in the commoditization of women to something more multi-dimensional. I must mention here a story told me in childhood by my father, Sudhiranjan Mukherjee, and one that I recall often. On one of his visits as a young writer to Shantiniketan to see Rabindranath Tagore, my father had the opportunity to ask him a question as Tagore sometimes took questions from visitors. "Gurudeb," said my father, "what is the meaning of romance?" Tagore paced back and forth uttering the word three times—"Romance, romance, romance. Romance," he said, "is the mystery of the unknown." I am, of course, translating from the Bengali conversation, although the word "romance" figured in it as I have quoted above.

32 *Introduction*

References

Abar Byomkesh. Dir. Anjan Dutt. Rana Sarkar. DAG Creative Media, 2012. Film.

Abohomaan (The Eternal). Dir. Rituparno Ghosh. Mahesh Ramanathan and Rajesh Sawhney. Reliance Big, 2009. Film.

Antarjali Jatra (The Voyage Beyond). Dir. Goutam Ghose. Ravi Malik. National Film Development Corporation, 1987. Film.

Anuranan (Resonance). Dir. Aniruddha Roy Chowdhury. Jeet Banerjee, Aniruddha Roy Chowdhury, and Indrani Mukherjee. Screenplay Films, 2006. Film.

Aranyer Din Ratri (Days and Nights in the Forest). Dir. Satyajit Ray. Asim Dutta and Nepal Dutta. Priya Films, 1969. Film.

Autograph. Dir. Srijit Mukherjee. Madhu Mantena, Shrikant Mohta, and Mahendra Soni. Shree Venkatesh Films, 2010. Film.

Bagchi, Jasodhara. "Representing Nationalism: Ideology of Motherhood in Colonial Bengal." *Economic and Political Weekly* October 20–29, 1990: WS 65–71. Web.

Bagchi, Jasodhara. "Socialising the Girl Child in Colonial Bengal." *Economic and Political Weekly* October 9, 1993: 2214–19. Web.

Banerjee, Sumanta. *India's Simmering Revolution: The Naxalite Uprising.* London: Zed, 1980. Print.

Bariwali (The Lady of the House). Dir. Rituparno Ghosh. Anupam Kher, 1999. Film.

Benjamin, Walter. "The Work of Art in the Age of Its Technological Reproducibility." *"The Work of Art in the Age of Its Technological Reproducibility" and Other Writings on Media.* Eds. Michael W. Jennings, Brigid Doherty, and Thomas Y. Levin. Trans. Edmund Jephcott, Rodney Livingstone, Howard Eiland, and Others. Cambridge, MA: Belknap-Harvard UP, 2008. 19–55. Print.

Bhaskaran, Gautaman. "Buddhadeb Dasgupta's *Quartet 1* Is Sheer Poetry." *Hindustan Times* December 12, 2012: Entertainment-regional. Online, available at: www.hindustan times.com/entertainment/regional/buddhadeb-dasgupta-s-quartet-1-is-sheer-poetry/ article1-971765.aspx. Accessed August 5, 2014. Web.

Byomkesh Bakshi. Dir. Anjan Dutt. Shibaji Panja and Kaustubh Roy. Red Molecule, 2010. Film.

Charachar (The Shelter of the Wings). Dir. Buddhadeb Dasgupta. Gita Gope and Shankar Gope. Gope Movies, 1994. Film.

Chiriakhana (The Zoo). Dir. Satyajit Ray. Harendranath Bhattacharya. Star Productions, 1967. Film.

Chokher Bali: A Passion Play. Dir. Rituparno Ghosh. Shrikant Mohta and Mahendra Soni. Shree Venkatesh Films, 2003. Film.

Dahan (Crossfire). Dir. Rituparno Ghosh. Vijay Agarwal and Kalpana Agarwal. Gee Pee Films Pvt. Ltd., 1997. Film.

Dakhal (The Occupation). Dir. Goutam Ghose. West Bengal Film Industry, 1982. Film.

Dasgupta, Buddhadeb. Personal interview. August 19, 2007.

Dasgupta, Buddhadeb. "Cinema Has a Language of Its Own." Interview by Fahmin Ferdous. *Daily Star* June 27, 2014: Entertainment. Online, available at: www.the dailystar.net/entertainment/cinema-has-a-language-of-its-own-buddhadeb-dasgupta-30548. Accessed August 1, 2014. Web.

Dasi, Binodini. *My Story and My Life as an Actress.* Ed. and trans. Rimli Bhattacharya. New Delhi: Kali for Women, 1998. Print.

Dekha (Seeing). Dir. Goutam Ghose. Ramesh Gandhi, 2001. Film.

Introduction 33

Deleuze, Gilles. *Cinema 2: The Time-Image.* Trans. Hugh Tomlinson and Robert Galeta. Minneapolis: U of Minnesota P, 1989. Print.

Devi, Mahasweta. "Breast-Giver." Trans. Gayatri Chakravorty Spivak. *In Other Worlds: Essays in Cultural Politics.* New York: Routledge, 1988. 222–40. Print.

Dosar (The Companion). Dir. Rituparno Ghosh. Arindam Chaudhuri. Planman Motion Pictures, 2006. Film.

Franda, Marcus F. *Radical Politics in West Bengal.* Cambridge, MA: MIT, 1971. Print.

Gandhi, M.K. "The Law of Suffering." *Non-Violent Resistance (Satyagraha).* New York: Schocken, 1961. 112–15. Print.

Ghose, Goutam. Personal interview. August 20, 2007.

Ghosh, Nandini. "Embodied Experiences: Being Female and Disabled." *Economic and Political Weekly* April 24, 2010, Review of Women's Studies sec.: 58–63. Web.

Ghosh, Rituparno. Personal interview. September 28, 2009.

Ghosh, Rituparno. "First Person." *Prōtidin-Rōbbar* June 9, 2013: 6–17. Print.

Gooptu, Sharmistha. *Bengali Cinema: "An Other Nation."* London: Routledge, 2011. Print.

Gooptu, Sharmistha. "'Bengali' Cinema: Its Making and Unmaking." *Routledge Handbook of Indian Cinemas.* Eds. K. Moti Gokulsing and Wimal Dissanayake. London: Routledge, 2013. 37–50. Print.

Habermas, Jürgen. *The Structural Transformation of the Public Sphere: An Inquiry into a Category of Bourgeois Society.* Trans. Thomas Burger with the Assistance of Frederick Lawrence. Cambridge: MIT, 1989. Print.

Kurian, Alka. *Narratives of Gendered Dissent in South Asian Cinemas.* New York: Routledge, 2012. Print.

Maa Bhoomi (Our Land). Dir. Goutam Ghose. Ravindranath G. and B. Narsing Rao. Chaitanya Chitra, 1979. Film.

Mandal, Somdatta. "Of 'Women' and 'Relationships' in Contemporary Bengali Cinema: Rituparno Ghosh's Oeuvre." *Asian Cinema* (USA) Fall/Winter 2002: 85–104. Online, available at: https://sites.google.com/site/mandalsomdatta/publications. Accessed February 1, 2015. Web.

Mon Amour: Shesher Kobita Revisited. Dir. Subhrajit Mitra. Men at Work. T. Sarkar Productions, 2008. DVD.

Mondo Meyer Upakhyan (A Tale of a Naughty Girl). Dir. Buddhadeb Dasgupta. Arya Bhattacharya. Arjoe Entertainment (India), 2002. Film.

Mukherjee, Madhuja. "En-gendering the Detective: Of Love, Longing and Feminine Follies." *South Asian History and Culture* Latest articles (ahead of print). Online, available at: www.tandfonline.com/doi/full/10.1080/19472498.2014.999441#.VNf7ifnF-So. Accessed February 1, 2015 via Temple University Libraries. Web.

Nandy, Ashis, ed. *The Secret Politics of Our Desires: Innocence, Culpability and Indian Popular Cinema.* London: Zed, 1998. Print.

Nietzsche, Friedrich. *The Anti-Christ, Ecce Homo, Twilight of the Idols, and Other Writings.* Eds. Aaron Ridley and Judith Norman. Trans. Judith Norman. Cambridge Texts in the History of Philosophy. Cambridge: CUP, 2005. Print.

Paar (The Crossing). Dir. Goutam Ghose. Swapan Sarkar. Orchid Films, 1984. Film.

Padma Nadir Majhi (The Boatman of the River Padma). Dir. Goutam Ghose. Ashirbad Chalchitra and Habibur Rahman Khan. Government of West Bengal, 1993. Film.

Prasad, M. Madhava. "From Cultural Backwardness to the Age of Imitation: An Essay on Film History." *Routledge Handbook of Indian Cinemas.* Eds. K. Moti Gokulsing and Wimal Dissanayake. London: Routledge, 2013. 7–18. Print.

34 *Introduction*

Rajadhyaksha, Ashish. *Indian Cinema in the Time of Celluloid: From Bollywood to the Emergency.* Bloomington: Indiana UP, 2009. Print.

Rajan, Rajeswari Sunder. *Real and Imagined Women: Gender, Culture and Postcolonialism.* London: Routledge, 1993. Print.

Roy, Srila. "The Everyday Life of the Revolution: Gender, Violence, and Memory." *South Asia Research* 27 (July 2007): 187–204. Print.

Rubin, Gayle. "The Traffic in Women: Notes on the 'Political Economy' of Sex." *Toward an Anthropology of Women.* Ed. Rayna R. Reiter. New York: Monthly Review P, 1975. 157–210. Print.

Sarkar, Bhaskar. *Mourning the Nation: Indian Cinema in the Wake of Partition.* Durham: Duke UP, 2009. Print.

Satyanweshi. Dir. Rituparno Ghosh. Shrikant Mohta and Mahendra Soni. Shree Venkatesh Films, 2013. Film.

Sen, Samar, Debabrata Panda, and Ashish Lahiri, eds. *Naxalbari and After: A Frontier Anthology.* Vols. I and II. Calcutta: Kathashilpa, 1978. Print.

Shubho Muharat (The First Shoot). Dir. Rituparno Ghosh. Bishu Chakraborty and Indrakumar Ghosh. Jagannath Productions, 2003. Film.

Spivak, Gayatri Chakravorty. "French Feminism in an International Frame." *In Other Worlds: Essays in Cultural Politics.* New York: Routledge, 1988. 134–53. Print.

Spivak, Gayatri Chakravorty. "Unmaking and Making in *To The Lighthouse*." In *Other Worlds: Essays in Cultural Politics.* New York: Routledge, 1988. 30–45. Print.

Tagore, Rabindranath. *Religion of Man. Rabindranath Tagore Omnibus II.* New Delhi: Rupa, 2003. 1–175. Print.

Thoraval, Yves. *The Cinemas of India.* New Delhi: Macmillan India, 2000. Print.

Utsab (Festival). Dir. Rituparno Ghosh. Tapan Biswas and Sutapa Ghosh. Cinemawallah, 2000. Film.

Virdi, Jyotika. *The Cinematic Imagination: Indian Popular Films as Social History.* New Brunswick: Rutgers UP, 2003. Print.

Wordsworth, William. "A Slumber Did My Spirit Seal." *The Complete Poetical Works of Wordsworth.* Cambridge Edition of the Poets. Ed. Andrew J. George. Boston: Houghton Mifflin, 1904. 113. Print.

Part I

Representations of disjuncture

Antithetical responses to resistance in public and private spheres

1 Feminism in a Kolkata context
Assault, appeasement, and assertion in *Dahan*

Rituparno Ghosh's cinematization of *Dahan* (*Crossfire*, 1997), based on the novel by Bengali writer Suchitra Bhattacharya, interrogates the intersections of a woman's molestation in a Kolkata subway station, the retribution she faces from community and husband, and the solidarity offered by another young woman, a radical schoolteacher, who is witness to the incident. At the same time that I trace the feminist overtones characteristic of most of Ghosh's films, I consider the overarching impact of class and privilege, as also masculinity, which stands as counterpoint to the expiatory feminist impulse. However, beyond textual critique, this chapter begins, also, a preliminary discussion of *Dahan*'s possible reception in international and particularly "First World" circles. I draw on Theodor W. Adorno's essay "Transparencies on Film," in which Adorno says, "Benjamin did not elaborate on how deeply some of the categories he postulated for film—exhibition, test—are imbricated with the commodity character which his theory opposes" (182),[1] to examine how *Dahan* (in some versions with English subtitles) enables the undercutting and reversing of both a facile commodification of Indian women and broad assumptions about "Third World" subjects' desire to relocate to countries such as the United States. Despite limited possibilities of reaching the masses as contrasted with the recent proliferation of Bollywood extravaganza in the United States, for instance, *Dahan* is effective in sending out its quiet message of feminist resilience.

In relation to the foci of this study, I analyze, in this chapter, how masculinist impulses in the private sphere, such as in the intimate spaces of the home, as also in sites of the public sphere not marked by large-scale public access, such as in a court-room, can be equated with Tagore's views on the repressive, stagnating aspects of tradition addressed in my Introduction. Further, this chapter traces how incipient or full-fledged feminist actions represented in Ghosh's film show a directorial impetus to bring us non-traditional, unexpected aspects of women's personalities that point to more exciting and dynamic possibilities within Bengali culture itself. Finally, the chapter addresses contradictory responses from agents of the public and private domains to women's resistance in order to exemplify how one contemporary director focuses on this rift.

38 *Representations of disjuncture*

Domestic and economic structures of domination

In the film, the newly married and attractive Romita Chowdhury is assaulted by a group of men on July 29, 1997 as she exits one of the Kolkata Metro (subway) stations with her husband on a rain-washed night. As the men attempt to drive away with her on a motorbike, a young schoolteacher, Srobona Sarkar, rushes to the motorbike and forcefully pulls one of the men off. Romita falls to the ground in the process, and the men ultimately manage to escape. Srobona, herself injured, holds the traumatized Romi and drapes her sari back over her as her husband, Palash lies bleeding on the ground.

The director of the film, Ghosh, foregrounds Srobona's resolve from the beginning. The class ten (tenth grade) students in her school want to acknowledge her courage formally, but she is firm in that she will be unable to attend the event if she has to identify the by then arrested men on that day. Ghosh layers this representation of the unyielding woman through the depiction of Srobona's grandmother,[2] who despite opposition from Srobona's mother and Srobona herself refuses to see her granddaughter's intervention in the assault as anything especially creditable. Her questions—"Is injustice normal? Is it normal not to respond to or protest what is wrong?"[3]—counteract the extensive media coverage that Srobona gets as the singular and daring interceptor.

Ghosh's representation of Romi is more divided. At the same time that she molds herself into the role of acquiescent housewife and then mourns how her marriage is rendered "stale" because of the assault, she resists the post-assault objectification by neighbors and relatives and questions where the self/identity goes under such circumstances. She takes vicarious pleasure in Srobona's agency, inquiring of Palash if like him, she, too, had gone to identify the men in jail.

Palash, however, turns savagely against the woman who rescues his wife, reading Srobona's incisive questions to him—"Did the press contact you? Why won't you talk?"—as twisted. "If she wants to be a heroine," he says to his wife, "why should it be at the expense of causing a scandal?" Yet, it is not just the undaunted female rescuer versus the beaten and ineffective husband polarity that *Dahan* presents to us, outlining the external/feminist "threats" to the mutuality in the marriage established in the opening scenes of the film through Romi and Palash's romantically charged camaraderie.[4]

Other demons stalk both Romi and Srobona's inter-personal relationships, signaling the unmitigated force of "multiple patriarchies" and social and "economic hegemonies" in the Bengali context (Grewal and Kaplan 17). In their introduction in *SCATTERED Hegemonies: Postmodernity and Transnational Feminist Practices*, Inderpal Grewal and Caren Kaplan note:

> Yet we know that there is an imperative need to address the concerns of women around the world in the historicized particularity of their relationship to multiple patriarchies as well as to international economic hegemonies. We seek creative ways to move beyond constructed oppositions without ignoring the histories that have informed these conflicts or the valid

Feminism in a Kolkata context 39

concerns about power relations that have represented or structured the conflicts up to this point. We need to articulate the relationship of gender to scattered hegemonies such as global economic structures, patriarchal nationalisms, "authentic" forms of tradition, local structures of domination, and legal-juridical oppression on multiple levels.

(17)

If we read the Indian institution of marriage as an "'authentic' (form) of tradition," then two scenes from *Dahan* illustrate the ineffectiveness of Romi's resistance to this particular hegemony. In the first of these charged bedroom scenes, Palash recounts to his wife that a colleague had asked him if there was a difference between molestation and rape. He adds that there was speculation that Romi had perhaps had an affair with one of the men before marriage, and he did not know what to believe. The tension initiated in this scene escalates in a scene shortly after when, following an altercation in which Palash objects to Romi standing in the verandah in a nightgown, he then proceeds to imprint his authority and rights on her. This scene is grotesquely reiterative in that it repeats the violence of the assault on Romi, the violence this time clearly shown to the audience, perhaps receiving its sanction because framed by the institution of marriage. In fact, at the close of the scene, Palash reminds Romi that he is her husband, a role ratified by the "ceremony" of marriage.

In *Dahan*, Ghosh does not hesitate to point out, however, that such masculinist manipulation and exploitation exist well beyond the frame of marriage in contemporary Bengal. Together with the insidious effects of the hierarchized Indian class structure, they operate to undermine seriously the opposing feminist impulse that the film captures. In a scene set in what appears to be a five-star hotel, Srobona's fiancé, Tunir, for instance, who is looking to make a job-related move to the United States, says to Srobona that although she had been elevated to celebrity status in Kolkata, by way of her attacking ruffians and hastening to the police, she would be redundant in that regard in California, since American women were capable of protecting themselves. Underlying the irrelevance of this comment, of course, is Tunir's effort to both ridicule and trivialize Srobona's gesture at a time when others, as the film shows us, had remained neutral or departed from the crime scene.[5]

Tunir also pleads with Srobona to not go to court as witness to Romi's assault. Although he predicates his request on his fear that the same men (released on bail) may now attack Srobona, we soon learn that Radheshyam Gupta, the father of one of the accused and a rich, influential promoter (one involved in the construction and sale of apartments in multi-storied complexes) in Kolkata, is a friend of Tunir's finance director at work. Together they negotiate with Tunir to dissuade his girlfriend from appearing in court, promising to facilitate his transfer to the United States. Tunir, generally empathetic of Srobona's assertiveness, in this instance, pleads on behalf of Gupta's son, saying he was repentant, had committed the crime in the heat of the moment, and had spent a week in jail.

40   *Representations of disjuncture*

However, even as Tunir outlines his interests in and obligations to his firm, as well as the incentive offered him, Srobona tells him she must move forward with what she has started. She asks him to give up his job and not consider moving to the United States. "We will stay here," she insists. "They can rape you," he warns. "They will have it done if they go to jail." "Look at me," he entreats Srobona. "Who is more important to you, Romita or I?" "Don't ask to hear," replies Srobona. "You will not like my answer."

Ghosh sets at least two such scenes with Srobona and Tunir in five-star hotels, making it clear to the audience that the milieu is Tunir's choice and suggesting his job is more lucrative than Srobona's one of school teacher. His possible transfer to the United States also hints at the firm's multinational connections. As Grewal and Kaplan would say, Srobona's is a gendered relationship to these "scattered hegemonies" such as "global economic structures" and "local structures of domination." Yet, it is a young, middle-class Bengali woman who unerringly resists Tunir's erotically charged appeals and is not hesitant to speak her mind, despite the possibility of falling out of favor with a fiancé who is more empowered financially and who offers her the possibility of migration to the West.

Silence, "honor," and the patriarchal legal system

What Grewal and Kaplan term "legal juridical oppression" is also very much a force that undermines Srobona's efforts. As I mentioned earlier, the accused are quickly released on bail; the police officer-in-charge, who had shown some integrity of character, is transferred after "pressure from above" (and the new officer-in-charge is hostile to Srobona); and in court, Romita, supposedly coerced by her in-laws, fails to identify the men who had assaulted her, claiming there was little visibility during the incident. In "Embodying the Self: Feminism, Sexual Violence and the Law,"[6] an essay on feminist (and legal) intervention in the area of sexual violence perpetrated on women in India, Nivedita Menon notes:

> Or, as another writer puts it, publicizing private injuries, that is, making them legally cognizable, politicizes them. "The specific legal strategy advocated here is that we publicize and thus politicize those injuries—those intimate intrusions into our lives—which we want to make legally cognizable." Law is seen as the primary legitimating discourse and it is believed therefore, that legal criminalization would socially delegitimise a practice.
>
> (78)

In *Dahan*, Ghosh suggests that it is not only the agents of law that capitulate to financial pressure and show leniency to the accused from the beginning. His directorial intent is to take us inside the Bengali household and markedly masculinist matrimonial structure to show how such "publicizing" of "private injuries," as Menon mentions, is suppressed.

Feminism in a Kolkata context 41

Within such a structure in general, the sexual violation of the housewife, if it is perceived as inflicting shame on the household, must remain private and not be vocalized. Of course, such silencing further facilitates the corrupt practices of the law I refer to in the previous paragraph. Thus, even though sexual assault could and possibly would be charged as a criminal act, "local structures of domination," in this case the patriarchal household that compels Romi to lie about her assailants, also enable the men to go free, resulting in fewer convictions. In a scene earlier to that of Romi's appearance in court, her father-in-law expresses anger that she had accepted the summons, an act that necessitates her presence as victim and witness in the trial. The family's initial intent, then, is to not collaborate in the legal process, in the hope that this non-involvement will preserve whatever "honor" remains and not foreground the housewife's sexuality and its violation. Romi's "disrupting" of such intent leads to her presence in court and subsequent lying. It is more than likely that the family believes this falsehood will help in the men's acquittal; will appease them; and stop them from avenging themselves through future attacks that may further "publicize" the family. It is precisely such publicizing that the household fears.[7]

In the trial scenes of *Dahan*, Srobona's vilification continues unabated. The defense attorney casts aspersions on her character by asking if she often returned home late as she had done on the night of Romi's assault. He attempts to invalidate her evidence by saying she surmises frequently; she had filed no police report on the physical assault on her; the victim herself and her husband could not identify the assailants; and no one else had reported the incident to the police. Romi's falsehood, then, undermines the strength of Srobona's testimony. The men are acquitted.

The defense attorney's attempts to defame Srobona and Romi's husband and his father's efforts to refrain from publicizing her assault, so that no serious retribution for the culprits is possible lead me to address another point in Menon's essay mentioned earlier. Menon says:

> Activists working in the area of sexual violence are increasingly coming to feel that there is a need to adopt strategies other than legal reform. Having conducted a workshop on sexual assault, a lawyer and feminist activist reports that the participants felt that they should shift focus from "mainstream remedies to a sense of justice within." This meant focusing on the victim's sense of self, denied to her by both the rapist and the enforcement agencies. More importantly, they felt they should work towards reinstating her within her community through gender education and awareness.
>
> (95–6)[8]

Although Romi is assaulted and not raped, her family's movement towards silence illustrates that they prioritize their own "honor" over her fractured sense of self. As I have discussed earlier, scenes in the film show that Romi's husband and father-in-law choose this silence, underscoring the patriarchal force within the household. Further, if it is expected that the defense attorney should protect

42   *Representations of disjuncture*

the assailants, what we do not expect are his unnecessary insinuations about Srobona's character. In fact, during the trial sequence, Ghosh depicts Srobona, traumatized by the events in court, as more of a victim of the system than a hero. Thus, it is not just the victim of the assault, but the woman who fights to save her who is also humiliated because of minimal attention to women's identities.[9]

In such a scenario, in which the woman's (or women's) sense of self is denied by assailants, the family, and the legal system, the importance of "gender education" can hardly be overemphasized. While one understands the general futility of such education for men who assault in the first place and the time it would take for the same to infiltrate the largely patriarchal Indian legal system, it could be valuable, in a more immediate sense, for traditional Bengali families such as Romita's. My question, at the moment, is how activists could effectively enter and address similar families, so that within them, women's identities are not totally marginalized and they are seen as occupying more subject positions than that of chaste housewife.[10]

As is evident from my preceding discussion, *Dahan* dramatizes the restrictive force of the masculinist on the one hand and feminist interventions on the other. These impulses are not limited to the public or private spheres exclusively, but can be noticed in either. For instance, although Srobona's feminist act is one that occurs in the public sphere, a feminist consciousness takes root in Romi even as the film depicts her as largely situated in a private, domestic space as a housewife. I will speak a bit more about this in the concluding sections of this chapter. Yet, in a different way, *Dahan* does hold up a clean split, what I call in my Introduction a disjuncture between the public sphere and the private. One of the most powerful apparatuses of the public domain, the media, lauds and, by extension, supports Srobona's courageous act of intervening during Romi's assault. An early series of shots in *Dahan* brings us newspaper headlines such as "teacher rescues young woman" and "teacher saves housewife from molestation."

Yet, this very public espousal of a woman's act of resistance is set in contradistinction to the hostility and rejection Srobona faces from Romi's husband and father-in-law, figures in the film who embody the patriarchal force within the private domain. In one sequence of the film, for instance, when Srobona attempts to contact Romi, Romi's father-in-law does not provide her with a number where his daughter-in-law can be reached; tells her brusquely not to call again regarding the court case in which their family is *not* interested; and hangs up on her.[11] Ghosh uses such contrary responses from agents of the public and private domains, responses to a singular yet atypical act of resistance from a woman to pinpoint that chasm that still exists between the two spheres. Formal approbation from without can be complicated and even negated when the resistor is silenced and humiliated in everyday interactions.

Refuting typical media representations of the "Third World"

I move now to a brief discussion of possible audience reception of *Dahan*. In my Introduction and towards the close of Chapter 5, I address how some of the directors covered in my study work to change audience expectations, both in Bengal and internationally, for viewers of Bengali cinema. In these sections, I focus on their attempts to associate Bengali film with distinctly identifiable characteristics; their innovativeness in transferring poetry and other canonical texts of Bengali literature to film; and their undercutting of global stereotypes of certain figures in Bengali/Indian culture, such as the widow. Similarly in this section of Chapter 1, I show how Ghosh's *Dahan* as also selected films by director Aparna Sen could help to change certain perceptions of Bengali women, not only for a domestic audience but for international and particularly "First World" audiences as well.

It is my fear, that just as my argument focuses considerably on masculinist, class-based, and juridical manipulation in *Dahan*, so also "First World" audiences will tend to foreground such as the "inadequacies" of India, and read Romi's initial interest in Srobona's involvement or Srobona's assertiveness in working against entrenched hegemonies as exceptions. Clearly, Ghosh's canon, which has been positively or negatively critiqued as always feminist, leads us to believe that feminism is the force in the interstices of the film and in its closing scene. But, why am I apprehensive that this will not receive as much attention in discussions of the film in the West as will the essentialism of Indian society and the corruption and bigotry of the legal-juridical system? I attempt to answer this question in the following paragraphs.

In a discussion of the film *Bandit Queen* (1994), which has received some exposure in the United States, Leela Fernandes[12] also focuses on the expectations of the Western audience; how the producers themselves meet such consumer expectations; and how the process inevitably results in the stereotyping of India. Fernandes notes:

> The film highlights particular forms of traditional culture, such as Phoolan Devi's child marriage, caste-based segregation, and passive villagers, which conform well with the Western imagination of oppressive Indian traditions.... The film juxtaposes such hierarchies with an individual view of Phoolan Devi's rebelliousness. While the film casts Phoolan Devi as a heroic woman striving against her culture, the audience is not provided with any context in which to place her actions; her rebelliousness is depicted as an aberration within a society that otherwise consists of active oppressors and passive victims.
>
> (55)

Fernandes also says that in *Bandit Queen*,

> All characters representing the modern Indian nation-state, ranging from policemen to doctors to state government officials, are depicted as violent or corrupt.... [T]he association of such images with corruption and violence clearly projects an Indian modernity marked by a failure to achieve Western standards of progress and democracy.
>
> (55–6)

44   *Representations of disjuncture*

Fernandes relates such cinematic representation to the flow of cultural capital encoded within power relationships between the First and Third Worlds that influences the production and consumption of the film (56). She mentions that the film was directed by an Indian, Shekhar Kapur, but was funded by a British public television channel (50). Even as *Bandit Queen* attempts to produce a "Third-World authenticity," it does so through a representation of "difference as otherness" and "difference as inferiority" (54–5). Fernandes reads such representation as being charged with a political undertone,

> given the historical relationship of colonialism. In the world of *Bandit Queen*, Phoolan Devi is trapped by a nation that has neither been able to discard the remnant of its oppressive cultural traditions nor to live up to the modern democratic institutions and traditions that India inherited through the legacies of colonialism.
>
> (56)

Unlike in *Bandit Queen*, in *Dahan*, Srobona's sustained counteracting of abuse and manipulation is not without context. Her outspoken grandmother's presence is a pivotal one in the film; she receives almost unanimous approbation from her colleagues (as also her students); and she impacts Romi despite the fact that the latter has all the markers of the traditional housewife. And if Ghosh presents the corruption that taints the Bengali juridical system, he makes it clear that Srobona's attempted resistance of that is as much a part of Indian modernity as the corruption itself. Backed by Indian producers, Vijay Agarwal and Kalpana Agarwal, Ghosh has no need to reproduce power differentials between "First" and "Third Worlds" by stereotyping or sensationalizing India for Western audiences. The problem here, then, is not perpetuation, but combating the impact of films such as *Bandit Queen* and progressively reversing a certain kind of audience expectation.

In her essay on *Bandit Queen*, Fernandes further addresses the representation of violence as another strategy of cinematic production to otherize the "Third World." She draws on Rey Chow to note that:

> Mainstream Western representations in film, television, and newspapers have a long history of representing the Third World as a site of violence and disorder—whether in relation to ancient primordial religious, tribal, and ethnic conflicts or revolution or state repression.... Such images link the production and consumption of a "Third-World" authenticity to the spectacle of violence. The violent, disordered, and repressive Third World is thus juxtaposed against the civilized, orderly, and democratic West.
>
> (57)[13]

On September 8, 1998, for instance, ABC's *World News Tonight*, as it covered the celebration of 50 years of Communism in North Korea, referred to that country's nuclear testing and missile launching over Japan as also its

Feminism in a Kolkata context   45

many starving or dead bodies, pointing out that the United States would stop North Korea and help with resources if it could. The news segment concluded with a reference to "a country that starves its people and lies about what it is doing."

I will also argue that mainstream Western media does not necessarily represent such violence in the "Third World" only in conjunction with "ancient primordial religious, tribal, and ethnic conflicts or revolution or state repression." It systematically associates such manifestations of violence with other crises in day-to-day living. On September 7, 1998, for instance, NBC's *Dateline* featured the capsizing of a boat in Indonesia, emphasizing how the two Americans involved, who knew how to swim, tried to rescue the drowning women, whereas the "native" men showed no such inclination in their agitation, pushing the women aside as they tried to return to the boat.

We would do well to remember that a large section of the "First World" audience that watches *Dahan* will have been pre-conditioned by similar media representations of the "Third World." However, if pre-conceptions of India are authenticated by the spectacles of violence and the oppressive corruption depicted in the film, then Ghosh's representation of Srobona is full and credible enough to have any audience consider that there are centers of consciousness in India that systematically counteract such forces. These sensibilities are not necessarily exceptions, and they are not necessarily of Indian subjects who want to relocate to a world that they consider more orderly and thus more conducive to their endeavors.

In a special issue of the journal *Public Culture* devoted to globalization, Arjun Appadurai, in his essay "Grassroots Globalization and the Research Imagination," addresses what he calls "'trait' geographies" and contrasts this with "'process' geographies" (7). In discussing area studies, particularly in the United States, Appadurai claims that thinking about regions "has been driven by conceptions of geographical, civilizational, and cultural coherence that rely on some sort of trait list—of values, languages, material practices, … and the like" (7). He argues that these approaches could be "sophisticated," but "they all tend to see 'areas' as relatively immobile aggregates of traits, with more or less durable historical boundaries and with a unity composed of more or less enduring properties" (Appadurai 7). He calls for a "shift" from such conceptualization to "process geographies," emphasizing that regions are not "fixed geographies marked by pregiven themes" (Appadurai 7–8).

Further on in his essay, Appadurai notes that due to the global flow of "migrants, media" etc., "the means for imagining areas is now itself globally widely distributed" (8). He poses the question—"how does the world look … from other locations (social, cultural, national)?" (Appadurai 8). He mentions that "areal worlds are globally produced …. in the public spheres of many societies" and involve "intellectuals" and "artists" (Appadurai 9). He urges us to take note of such activities and persons, so that our notion of "areas" is not limited to pre-determined "world pictures." He argues that the "potential payoff is a critical dialogue between world pictures" (Appadurai 9).

46 *Representations of disjuncture*

The directors covered in this study are public intellectuals of West Bengal who have repeatedly brought us films in the late twentieth and early twenty-first century that help audiences, both national and international, deconstruct pre-formed notions of (the Indian) woman. They are a group of artists who by giving us "pictures" of Bengali women from the contemporary space of Bengal itself facilitate the conceptual move from "trait geographies" to "process geographies," undoing the easy equating of "areas" with "relatively immobile aggregates of traits." This is one way in which their work is dynamic and merits wide circulation in countries other than their own, both for purposes of entertainment and education.

In countries of the "First World," a film such as *Dahan* can work to change audience expectations that have, to a considerable degree, been shaped by mainstream film and media and abetted by the financial power of Western producers who frequently reproduce the "First World–Third World" hierarchy in cinematic representation. However, minimal distribution and circulation of such films in the West can also pose a problem. Unlike the extensive showings and reproductions, via video and DVD, of popular Indian (read mostly Bollywood) films in the United States, *Dahan's* circulation has been limited, even when contrasted with films such as *Bandit Queen* or *Monsoon Wedding*, which, in themselves, are not of the Bollywood genre. I, myself, saw the special screening organized at a Convention for Bengalis in Atlanta in July 2002,[14] and although reproductions are available, they are difficult to locate even in Indian stores in the United States. One reason, of course, could be that Bengali is more of a peripheral language as compared to Hindi, and the immigrant audience, itself, for *Dahan* would be limited. (In this regard, I am thinking exclusively of an Indian immigrant audience in the United States and not, necessarily, a Bangladeshi immigrant one, who, in general and understandably, are more drawn to films produced in Bangladesh.) However, it is by now a known truth that Bollywood films in the United States are not just consumed by Hindi-speaking audiences. By extension, one could argue that *Dahan's* audience need not necessarily be a Bengali one.

We need only consider a few of the comments from an established film critic to evaluate the impact of Bollywood cinema in the United States at the beginning of the twenty-first century. Richard Corliss's June 2003 article for *Time* is titled "That Old Feeling: Bollywood Fever," and the following explanatory sentence reads, "Richard Corliss rekindles his obsession with the seductive madness of Indian musicals."[15] Corliss begins the article with, "It was a delirium, so in retrospect some of the details are hazy, but this I clearly recall: for four months last year I was in the grip of Bollywood fever." He continues,

I'm not the only American of non-Indian descent who's caught the jolly folly of Bollywood. A few other critic types, notably the trend-setting, retrospective-begetting David Chute, have found in Indian-pop cinema some of the same exuberance and craft they earlier detected in Hong Kong movies.

As regards the spreading of "Bollywood fever" and his role in it, Corliss says,

> Now Bollywood has eyes to conquer the firangis—Hindi for "foreigners."
> US viewers may have seen fragments of Bollywood films at their local
> Indian restaurants, which often have a video playing for atmosphere; I know
> one gourmand who chooses her Indian restaurants based on the films shown
> there.... But can the real thing make it here? Can Americans open up to the
> real Bollywood? They will if I have anything to do with it.[16]

Corliss seems determined to facilitate further popularizing of Bollywood films, no matter that they make him delirious and feverish. After his categorical declaration of intent, he attempts to explain to the as yet uninitiated American viewer the "divine madness that is Bollywood," of course resorting to an American example for clarification:

> The Bollywood masala—savory cultural stew—restores melodrama to its
> Greek-tragedy and Italian-opera roots: melody-drama, in which emotions
> too deep to be spoken must be sung. Imagine Julia Roberts in "Erin Brocko-
> vich" [sic] dancing around the utility company's lawyers while lip-synching
> a tune sung by Faith Hill, and you have a hint of the divine madness that is
> Bollywood.[17]

A different kind of woman

Such Eastern lure that renders the viewer feverish and drives him to the edge of insanity is, of course, absent in *Dahan*. And neither one of its "heroines" has any time to sing or dance. In the film's last scene, we learn that Srobona's wedding date with Tunir is set, and yet she verbalizes her fears regarding entering into matrimony with someone who had succumbed to manipulative coercions, and decides to return home alone from visiting her grandmother, without waiting for Tunir. The scene shows her walking away from us, but the voice-over is that of Romita who has decided to visit her sister in Canada, also alone, hoping to pursue a course of study or find a job there, claiming "let my relationships here remain as they are for the moment."

Of course, it is relevant to mention that Ghosh had a context to draw from here—specifically films such as *Paroma* (*The Ultimate Woman*, 1984) directed by Aparna Sen. In a feminist-reform genre film such as *Paroma*, Sen squarely foregrounded for the Bengali film-going public a housewife's erotic desires, but also her distinctly individualized memories, rights, and unique gifts. Rahul, a much younger man and professional photographer visiting from the United States and with whom the eponymous Paroma has a passionate affair, is the figure who draws her out of the private sphere of endless domestic chores that she has lived in as a married woman and into the public realm of the city. Although at this point in the film, Paroma is not a working woman, as Srobona is in *Dahan*, and therefore not an active participant in the public domain, Rahul encourages her to take her time in enjoying the sites and views of Kolkata.

48 *Representations of disjuncture*

In this regard, a particularly significant sequence is one in which Paroma and Rahul look at the city of Kolkata. Sen uses high-angle, panoramic shots to capture the city spread out beneath the couple in its infinite potential. Rahul says to Paroma, "Look, your city. Have you ever seen it in this way?"[18] This prompts Paroma to recite a poem by Premendra Mitra with the words "my city"[19] as she looks slowly at Kolkata through the lens of one of Rahul's cameras. The camera for the sequence itself tracks from left to right, continuing to give us high-angle shots of Kolkata, as the poem details how the city suddenly descended to the river and the merchant-boats in its mud-caked feet and also how it looked out through the eyes of dust-covered leaves, eyes dimmed by much smoke. The last line recited by Paroma is "My city has forgotten the original and ultimate verse of its life."[20]

It is easy for the spectator to equate these lines with Paroma herself, with the image of merchant-boats evoking the idea of exchange and relatable to her "transaction" through marriage.[21] The dimming of the city's vision suggests the limiting of her perspective, daily immersed in domesticity in the private sphere. If one function of high-angle shots is to suggest the vulnerability of the subject, then these shots could very well imply not the city's, but Paroma's own diminution, caught in the many responsibilities of marriage. When Rahul says confidently that she must love reading poetry, Paroma responds that she used to, but today it is irrelevant to people what she loved or did not love. Like the city, she has relinquished, if not forgotten, these pleasures of her life.

While Rahul pulls Paroma out into the public realm, her friend Shila, who runs a school for disabled children, and which role is played by director Aparna Sen herself, consolidates her position in it by motivating her to apply for a job. Earlier in the film, Shila encourages Paroma to consider just how much she needed the romantic relationship with Rahul for her own validation. The Shila–Paroma duo in this film is very possibly one model for Ghosh's Srobona–Romita duo in *Dahan*. In each case, the pairing represents the feminist impulse against the restrictive masculinist in the private sphere. Other than all the censure Paroma takes at the end of the film for her affair, her husband cannot understand why she decides to go out and work when she is "Bhaskar Chowdhury's wife"; he has the employment he has; and can easily increase the spending money she needs. Paroma's imminent entry into the public domain at the end of the film corresponds to Romita's leaving the private sphere for Canada and a possible job at the end of Rituparno Ghosh's *Dahan*.

Since it is well-known in Bengali film circles that Ghosh and Sen were friends and mutually inspired by each other's ideas, it is appropriate to mention Sen's film *Paromitar Ek Din* (*House of Memories*, 2000). This once again brought before audiences the strong friendship and bond between two women, and charted one of these women's movement out from a prescriptive, patriarchal private realm to the public domain of work and self-affirmation. In this film, Paromita, initially the traditional acquiescent housewife, not only takes a job at an advertisement agency suggested by the man attracted to her, but also fearlessly leaves her repressive, meaningless first marriage and the house of her in-laws to marry her lover.

Feminism in a Kolkata context 49

What is even more interesting about this film, however, is that the woman she develops the friendship with is her mother-in-law from her first marriage, Sanaka, another role played by director Sen herself. Sanaka is confined in a marriage in which she feels no emotional connection to her husband. By her own aggrieved admission to her daughter-in-law, she is totally entrapped in the domestic realm, largely because she has to tend ceaselessly to her grown but disabled daughter. Paromita draws her mother-in-law out into the public sphere, taking her with her to a school for disabled children that her own son attends; for shopping; and to a restaurant.

Sen brings us a rather unusual representation of women's cross-generational mutuality not only in the restaurant sequence, where Paromita encourages her widowed mother-in-law to eat fish and Sanaka agrees, but also in other sequences where the audience understands or Sanaka explicitly states that she has never objected to Paromita's relationship with her lover.[22] Although Sanaka, in one of the last sequences of the film, tells Paromita that she realized soon after the marriage that there was "no glue"[23] between her son and daughter-in-law, she is also aware that he tends to be crude and is verbally abusive.

A singularly striking aspect of *Paromitar Ek Din* is that the main reason Sanaka lashes out at Paromita prior to her departure from her in-laws' house is that she will be left alone and abandoned to the sphere of the domestic. Sen captures beautifully the older woman's fear of being relegated once more to the private realm, and indicates how much she valued moving out of it with the help of her daughter-in-law. Here, Sen's film helps substantiate my argument that certain directors of Bengali cinema are clearly invested in representing women as rejecting aspects of a restrictive tradition and embodying the shifting, dynamic possibilities of a culture. While *Paroma* and *Dahan* bring us such possibilities in the figures of younger women, Sen's *Paromitar Ek Din* moves a step further, dramatizing how openness to such change works across generations.[24]

It is my hope, and here, I go back to Adorno's terms from Benjamin— "exhibition," "test"—that if Bollywood films, as also to some extent films such as *Bandit Queen* in the "First World," are a part of the exhibition/spectacle that continues to conveniently commodify India for Western audiences, films such as *Dahan, Paroma, Paromitar Ek Din,* and others will serve as the test in an attempt to work against such tendencies. To this end, serious and committed directors of Bengali cinema must work to ensure better distribution and showing of these films. If not, we are faced with an audience watching sometimes half-naked, sometimes vulnerable (and sometimes both) Indian women rescued from corrupt villains by valiant men,[25] a "renunciation," as Adorno calls it in the same essay, "Transparencies on Film," "of all interference with the syrupy substance of the current idiom, and, as a result, with the reified consciousness of the audience" (185).[26]

In the above essay, Adorno speaks of how the "Oberhauseners attacked the nearly sixty-year-old trash production of the [German] film industry with the epithet 'Daddy's Cinema'" (178).[27] He continues that this cinema produces what the consumers want or rather insidiously encourages them never to want

50 *Representations of disjuncture*

something different from what they are being given. By repeatedly pandering to the "reified consciousness" of the spectators, the "culture industry" prevents the consumers from being critical thinkers. He concludes that in this sense, the "culture industry is … the projection of the will of those in control onto their victims" (Adorno 185).[28] Further, in "Transparencies," Adorno claims that the "liberated film would have to wrest its *a priori* collectivity from the mechanisms of unconscious and irrational influence and enlist this collectivity in the service of emancipatory intentions" (183–4).[29]

We clearly see such non-conformist, individualized work in Bengali cinema in the period covered by this study. At the turn of the twenty-first century, Sen and Ghosh bring to Bengali film multiple representations of the female duo, one of whom inspires or helps the other leave the private domain and enter the public. A cluster of such films helps demonstrate to Bengali and global audiences of Bengali cinema that these women are not necessarily exceptions. As mentioned earlier in this chapter, Leela Fernandes alerts us to how a film such as *Bandit Queen* can feed Western audiences' expectations about the "exceptional" nature of an Indian woman's rebelliousness; "active oppressors" and "passive victims" in Indian society; and daily eruptions of violence. However, films made by Ghosh and Sen in Bengal around the same time as or even a decade before *Bandit Queen* illustrate reiteratively that women act as agents, moving out of the private sphere into the public, and have the courage to resist and stand up against forms of masculinist violence and obliviousness. What is ultimately desirable is a world audience's association of Bengali (and Indian) feature films with such feminist impulses.

What I have tried to show in this chapter is how contemporary Bengali directors such as Ghosh (and of course Sen) bring us the rift between repressive, debilitating forms of tradition and possibilities within a culture that could eventually effect a broader conceptual shift. In *Dahan*, these antithetical tendencies are embodied in the masculinist and the feminist respectively. The chapter also addresses a different kind of chasm that exists between public and private spheres by reason of which validation from the former and rejection from the latter can leave a feminist feeling confused and depleted.

My 2009 interviews of feminist activists in Kolkata revealed that even 12 years after *Dahan*'s release, sexual assault of women is often followed by silence, either on the part of the victim's family or the victim herself, or both.[30] One of the more heartening features of these discussions was that two of these interviewees, Rajashri Dasgupta and Soma Marik, spoke of the University Grants Commission in India, which, since 1986, has funded Women's Studies programs in colleges and universities and continues to promote the development of this area of study through various initiatives. Dasgupta further mentioned *Ebong Alap*, a group in which she is involved, which through workshops, seeks to educate students on a range of issues, one being violence against women. These workshops are mostly targeted at students who live outside the urban metropolis of Kolkata. Dasgupta noted that students are very receptive to the group's work and eager to discuss issues surrounding sex and sexuality.

Feminism in a Kolkata context 51

I suggest here that the pioneering work of directors such as Ghosh in *Dahan* parallels the efforts of governmental bodies, such as the UGC, and the commitment of women's rights activists in Kolkata to emphasize women's progressively changing roles and self-perceptions within Indian or Bengali culture. Thus, as I argue in my Introduction, the filmic rhetoric of a number of contemporary Bengali directors such as Ghosh foregrounds a shifting, dynamic cultural terrain in which women reject forms of tradition that stigmatize or stifle them. In light of this, it is contextually significant that at the close of *Dahan*, Srobona walks away alone, refusing to wait for her fiancé, and Romi relinquishes the traditional ties of the housewife to move to Canada, even if temporarily. Additionally, Romi's voiceover that we hear as Srobona walks away effects an on-screen fusion of the protagonists, Ghosh ending the film with an intangible bond between the two women, even if they have been driven apart by family and in the spotlight of the patriarchal juridical system. So, while the director presents one kind of rupture in the relationship of the women, he underscores another association, a suggested association in understanding. By ending *Dahan* with the suggestion of an unexpected synchronicity in the thought processes of a housewife and a career-woman, Ghosh points to the possibility of change in women's consciousness across the socio-cultural spectrum.

Notes

1 In *The Culture Industry: Selected Essays on Mass Culture*. Ed. and introd. J.M. Bernstein. London: Routledge, 1991. 178–86.
2 In *Dahan*, this role is played by Suchitra Mitra, a leading exponent of Rabindranath Tagore's songs in Kolkata. Mitra herself was a political activist in her youth. She passed away on January 3, 2011.
3 All translation of dialogue from the film is mine.
4 Much of Romi and Palash's playful dialogue takes place as they are shopping for clothes in the New Market area of Kolkata, a section known for its variety of shops.

   Dahan (both print text and film) is based on a real-life incident. Somdatta Mandal, in "Of 'Women' and 'Relationships' in Contemporary Bengali Cinema," alerts us to the fact that the journalist, Ananya Chatterjee, who helped the couple in actuality protested the negative depiction of the husband in Ghosh's film. In reality, the man stood by the woman all through and married her. They were college students when the assault happened.
5 Ghosh shows us at least three instances, during the attack and molestation sequence, of groups of people in taxis, cars, and autotaxis who choose to remain uninvolved and leave the crime scene.
6 In *Subaltern Studies XI: Community, Gender, and Violence*. Eds. Partha Chatterjee and Pradeep Jeganathan. New York: Columbia UP, 2000. 66–105.
7 In this regard, I was fortunate to be able to interview Madhuchhanda Karlekar, Rajashri Dasgupta, and Soma Marik, all activists for women's rights, in Kolkata in 2009. In response to my questions on notions of "honor" and the need to maintain silence within households in which women had been sexually assaulted, Karlekar and Dasgupta noted that women were much more ready to talk if the "sex" was taken out of a discussion of violence perpetrated against them. Karlekar added that the thought of "losing face" prevailed more in middle-class households. So at times, the activist's efforts may "boomerang," with the middle-class woman whom she tried to help

52 *Representations of disjuncture*

asking why she proceeded so fast. Marik, also speaking of contemporary cases, observed that there was a general tendency towards silence (in victims or their families) after incidents of sexual assault against girls/women. She addressed a range of reasons for this silence: fear in girls that their mobility would be taken away; a communication gap with family members; pressure from family to hush up the incident even when the victim was ready to go to court.

8 Menon, "Embodying the Self."

9 The interviews mentioned in Note 7 also helped me understand better current conservative perceptions (in India) about the one who intervenes, such as Srobona in *Dahan*, or the female activist. According to Dasgupta, the activist signifies one who questions, one who will not take the status quo. Unfortunately, she is also the one who often takes the bad-mouthing, sometimes activists being pejoratively called "*balkattis*" ("those who cut their hair" (in imitation of Western women)). Whenever the woman protests, whenever she finds something to discredit in the socio-cultural construct, whenever she stands beside the victim and mobilizes forces to help her, it is possible that she may become the center of attack and be subjected to character assassination (as was Srobona in *Dahan*), even today (Dasgupta). Both Karlekar and Dasgupta observed, however, that the encouraging aspect was that it was now no longer the lone woman (the victim) going to court, but increasingly, a community of protesters. Further, Karlekar added that empowerment was not necessarily getting help from women activists with formal education: across class lines, women were forming self-help groups; police took notice of these groups; and it was easier to file First Investigative Reports after incidents of assault.

Marik felt that the female activist was still more of a marginal figure, at times without familial support or encouragement from the workplace if she was also a working woman. A wonderful suggestion from Marik was that victims of sexual assault should be encouraged to become members of groups that fought for women's rights so they had a sense of solidarity and fought back. She suggested that non-governmental organizations, for instance, could also help form groups with such victims.

10 In *Unthinking Eurocentrism: Multiculturalism and the Media* (London: Routledge, 1994), Ella Shohat and Robert Stam make a point about the role of film in such contexts:

> The minoritarian/Third World films of the 1980s and 1990s ... do not so much reject the "nation" as interrogate its repressions and limits. While often embedded in the autobiographical, they are not always narrated in the first person, nor are they "merely" personal; rather, the boundaries between the personal and the communal, like the generic boundaries between documentary and fiction, are constantly blurred.... While early Third Worldist films documented alternative histories through archival footage, interviews, testimonials, and historical reconstructions, generally limiting their attention to the public sphere, the films of the 1980s and 1990s use the camera less as revolutionary weapon than as monitor of the gendered and sexualized realms of the personal and the domestic, seen as integral but repressed aspects of collective history.
>
> (288)

Ghosh, even as his film narrates Romi's violation, shifts the focus beyond the merely personal to a growing sense of community or solidarity between certain women. Further, *Dahan* explores different facets of Romi's personality despite the fact that she is situated within a traditional Bengali household.

11 I should point out here that initially in the film, Romi's father-in-law does congratulate and thank Srobona for preserving the "honor" of his daughter-in-law. It is when the incident is highlighted in the media and when the court-case ensues, that he turns against her.

Feminism in a Kolkata context 53

12 Leela Fernandes "Reading 'India's Bandit Queen': A Trans/National Feminist Perspective on the Discrepancies of Representation." In *Haunting Violations: Feminist Criticism and the Crisis of the "Real."* Eds. Wendy S. Hesford and Wendy Kozol. Urbana: U of Illinois P, 2001. 47–75.
13 Fernandes, "Reading 'India's Bandit Queen'." For interesting facts on negotiations between Britain's Channel 4, which produced this film by Shekhar Kapur, and Phoolan Devi as also the English press's attitude towards her when she was elected to Parliament, see Virdi, *Cinematic Imagination,* page 176.
14 This convention, called *Banga Sankskriti Sammelan,* is an annual event, organized by Bengalis in the United States or Canada and held in a different city each year. The organizers invite renowned Kolkata based artists and film directors to the convention, and current Bengali films are screened.
15 In *Time,* June 19, 2003. Online, available at: www.time.com/time/arts/article/0,8599, 459899,00.html.
16 Ibid.
17 Ibid.
18 Translation mine.
19 The words in Bengali are "*amar shohōr.*"
20 Translation mine.
21 For a more detailed discussion of this notion, see my Introduction and Chapter 2.
22 The film presents this relationship as more romantic than sexual before Paromita leaves her in-laws' house to marry again.
23 Translation mine. The original Bengali words are "*ata nei.*"
24 I should mention here that Sanaka's entry into the public realm is not only about her enjoying shopping or eating out. Sen deliberately inserts a sequence in which Sanaka tells Paromita that she would never have known how the dormant talents of disabled children were made to flourish if she had not visited or spent time at their school.
25 This has been a standard theme and/or ending of Bollywood films for several decades now.
26 Adorno, "Transparencies on Film."
27 Ibid.
28 Ibid.
29 Ibid.
30 See Note 7 of this chapter.

References

Adorno, Theodor W. "Transparencies on Film." *The Culture Industry: Selected Essays on Mass Culture.* Ed. and introd. J.M. Bernstein. London: Routledge, 1991. 178–86. Print.
Appadurai, Arjun. "Grassroots Globalization and the Research Imagination." *Public Culture* Special Issue on Globalization. Ed. Arjun Appadurai. 12.1 (2000): 1–19. Print.
Bandit Queen. Dir. Shekhar Kapur. Channel Four Films, 1994. Film.
Corliss, Richard. "That Old Feeling: Bollywood Fever." *Time,* June 19, 2003. Online, available at: www.time.com/time/arts/article/0,8599,459899,00.html. Accessed January 14, 2004. Web.
Dahan (Crossfire). Dir. Rituparno Ghosh. Vijay Agarwal and Kalpana Agarwal. Gee Pee Films Pvt. Ltd., 1997. Film.
Dateline. NBC. 7 Sep. 1998. Television.
Fernandes, Leela. "Reading 'India's Bandit Queen': A Trans/National Feminist Perspective on the Discrepancies of Representation." *Haunting Violations: Feminist Criticism and the Crisis of the "Real."* Eds. Wendy S. Hesford and Wendy Kozol. Urbana: U of Illinois P, 2001. 47–75. Print.

54 Representations of disjuncture

Grewal, Inderpal and Caren Kaplan. "Introduction: Transnational Feminist Practices and Questions of Postmodernity." *SCATTERED Hegemonies: Postmodernity and Transnational Feminist Practices*. Eds. Inderpal Grewal and Caren Kaplan. Minneapolis: U of Minnesota P, 1994. 1–33. Print.

Karlekar, Madhuchhanda and Rajashri Dasgupta. Personal interview. October 3, 2009.

Marik, Soma. Personal interview. October 7, 2009.

Menon, Nivedita. "Embodying the Self: Feminism, Sexual Violence and the Law." *Subaltern Studies XI: Community, Gender, and Violence*. Eds. Partha Chatterjee and Pradeep Jeganathan. New York: Columbia UP, 2000. 66–105. Print.

Monsoon Wedding. Dir. Mira Nair. IFC Productions; Mirabai Films, 2001. Film.

Paroma (The Ultimate Woman). Dir. Aparna Sen. Nirmal Kumar. Usha Enterprises, 1984. Film.

Paromitar Ek Din (House of Memories). Dir. Aparna Sen. Rajesh Agarwal. Suravi, 2000. Film.

Shohat, Ella and Robert Stam. *Unthinking Eurocentrism: Multiculturalism and the Media*. London: Routledge, 1994. Print.

Virdi, Jyotika. *The Cinematic Imagination: Indian Popular Films as Social History*. New Brunswick: Rutgers UP, 2003. Print.

World News Tonight. ABC. September 8, 1998. Television.

2 The impossibility of incestuous love

Woman's captivity and national liberation in *Utsab*

If *Dahan* dramatizes how a marriage structure permeated by the force of patriarchy silences and suppresses a woman assaulted by outsiders, *Utsab* details how "aberrations" within the family are brought under control. This chapter addresses contradictory responses to resistance within the private sphere itself, discussing how one supports and glorifies nationalist struggle, but represses a woman who fights against traditional structures of domination within the domain of "home." Released 53 years after the gaining of Indian independence, Rituparno Ghosh's *Utsab* (*Festival*, 2000) traces possibilities of incest through two successive generations of a single family, not only to convey that what is most true for two women must remain framed in secrecy and silence, but, in my reading, to remind us that paradigms of liberation must be more inclusive. The film's narratives shift easily from those of captivity, subjugation, or conformity, on the one hand, to those of personal mobility or India's national liberation on the other, but not without having us question the grave implications of such directorial juxtapositions. To me, it is also significant that *Utsab* offers its audience these stories of imprisonment or freedom through speech acts of women as they relive these events in memory and articulate them before an other or others.

Unmaking and making in the maternal figure

This chapter addresses the co-presence of antithetical strains in *Utsab* as manifested in individual scenes, sequences, and characters in an attempt to unravel the purpose of such contrast. One of the last scenes of *Utsab* is a love scene between a couple who have been persistently presented in the film as having marital problems. The wife, Keya, is one of two daughters/sisters in the family around which Ghosh's film revolves. As the husband makes love to the wife, he speaks of the annual immersion of the Goddess Durga in the Ganges, a rite that, obviously, returns the clay image of the female deity to the condition of mud and water, elements from which it was originally made.[1] In rhythm with his love-making, and in reference to the immersion, the husband utters the words "construction, deconstruction; construction, deconstruction," but what remains unspoken, although embedded in his thought, is the word "reconstruction," a "reconstruction" that he looks to in this relationship. Such reconstruction of

56 Representations of disjuncture

desire and romance in a lived, day-to-day scenario is impossible for Parul, the other daughter/sister who had felt "incestuous" love for her cousin, Shishir, several years ago. What she reconstructs in the sequence of her explosive narrative in *Utsab* is something to which I will return a little further on in this chapter.

A reconstruction of a different kind of desire may, perhaps, be charted through addressing aspects of the mother's narrative about her husband's commitment to India's struggle for liberation. We learn from this narrative that the father, a fugitive during the nationalist movement, was absent, in phases, from the family, and, of course, he is totally absent as a character in Ghosh's film. The mother's narrativizing of his acts, however, gives them a kind of embodiment, so that even as he is not seen cinematically, her words re-enact his return to the house in a long past Durga Puja. She finds his body burning with fever as she touches him; she learns there is a warrant out for his arrest. He asks for her jewelry (something commonly sold to obtain money for arms during the freedom movement), and she gives almost all, unhesitatingly, before he swims across the pond in the back of the house to disappear once again.

In speaking of the father's commitment to the nationalist cause to Keya, the daughter, the mother mobilizes and reinvigorates this political narrative for the next generation. But what is a key factor in this sequence is how Ghosh utilizes the speech act to show transference in desire. For according to the mother's narrative, even prior to the father's arrival, the ceremonial drums in the background, before the image of the Goddess Durga, on the fourth and final day of worship, play out *"Thakur thakbé kotōkhōn?"* ("How much longer will the goddess remain?"), but the then young mother hears instead, in their iteration, *"bondé mataram"* ("hail motherland").[2] What is deliberately left slippery here is whether the father's unquestionable dedication to nationalism transfers over to the mother or whether Ghosh, through shots of the mother's impassioned verbalization, and thus embodying, of the father's acts presents a different kind of transference: a woman's conceptual re-situating of herself in the realm of the political, provisionally away from the domestic or maternal commitments in which she is grounded.

Of not little significance here, then, is how the woman/mother hears the beating of the drums. The full verbal chant that the drums recreate is *"Thakur thakbé kotōkhōn?/Thakur jabé bishorjōn"* ("How long will the goddess remain?/ The goddess will be immersed"). Played reiteratively on the final day of worship, this beat adumbrates the immersion and, by extension, the annual disintegration of the image of the Mother Goddess. The dialogue in this sequence of the film, however, moves us even further than what this suggests, as the mother notes that the musical foreshadowing of immersion gives over in her mind to a phrase commonly used in the political rhetoric of the day, *"bondé mataram."*[3] In a sense, then, this sequence looks ahead to the love-making scene with its notions of "construction, deconstruction," except here, Ghosh focuses on the woman's imaginative unmaking and making of herself through her verbalization of past political acts. What she gives herself here, perhaps through articulating her own

The impossibility of incestuous love   57

once occluded desire, is a freedom, a mobility to shift from one conceptualization of herself to another less expected one.

What confounds the viewer of *Utsab* then is that this same mother is complicit in silencing and imprisoning her daughter, Parul, within the home. As she lauds her husband's involvement in the freedom movement on one level and exposes, at least for some audiences, her own unrealized desire for fighting for political liberation on another, she remains responsible for repressing and circumscribing romantic desire because it happens to be incestuous. Judith Butler reminds us, in "Quandaries of the Incest Taboo,"[4] that incest is not always a violation. "I do think that there are probably forms of incest that are not necessarily traumatic or which gain their traumatic character by virtue of the consciousness of social shame that they produce" (Butler 157). Together with Parul's brothers, her mother is one agent who converts her romantic experience to a traumatic one. The inclination towards liberating (as in the nation and herself) and the brutally real act of confining converge in the mother to give us a paradoxical character who, other than in scenes following which she reminisces about political acts, is shown in several shots as strangely immobile. Although in the majority of shots, Ghosh situates her in the balcony, a largely open space, this openness that frames her figure seems to be canceled out as the camera closes in on her often troubled expression and inert body.

It is clear that in *Utsab*, the mother, Bhagabati, exemplifies processes of unmaking and making in her identification with the mission of a freedom fighter in India's nationalist struggle. In my reading, Ghosh's presentation of her imaginative transformation of the ceremonial drumbeat into a political message connotes more than just spousal support and love and is also evidence of her investment in matters of the public sphere. In this, she moves beyond the space of a wife and mother as nurturer only. Yet, she is also a figure who helps illustrate another theme of this study: a paradoxical response to revolution and resistance in the public and private domains. As a woman who was both impassioned about India's freedom struggle and in all likelihood would not have been able to engage actively in it if she wanted to because of gendered familial responsibilities, she should have connected with her daughter's need for liberation from dominating constructs of tradition and empathized with the particular difficulties of a woman struggling against such constructs. Bhagabati, however, fails in this regard, unable to offer support in her daughter's attempt at resisting "traditional" power structures within the home even as she is committed to revolution in the public domain.

"Tradition" and the circulation of woman

It is in the balcony, as the two brothers of this family and their wives sit with the mother, that Ghosh also situates Parul's outburst about her confinement. In marked contrast to the cinematic representations of the mother's stillness, Parul's bitter denunciation of her family is captured in shots that highlight her rapid changes of expression and agitated body movements. Yet, what she speaks, or

58 *Representations of disjuncture*

re-enacts through this speech act, is a narrative of captivity and destruction. Unrelentingly, she reminds the family that they shut her up in a room as they threw her cousin, Shishir (also their childhood companion who had received shelter in their home), out of the house. Thus, even as Ghosh makes prominently visible the mobility of Parul's face and body, her narrative speaks the immobilization and freezing of desire, reminding viewers how antithetical strains are woven through the texture of this film. Here, I would also like to go back to Butler who notes, in "Quandaries of the Incest Taboo," "It might, then, be necessary to rethink the prohibition on incest as that which sometimes protects against a violation, and sometimes becomes the very instrument of a violation" (160).[5]

Parul's rights to freedom and love are violated of course in order to keep traditional kinship structures intact. Familiar to many of us is Gayle Rubin's discussion of Claude Lévi-Strauss' *The Elementary Structures of Kinship* in her essay "The Traffic in Women: Notes on the 'Political Economy' of Sex." According to Rubin:

> Lévi-Strauss adds to the theory of primitive reciprocity the idea that marriages are a most basic form of gift exchange, in which it is women who are the most precious of gifts. He argues that the incest taboo should best be understood as a mechanism to insure that such exchanges take place *between* families and *between* groups.
>
> (173)[6]

> If it is women who are being transacted, then it is the men who give and take them who are linked, the woman being a conduit of a relationship rather than a partner to it.... The relations of such a system are such that women are in no position to realize the benefits of their own circulation. As long as the relations specify that men exchange women, it is men who are the beneficiaries of the product of such exchanges—social organization.
>
> (174)[7]

Ghosh's *Utsab*, however, introduces possibilities of a different kind of transaction, other than Parul's arranged marriage, which is referred to as an event in the past, one more pertinent to the immediate present of the film. And it is Shishir, the cousin who was cast out, who returns with the prospect of this new transaction—an offer to the family to buy the house (property), undoubtedly charged with memories of repression, denial, and exclusion for him and Parul. Parul's outburst, which I referred to earlier, begins with a rejoinder to her mother who expresses her wish to invite Shishir for lunch (possibly to discuss further this new transaction), clarifying she would not do so if Parul objected. The daughter's outburst thus begins, "To what objection of mine have you [the family] ever listened?"[8]

If we return to Gayle Rubin's reading of Lévi-Strauss, in which she specifies that "The relations of such a system are such that women are in no position to realize the benefits of their own circulation" (174),[9] it seems that Parul is about

The impossibility of incestuous love 59

to be exploited not once but twice in such a system of circulation. For other than the charge of confinement, she now accuses her family of material greed and opportunism, crying out that they wanted to *bring her forth*, before Shishir, in order to facilitate the finalization of the deal. Her question to her family that concludes this outburst hangs in the air ominously for the audience "If he had been this prosperous materially *then*,[10] would you have been able to cast him out, would you have been able to arrange my marriage elsewhere?"

Thus, in the first instance, after she is enclosed in a room of the family home, Parul's "circulation" through marriage perpetuates a system of "social organization" (Rubin 174),[11] whereas in the second, bringing her forth before her (ex-) lover will, in her perception, hasten an expedient material transaction. However, what is amply clear as regards both the above is that Parul understands the advantages of her own "circulation." Even though it is possible that she exaggerates her family's intentions of "using" her in the context of the film's immediate present, Ghosh depicts her as unafraid to voice her thoughts. While the mother's discourse with the younger daughter, Keya, brings us a narrative that highlights the sentimentalized aspects of a struggle for political liberation[12] or projects a desire that remains dormant in the speaker, Parul's verbal outburst is markedly unsentimental and explicit in its accusations.

Ghosh empowers Parul's character through different cinematic strategies. A slight digression will help elaborate my point here. Towards the end of a difficult essay entitled "Subaltern Studies: Deconstructing Historiography," Gayatri Chakravorty Spivak makes observations similar to the ones I discussed from Rubin. Expanding on the notions of "territoriality," "kinship," and "woman," Spivak notes, "On the simplest possible level, it is evident that notions of kinship are anchored and consolidated by the exchange of women" (217).[13] I should clarify here that in this piece Spivak speaks specifically about subaltern insurgency in India in the context of British colonialism. Nonetheless, the following excerpt is helpful in addressing Parul's character:

> My point is, of course, that through all of these heterogeneous examples of territoriality and the communal mode of power, the figure of the woman, moving from clan to clan, and family to family as daughter/sister and wife/ mother, syntaxes patriarchal continuity even as she is herself drained of proper identity. In this particular area, the continuity of community or history ... is produced on ... the dissimulation of her discontinuity, on the repeated emptying of her meaning as instrument.
>
> (Spivak 220)[14]

Although Spivak and Ghosh focus on different contexts, both interrogate not just the solidifying of masculinist systems, but that such solidification is dependent on negating woman's agency. In using Spivak's ideas in an analysis of *Utsab*, of particular interest to me is the phrase "the dissimulation of her discontinuity." For no matter what the family might feign or wish to believe, Parul does not disappear into her marriage, and Ghosh foregrounds the animated

60 *Representations of disjuncture*

nature of her outburst to underscore, as in several other scenes in the film, that she retains the force of her identity. This animated quality is not only in contrast to her mother's immobility but helps throw into relief the general passivity of her two brothers. No matter that they were complicit in in the past, the brothers come through in the film's present as considerably less forceful than their wives or sister, Parul.

Contradictions within the domain of home and many struggles for liberation

It is no accident that Ghosh also deploys the concept of absence to signal the attenuation of the force of masculinity, at least as this force is operative within the context of his film. We only hear of Parul's husband, for instance, from her, who says he will forcibly stop her from re-visiting the house if he knows of Shishir coming back there, or from their son, who speaks of overhearing the father verbally abusing the mother for her past romantic relationship with her cousin. Yet this husband remains a disembodied presence or, more specifically, an absence. Thus, even though he possesses some kind of brute force, by not allowing him to materialize physically before us on the screen, Ghosh suggests, to quote from Spivak again, his "discontinuity," his general and ultimate irrelevance to the messages of *Utsab*.[15]

While it is true that the absent father, because of his involvement in the nationalist cause, does not elicit a negative response from *Utsab*'s audiences as Parul's husband does, his absence, within the structural scheme of this film, also helps Ghosh convey his messages. For just as it cannot be denied that the freedom movement was imperative for India in the pre-Independence period, so also glorifying one kind of struggle for autonomy while curbing other expressions of selfhood is not a disposition that should go unchallenged. The fact that the father is missing in this film while Parul is very much a vocal presence perhaps indicates that one struggle for liberation, once its objectives have been attained, should make way for others, and, in fact, should help, by example, in mobilizing others.

Unfortunately, Parul's upbraiding of her family clarifies for us that this is not always the case, that the momentum of the nation-wide freedom movement, witnessed over a half a century before the film's release, has not, in the twenty-first century, entered areas of domestic life where certain individuals continue to struggle for self-expression and attempt to bring their own truth out into the open. It is clearly to emphasize this hiatus that Ghosh has Parul articulate one after another the values her family claims the father taught them to cherish—tolerance, forgiveness, sacrifice—and has her indicate that they have not really internalized these values. Thus, the domain of home remains fraught with contradictions for citizens whose desire, in the case of *Utsab*, does not cohere with prescriptive norms.

In a book chapter in which she addresses Chen Kaige's *Temptress Moon*, "The Seductions of Homecoming: *Temptress Moon* and the Question of

The impossibility of incestuous love   61

Origins," Rey Chow explains why for the male protagonist, Zhongliang, "homecoming itself is always (the repetition of) a going astray, a departure that already began some time ago" (38).[16] In this film, the recently orphaned Zhongliang arrives at the house of his sister and brother-in-law and sometime after, is asked by his opium-taking brother-in-law to kiss his sister, who is a willing participant in this process. Zhongliang is in shock, and in her analysis of this particular scene in the film, Chow notes that "(t)he place that is supposed to be a home for the displaced orphan child thus serves, in terms of narrative structure, as the unbearable site of infantile seduction" (32).[17] In *Utsab*, what "incestuous" desire the cousins felt for each other is, of course, not tied to any form of coercion, but the relentless suppression of this desire by family would render any future "homecoming" a complicated process for Parul and Shishir.

For them, "homecoming" would continue to evoke memories not of inclusion but of marginalization and what was prohibited. For me, the most fascinating part of Chow's reading of Chen's film is how she draws together the concept of homecoming with the notion of "going astray." Although, as I point out above, Parul's incestuous relationship is very unlike Zhongliang's forced encounter with incest, for both, returning "home" is a re-enactment in memory of ways of "going astray," whether this was forced or categorized as such by family.

And just as Rey Chow details how Zhongliang, in *Temptress Moon*, later recognizes "a frightful mirror image" of his own incestuous relationship in the relationship of two other characters (36),[18] so also Parul, in *Utsab*, faces (and attempts to undo) the erotic pull felt by her son, Joy, towards his cousin Shompa. The fact that despite her own sense of being betrayed by her family, she is sharply apprehensive and disapproving of a possible incestuous romance in the next generation shows an ossification in her of a conventional way of thinking, a rigidity whose force triumphs over her personal memory of romantic desire.[19] So, even though Ghosh positions Parul's courage and the animated nature of her outburst, as discussed earlier, as foils to the traditional mindset of most of her family, he does not hesitate to portray contradictions within her as well.

Breaking the hold of "tradition" and the "instrument" of transformation

Yet, it is to his credit as director that in *Utsab*, Ghosh does not remain caught in an endless vicious circle where the merits or dynamic traits of one character after another give way to dead-end ways of thinking governed by the dictates of custom. In my mind, it is precisely to avoid such repetition that he moves away from the emotional stalemate implicit in the relationship between Parul and her mother and gestures towards a link between Parul's withheld though still intensely felt emotion for Shishir and her son's more openly expressed attraction for his cousin.

Ghosh makes brilliant use of something frequently a part of his oeuvre, a song by Rabindranath Tagore to suggest a link between the incestuous desire felt by the mother and that felt by the son. This particular song, broadly translated, is

62   *Representations of disjuncture*

Pure, white sails are filled by a slow, sweet breeze/(I) have never seen such (wondrous) rowing/What distant treasure does this (rowing) bring, from what seashore?/The mind wishes to float away,/It wishes to leave behind, on this bank, all one has wanted, all one has received.[20]

Ghosh's filmic language renders this point in the song as crucial for his narrative. It is being sung by Shompa, the cousin who is the focus of Joy's romantic interest, as he stands intimately close behind her, arms on either side of her body, face gazing down intensely into her face. But this scene, with the younger couple at center, as also the music fade away; and as we hear rather indistinctly the song—"Incessant, the rains fall behind, the thunder calls intermittently,/A ray of sunshine, breaking through scattered clouds, falls on the face"—heard more distinctly are footsteps approaching the house as Parul stands with her back to us lighting an earthen oil lamp. "Who (is it)?" she asks.[21] "I'm Shishir," comes the reply as the viewer sees him for the first time towards the very end of the film. "I left my sunglasses behind this morning."[22] "I know. They are upstairs.... I'll send them down," says Parul.

Ghosh keeps the last of the song in the background as Parul and Shishir speak about Joy, and she asks if he would go upstairs to see her son. The song concludes, "Who are you oh boatman, the sum of whose laughter and tears?/My mind wonders endlessly./How will you tune your instrument today, what *mantra* will be sung?" What Parul also says, in this one conversation with Shishir that the audience is able to hear, is "Please don't tell anyone that you saw me." "Let it be, then," replies Shishir, preparing to walk away without his sunglasses. "Let it be," says Parul. Yet, they use the same words for different reasons, Parul to keep their coincidental meeting secret and Shishir because he is tired of such covertness. In this way, even though he is long married to another woman and has a teenage daughter with her, Ghosh draws Shishir close to the younger couple, Joy and Shompa, who are far more daring in keeping each other's company, even when surrounded by family. Further, several scenes in *Utsab* make the erotic attraction between them explicit for the viewer as when Joy grabs Shompa's foot or says he wants to hold her hand openly, unlike many years ago in a darkened planetarium where, in the company of family, he held it secretly.[23]

Shishir's rejection of Parul's plea for secrecy and silence may very well be a controlled expression of his frustration at what he has kept buried through the years, what, in the manner of Joy and Shompa, he would have liked to express. It is the playing field of romantic and erotic desire that Ghosh brings back at the end of *Utsab* to forge a link between the two generations. How, then, is Parul linked to her son? When the expression or consummation of desire has been forbidden one generation, pleasure from only what is possible, in this case the verbal, must suffice. One impression we have of Parul in the film is as a prohibitive figure in the relationship of her son and Shompa. Yet, the image of Parul we come away with at the end of her meeting with Shishir, and close to the end of the film, is of a woman suffused with pleasure, a pleasure not very different from that which Joy experienced in Shompa's company.

The impossibility of incestuous love 63

Here, it is necessary to address, even if briefly, Parul and Shishir's last words together. Before he leaves, Shishir says to Parul, "I enjoyed the French toast, the tea you made this morning." "Did you come back all this way to tell me this?" asks Parul. Shishir nods slowly. "Are you happy?" he inquires. Parul looks at him quietly before he walks away. Parul's question here, "Did you come back all this way to tell me this?" embodies not just her hope, but his, in the process of his return, as well. For Shishir's return has nothing to do with the material transaction he is negotiating with the family. Apparently, it has to do with some-thing he left behind in the morning—his sunglasses—but something he also chooses to go back without.[24] More likely, it is a return for something he left behind at the house many years ago; a return whose possible outcome he does not know but one undertaken in hope.

If this is the case, then Tagore's song, although sung by Shompa, signifies more poignantly the predicament of the older couple than the younger at this point in *Utsab*.[25] Even other than phrases such as "what distant treasure" or lines such as "[a] ray of sunshine, breaking through scattered clouds, falls on the face," the concluding line of the song, "[h]ow will you tune your instrument today, what *mantra* will be sung?" suggests more pointedly the mindset of Shishir and Parul, I will argue, than that of Joy and Shompa.[26] I have already discussed above the uncertainty of outcome that marks Shishir's return. If we go back to Ghosh's representation of Parul's sense of pleasure at the end of this sequence, then the sequence can be read as signaling the return, late in life, of something that was once forbidden but now has the potential to transform. Once Shishir has conveyed his message to her, Parul can choose the "*mantra*" to be "sung."

On the images of confinement that were evoked previously by Parul's out-burst and that lurk in our minds as viewers, Ghosh now superimposes actual images of space and mobility. As Shishir walks away from the camera, the shot transforms into a top angle one. Parul's older sister-in-law, who has been empa-thetic to her past romance, stands watching her and Shishir from the upper level balcony of the house. Ghosh keeps her in the foreground, while the shot, also changing to a wide one, gives us a smaller figure of Parul behind her, as she gazes at a departing Shishir walking down the long entrance-way to the house. Although Parul stands still here, there is no sense of arrested movement, as in several shots of her mother, and the viewer feels her moving with Shishir in her imagination. This return, of her lover from the past, is hers to do with as she pleases, an "instrument" only she can, and should, "tune" herself.[27] Ghosh sug-gests the magnitude of this possibility by framing Parul, in this shot, by space that is both expansive and multi-leveled.

He gives us in Parul a character who has been confined and subjugated by a "normative" and patriarchal household and forced to enter the institution of arranged marriage. But perhaps more importantly, he gives us here a character for whom, in youth, no possibilities could come into play at the site of desire. Although in his 2009 interview with me, in a reference to the Parul–Shishir sequence in *Utsab*, Ghosh spoke of it as "their story of one evening," I read it as

64 *Representations of disjuncture*

much more integrally connected to the thematic and ideological concerns manifest in his canon. Even other than the point on pleasure mentioned above, by positioning Parul as contemplative spectator looking down the path of her ex-lover's departure, Ghosh aligns our gaze with hers in a different way than in the rest of *Utsab*.

For at the end of this film, we no longer imagine her as merely caught in a post-marriage space subject to verbal abuse. Even though she takes no action, her perspective and gazing in this long shot enable the viewer to move out with her from such spaces of confinement, whether pre or post-marriage, and look with her at the possibilities offered by imagination. I will add that in my view, Ghosh also offers us the option of re-situating her at the site of desire. Herein, this suggestive yet clearly forceful sequence in *Utsab* connects to his broader objectives regarding the representation of women and to one of the major themes of my study: how selected contemporary directors of Bengali cinema dramatize processes of unmaking and making in women. In this particular instance, since action is minimized and seeing underscored in a sustained way towards the end of the sequence, the spectator is almost immediately drawn in into this process of imaginative unmaking and making as well.

Thus Parul, a character we almost ineluctably associate with her memory of captivity, is presented towards the end of *Utsab* as liberated in imagination, whereas the mother, Bhagabati, whom "time has taught the value of independence,"[28] is largely shown as a static, immobile figure. Yet, as I argue earlier in this chapter, the film is rife with such contraries, these being an integral part of Ghosh's cinematic message in *Utsab*.

A freedom incomplete

For although India gained political independence from the British in 1947, the work of liberation, within the country itself, remains incomplete. This work, *Utsab* suggests, needs to be expanded to include situations in the realm of private life, an area in which repression takes hold reiteratively. Perhaps this is one reason Rituparno Ghosh traces the potential of incestuous romance as also its repression through two successive generations. And if the family in *Utsab* is paradigmatic of the nation, then the film posits that such romance is not a sporadic phenomenon in the cultural fabric. Yet, the knowledge of its existence incites considerable conflict within certain spaces, such as the nuclear or extended family. As in one of his preceding films—*Dahan*—in *Utsab*, Ghosh uses cinema to probe into these cultural spaces temporarily threatened by a "crisis"; explores the tensions inherent in them; and invites us to consider the legitimacy of such dynamics.

With regards to cross-generational desire and possibilities of the "incestuous," a more muted and lighter treatment of the issues is seen in *Titli* (*The First Monsoon Day*, 2002), a Ghosh film following shortly after *Utsab*. Titli, the adolescent girl after whom the film is named, claims she wants to marry the Mumbai film star Rohit, with whom she is obsessed. Coincidentally, while traveling

The impossibility of incestuous love 65

through the mountains to pick up her father,[29] Titli and her mother, Urmila, give a ride to Rohit, and Titli discovers there had been a romantic relationship in the past between her mother and the star of her dreams.

While portraying the tension in family dynamics following Titli's discovery, Ghosh also uses the possibility of the incestuous in this film to show precisely how desire is *not* articulated in a certain generation and class of Bengali women. Thus, the daughter's desire in *Titli* becomes a vehicle for the mother to express the desire she has not verbalized for years. In a sequence in which Urmila and Rohit are portrayed together as Titli and the family's driver go on quick errands, Rohit asks Urmila if she herself watches his films. This is in response to Urmila's comment that both her daughter and husband watch his films regularly. "I watch Titli," responds Urmila.

> I gaze at her as long as she looks at you. Her face changes when you appear on screen. When the villain beats you up, she chews gum loudly. When you embrace your heroine, her face fills with anger and jealousy. I watch everything.[30]

Rohit inquires if Urmila feels jealous. She does not respond, but comes up with the unexpected disclosure that her daughter wants to marry him. The couple laughs loudly at this.

Once again, as in *Utsab*, Ghosh uses the more unreserved expression of desire in a member of the succeeding generation to capture the unexpressed though strong desire in a woman from the previous generation. In *Titli*, Urmila is also marked as a highly literate, middle to upper-middle class Bengali woman who came of age in the mid- to late 1960s.[31] As is usual for such women in Bengali culture, she is capable of reciting poetry effortlessly and rendering Tagore's songs movingly. Ghosh represents her as using these media to subtly convey her emotions to Rohit as well.

Yet, although much more content in her marriage than Parul in *Utsab*, displacement is not the only way Urmila vocalizes her emotions for her past lover in *Titli*. Particularly evocative is a sequence towards the end of the film when the daughter asks the mother why she never told her or her father about her emotions for Rohit. Ghosh uses a blown-up picture of the star in the background as Urmila and Titli talk in this sequence. More than once, the mother is situated between the picture on the wall and the daughter on her bed. As Urmila rises to close Titli's window through which rain is pouring into her room, her shawl falls partly off, revealing her bare back to her daughter.[32] The camera moves back and forth between shots of Urmila and Titli, capturing the daughter's tormented expression at the recognition of the mother's body as an object of erotic desire. The mother is sharply illuminated by a flash of lightning as she suddenly sees her own body, now from her daughter's perspective, and quickly pulls the shawl over it.

While in Urmila's conversation with Rohit addressed above, she placed her daughter's body and expressions center-stage and conveyed unarticulated

66 *Representations of disjuncture*

emotions through her, in this later sequence, Ghosh foregrounds the mother's body and past, as Titli comes to terms with the reality of what had been between Urmila and Rohit. In response to Titli's suspicious comments about Urmila's current feelings for Rohit, the mother squarely puts the daughter in her place. "This is not a Hindi film, Titli, in which you will force me to be your rival," says Urmila.[33] "If I had married him, you could have been his daughter. Do you still feel like having a romance with him?"[34] Subsequently, she lies to her daughter, saying that although she did not mention to Rohit Titli's desire to marry him, it would be terribly embarrassing if she had done so. This lie, told unflinchingly, is a form of betrayal of the mother–daughter trust. The fact that Urmila had, indeed, revealed her daughter's wish indicates a degree of intimacy she still shares with Rohit that remains hidden from Titli. Ghosh deliberately accords the housewife this privilege, as also the upper hand, as Urmila tells Titli that hers is not the desire of a fan for a star, but the story of an ordinary girl who loved an ordinary boy.

Urmila's assertiveness, an assertiveness that almost borders on aggression, in this sequence comes as a surprise to the spectator considering how Ghosh presents her as the mild-mannered housewife all through and how he prioritizes the mother–daughter dyad over everything else at the end of the film.[35] The dismissal of the daughter's desire as idol-worship and Urmila's explanation that a socio-economic hiatus and Rohit's film career-oriented "craziness" prevented them from getting married give the mother's emotional claim on Rohit much more credibility.[36] In fact, by the end of the sequence, Urmila blames Titli for not letting her forget, saying she had played film after film of Rohit's in the house and kept his image and voice alive at all times for Urmila.

As mentioned in my Introduction, Goutam Ghose and Buddhadeb Dasgupta undo traditional conceptions of motherhood in selected films such as *Dekha* and *Mondo Meyer Upakhyan*. I address such representations at greater length in Chapters 3 and 6 respectively. In *Titli*, Rituparno Ghosh brings us a sequence in which Urmila briefly steps out of her role as conventional, accommodating housewife and always agreeable, always relenting mother. She de-prioritizes her teenage daughter's star-worship; addresses bluntly the reality of her past relationship with Rohit; and lies to her daughter about her shared secret with him. The portrayal of such assertiveness and the right of concealment, in sharp contrast to how Urmila is represented in the rest of *Titli*, demonstrates how Ghosh, like Ghose and Dasgupta, is invested in the theme of rupture in his representation of women characters, one of the four themes covered by my study.

The possibility of "incest" and transgressive desire that repeats across generations and time are also present in one of Ghosh's later films—*Abohomaan*. As mentioned in one of the notes to my Introduction, this film captures the development of an extra-marital romance for Aniket with the female lead of the film he is directing—Srimati. The latter plays the role of Nõtee Binodini, a famed nineteenth-century actress and also prostitute, in his film. Aniket is significantly older than Srimati, and following his death Ghosh brings us two sequences that suggest his son, Apratim's, desire for Srimati and vice versa.

The impossibility of incestuous love 67

Ghosh adds to the complexity of the dynamics in the first sequence by blurring distinctions between truth and falsehood. Srimati mentions to Apratim, when he visits her, that his father had considered re-makes of noted Bengali classics such as *Nishi Padma* and *Debdas*.[37] Yet, she claims that Aniket planned to cast his wife (Apratim's mother and a former actress) in the role of the prostitute, Pushpa, in the first film and as the courtesan, Chandramukhi, in the latter. She says that in *Debdas*, she would have played Parboti, the hero's life-long love interest. Any discerning spectator would question the validity of Srimati's pronouncements here, since Aniket is absent and Srimati could be voicing latent wishes. What concludes the sequence, however, leading from Srimati's claims, accentuates the notion of cross-generational, cross-temporal desire with strong undertones of incest. Srimati says that *Debdas* was never made since an appropriate actor for the title role could not be found. She had suggested someone, but Aniket said, "No." "Who?" asks Apratim. "You," responds Srimati, "don't you think I do good casting?"[38]

Although the truth of Srimati's statements about Aniket's career ambitions remains equivocal in this section of *Abohomaan*, what does emerge is her desire that Aniket's son should play Debdas against her Parboti, the woman Debdas loves all his life and at whose door he dies. Her linking of Apratim's mother with the roles of a courtesan and prostitute are also unexpected, if not shocking, for the viewer of *Abohomaan* as this character, Deepti, is progressively built up in Ghosh's film as one totally dedicated to her husband and devastated by his affair. Yet, such linking by Srimati effects a conceptual displacement of sorts for the audience by way of which she and Deepti exchange roles, and the mother's place in Apratim's life opens for Srimati to step into. It is at the crossroads of this space of motherhood that Srimati does not yet occupy and her (vocalized) desire to play Parboti to Apratim's Debdas that Ghosh introduces undercurrents of incest.

As transgressive as this is, what complicates it further is Apratim's reciprocal emotion and the fact that he himself is married and about to become a father. The second of these sequences again locates Srimati and Apratim together, this time with the former listing her grievances against the father; clearly putting before the son what she perceives as Aniket's ultimate insensitivity to and rejection of her. Ghosh makes Apratim's empathy for Srimati obvious in this sequence through the actor's expressions.

Evidence from preceding sequences leads the viewer to suppose that Apratim is discussing a film he is about to make on his father's life as Srimati comments, "It's a very difficult role. No one will be able to play it as well as me, don't you think?" "I don't believe so," responds Apratim. "Do you like my acting?" asks Srimati. "I do," says Apratim. "And me?" questions Srimati.[39] Apratim nods slowly in affirmation. In this final part of the second sequence, Ghosh frames the two characters against images that suggest both imprisonment and space. Srimati leans against the railing of a balcony as she talks, and crisscrossing wires move upwards from it to the ceiling, closing her off from the expanse of the outside world and yet leaving that world visible to her and the spectator. "Do you ever want to have a romance with me?" she asks Apratim.[40]

68 *Representations of disjuncture*

As the camera cuts to a solo shot of Apratim, the viewer notices that he is partly framed by a window panel with the same crisscrossing wires but more by an expanse of open space. He indicates that he does not want to have a romance with Srimati. The following shots are quick alternating ones of Apratim and Srimati as she asks him question after question: "Is it because your mother will scold you?" "Your wife will?" "Is it because you will get a bad reputation?" Apratim answers "No" to each of these.[41] He elaborates that the problem is Srimati will just have a romance. She will neither love him nor trust him. He clarifies that he does not blame her; he would do the same in her position. However, she would playact so brilliantly, that he would believe she really loved him. Srimati does not refute him, and the sequence ends inconclusively at this point.

That both Srimati and Apratim are framed by images suggesting enclosure and space indicates the difficulty of choices involved. Although visually, the sequence presents Srimati with less possibility of access to the outside world, it becomes clear by its end that Apratim has more emotional investment in her than she does in him and thus is more tormented within. He conveys that he understands her feelings for him will not equal those she had for his father, and her perceived sense of abandonment will most likely complicate things for them.

If indeed Srimati is more rooted in the past and burdened with grievances, Ghosh's depiction of her as more "captive" through the images in this sequence becomes understandable. In the face of a possible incestuous relationship, Apratim implies he has more of a readiness and perhaps more serious intent. Hence, in shots with him, the open space in the background is highlighted rather than the crisscrossing wires on the window. As in his representation of incestuous desire in *Utsab*, Ghosh deploys images of enclosure and space, except that in *Abohomaan* there is far less of a sense of resolution than in the sequence in *Utsab* in which he aligns our gaze with Parul's and helps us move out with her conceptually from a space of repression.

As I return to my discussion of *Utsab*, I close with one last thought. If we are to read the family in *Utsab* as symptomatic of the nation, then another of the film's messages could very likely be that while India has successfully eliminated a foreign political presence some 50 years before *Utsab*'s release, what is domestic, what is familiar, what is initially beloved can also become an agent of considerable repression. Certainly for Parul, to some extent, her family signifies in this way. What brings her a measure of relief and happiness, after years of denial and fear, is the sheer simplicity of Shishir's words. She asks if he came back a long way only to tell her what he does. At least up to this point in his career, Rituparno Ghosh's trajectory as director showed characteristics similar to Shishir's return. He came a long way since his first feature in 1992, and made film after film, often to tell us something very simple: that those who are close to us, those who are our fellow citizens, no matter how different from the majority because of inclination or circumstance, need *not* censure but words of love. Like Parul, it is up to us to do what we will with this message.

Notes

1 *Utsab* unfolds during the celebration of the four-day autumn festival, *Durga Puja*, in West Bengal. The family, two daughters and two sons who have moved away because of marriage, job opportunities, and so forth, return with their spouses and/or children to the ancestral home in which the mother still lives to take part in the festivities together.

2 Translation mine.

3 This discussion can be complicated even further because of two factors. First, the mother's name in the film is Bhagabati, also one of Goddess *Durga*'s many names. Second, *Durga* herself connotes not just the nurture typically associated with motherhood, but is also depicted, as idol, killing the demon *mahishashur*. Hence, another one of her names is *mahishashurmardini* (the destroyer of *mahishashur*, the force of evil). Thus, as Bengalis conceptualize *Durga* as Mother Goddess, they simultaneously think of her as an embodiment of supreme strength, this suggesting the many dimensions of motherhood.

Before Bhagabati mentions how the beat of the drums transforms for her, she notes in her narrative that the face of the Mother Goddess seemed to blur through her tears (this grief brought about because of her husband's absence). Although my reading in this chapter suggests that (such blurring and) the thought of immersion is a transition into Bhagabati's re-conceptualization of herself as a political fighter, it is possible, also, to read such signifiers as pointing to the various possibilities within a mother herself. It is very likely that Ghosh wishes to underscore the fluidity of concepts such as motherhood by establishing parallels with *Durga*. This second reading becomes more meaningful if we see the British occupation in India as an "evil" that Bhagabati (and her husband) feel compelled to eliminate.

For a different discussion of the "rhetoric of nationalism," "Bharat Mata" (Mother India) as "deity" in Ghosh's film, and "the holy trinity of mother–goddess–nation," see Romita Ray, "At Home with Durga: The Goddess in a Palace and Corporeal Identity in Rituparno Ghosh's *Utsab*." *Religions* 5.2 (2014): 334–60.

4 In *Undoing Gender*. New York: Routledge, 2004. 152–60.

5 Butler, "Quandaries of the Incest Taboo."

6 Emphases mine.

7 Rubin, "The Traffic in Women."

8 All translations of dialogue from the film are mine.

9 Rubin, "The Traffic in Women."

10 Emphasis mine.

11 Rubin, "The Traffic in Women."

12 Previously in this chapter, I refer to how Bhagabati, the mother, in her narrative, recollects the father's high fever, his simultaneous fugitive status, the giving of jewelry (material items) for the nationalist cause, and the father's valiant escape from his pursuers despite the condition of his health. Clearly, as director, Ghosh suggests that in this instance at least, Bhagabati sees the freedom movement through a lens that romanticizes.

13 In *In Other Worlds: Essays in Cultural Politics*. New York: Routledge, 1988. 197–221. In this particular essay, Spivak critiques the volume *Subaltern Studies III: Writings on South Asian History and Society* edited by Ranajit Guha.

14 Ibid.

15 Parul's brief meeting with Shishir inserted by Ghosh towards the very end of *Utsab* underscores that the power of patriarchy can only go so far in curbing what is desired and beautiful.

16 In *Sentimental Fabulations, Contemporary Chinese Films: Attachment in the Age of Global Visibility*. New York: Columbia UP, 2007.

17 Ibid.

70 *Representations of disjuncture*

18 Ibid.

19 In the 2009 interview with me, when I asked him to expand on why Parul behaves in this manner, Ghosh responded that for her, experience has not translated into wisdom.

20 Translation of this song is mine.

21 In the same interview as mentioned in Note 19 above, Ghosh alerted me to the fact that this is the only instance in the film in which we see Parul wearing her hair in a braid, a way of taking the audience back to her youth.

22 Shishir does, actually, visit the house during Parul's stay there, although Parul does not appear before him. The mother had sought Parul's permission to invite him over for lunch *after* this first visit. In fact, all three events—Shishir's visit, Parul's outburst, and Shishir's return—occur on the same day.

23 What is surprising in the representation of this relationship, however, is that Joy talks unhesitatingly about his imminent departure to the United States to pursue an MBA degree, and both he and Shompa speak about her future marriage to someone else. Thus, even while they are much more unreserved about expressing the erotic pull between them, they are more resigned to their separate futures, unlike how, the audience surmises, Parul and Shishir had been in their youth. In a way, this could be a capitulation to a familial conformity.

24 I might not be stretching a point here if I say that it is appropriate he leaves without an object that shades or partly obfuscates the clarity of his vision.

25 I am grateful to Rituparno Ghosh for mentioning to me in this connection that this is a song of morning images, but it is sung at night in his film. (2009 interview with Ghosh.)

26 In Tagore's song, however, the "boatman" who will be "tun[ing]" the "instrument" is probably a reference to destiny or a higher power.

27 When a bit later, Parul lies to her older brother that no one had come to the house that evening, it is not, I believe, out of fear now, but because this is a "moment" of imaginative liberation for her, and she associates her brother with repression and denial in her past.

28 I am indebted to Rituparno Ghosh for this wonderful phrase, which he used during my 2009 interview with him. His original Bengali, which I have translated in this chapter, was "*Sōmoy Bhogōbōtiké swadhinota shikhiyeché.*" He is, of course, referring to the period of India's struggle for liberation from the British.

29 Titli's father is the manager of a tea garden in Kurseong in North Bengal.

30 Translation mine.

31 We are told in *Titli* that Urmila was her daughter's age—a teenager—when the film *Aradhana*, a Bollywood commercial hit, was released. This film was released in 1969.

32 It is a night sequence, and Urmila is in her nightgown.

33 Here, Ghosh has in mind the commercial Bollywood film sometimes known to have highly charged, melodramatic plots in which two women vie for the hero's attention.

34 Translation mine.

35 In a beautiful move at the close of *Titli*, Ghosh has the daughter ask the mother to recite the poem she overheard her recite to Rohit. A Tagore work titled "Ek Gayé" ("In the Same Village"), the poem shows, through its speaker, how living in the same village is the only joy for two lovers. It captures also how emotion for the beloved is expressed by transferring it to elements of nature. As Urmila and Titli together absorb news of Rohit's forthcoming marriage, the former's recitation of this poem transforms its contextual significance for the film's audience. No longer just signifying a space shared by lovers, the poem resonates as a tie between mother and daughter in the face of their felt sense of loss.

36 Urmila mentions that Rohit lived in a "refugee colony"; was not looking for a (conventional) job; and her parents were searching for a groom who could provide her economic security.

The impossibility of incestuous love   71

37 The Bengali film *Nishi Padma* (1970) is based on a short story, "Hinger Kōchuri," by Bibhutibhushan Bandopadhyay. The main female role is that of a prostitute, Pushpa. *Debdas*, based on the novel by Sarat Chandra Chattopadhyay, has been cinematized in many Indian languages through the twentieth century and into the twenty-first.
38 Translation mine.
39 Translation mine.
40 Translation mine.
41 Translation mine.

References

Abohomaan (The Eternal). Dir. Rituparno Ghosh. Mahesh Ramanathan and Rajesh Sawhney. Reliance Big, 2009. Film.

Butler, Judith. "Quandaries of the Incest Taboo." *Undoing Gender*. New York: Routledge, 2004. 152–60. Print.

Chow, Rey. *Sentimental Fabulations, Contemporary Chinese Films: Attachment in the Age of Global Visibility*. New York: Columbia UP, 2007. Print.

Dahan (Crossfire). Dir. Rituparno Ghosh. Vijay Agarwal and Kalpana Agarwal. Gee Pee Films Pvt. Ltd., 1997. Film.

Dekha (Seeing). Dir. Goutam Ghose. Ramesh Gandhi, 2001. Film.

Ghosh, Rituparno. Personal interview. September 28, 2009.

Ray, Romita. "At Home with Durga: The Goddess in a Palace and Corporeal Identity in Rituparno Ghosh's *Utsab*. *Religions* 5.2 (2014): 334–60. doi10.3390/rel5020334 Online, available at: www.mdpi.com/2077-1444/5/2/334/htm. Accessed February 8, 2015. Web.

Rubin, Gayle. "The Traffic in Women: Notes on the 'Political Economy' of Sex." *Toward an Anthropology of Women*. Ed. Rayna R. Reiter. New York: Monthly Review P, 1975. 157–210. Print.

Spivak, Gayatri Chakravorty. "Subaltern Studies: Deconstructing Historiography." *In Other Worlds: Essays in Cultural Politics*. New York: Routledge, 1988. 197–221. Print.

Titli (The First Monsoon Day). Dir. Rituparno Ghosh. Tapan Biswas and Sutapa Ghosh. Cinemawallah, 2002. Film.

Utsab (Festival). Dir. Rituparno Ghosh. Tapan Biswas and Sutapa Ghosh. Cinemawallah, 2000. Film.

3 Impermanence in *Dekha*

The fragility of the present and the passing of a "traditional" perspective

In a 2007 interview in Kolkata, Goutam Ghose noted that *Dekha* (*Seeing*, 2001) was made shortly after he lost both his parents.[1] In fact, the film is dedicated to his mother and father as also to the memory of a friend, Ayan Rashid. In the interview, Ghose mentioned that that time marked what he felt was the removal of "umbrella" presences or influences in his life. Perhaps because of this comment, I read the film, among other things, as a questioning and an exploration of the strength or tenuousness, as the case may be, of those things we consider of paramount importance in our lives. Hence, I claim that motifs or characters that seem to have overarching significance at points in the film are also those that end up having little validity in and of themselves by the end. In my view, *Dekha* becomes a critique, a laying bare, even an undoing of some of the major thematic elements that help structure it.

One other thing that comes through as an undercurrent in the film is the director's mulling over temporality. In the same interview mentioned above, Ghose noted that in the face of real loss, "the present becomes a fraction [of time] between the past and the future." I will argue that what *Dekha* tries to capture is such a "present," located as only a part of a continuum, as shifting, unstable, and perhaps, ultimately, without much significance. This keen awareness of the impermanence of the present is obvious in Ghose's cinematic technique in *Dekha*, chiefly in his repeated use of what Gilles Deleuze terms the "time-image," as opposed to the "action image," in his magnificent study of post-World War II cinema.[2] In this chapter, I will elaborate on Ghose's exploration of this sense of impermanence, as manifested both in his treatment of time through the use of certain kinds of cinematic images and as evident in the way in which he empties out the significance of his central character and major motifs. Finally, I will argue that Ghose makes a broader point through his focus on impermanence. For me, his film suggests that a primarily masculinist culture's perceptions of women are also, ultimately, impermanent. Like the present of *Dekha*, they are only part of a continuum; they can be emptied of their significance and supplanted by other perceptions more appropriate to the times.

Ghose's central character in the film, Sashibhushan, is male, filtered through whose perspective we come to know the female characters in *Dekha*, but he suffers from glaucoma or what he calls "tunnel vision," which deteriorates to near-total blindness. I believe that at strategic points in the film, Ghose uses this illness to suggest that Sashi's understanding of women is, at best, limited. Further, a number of key sequences foreground the inescapable allure of the maternal for Sashi, and yet Ghose makes the statement that motherhood is not everything for the contemporary Bengali woman. It is precisely Sashi's idealization of motherhood that is undercut through the thoughts and actions of the primary female characters in *Dekha*. As regards women in whom he is erotically interested, Ghose reiteratively gives us two scenarios as possible points of entry into Sashi's psyche. First, even in days that pre-date his visual affliction, he is shown to touch, lingeringly, women's bodies. Second, a proximity to the wilderness arouses his desire for erotic interaction with women, hinting at an associative fantasy that links women to the primal and an imagination that refuses to consider how contemporary women have broken from traditional structures of domination.

If we consider the context of *Dekha*, a film set in the heart of Kolkata in the late twentieth century and a film in which the three major female characters are presented as educated, working, independent women, Sashi's proclivities detailed above certainly seem anachronistic. Yet, as I address before, in my reading, the film opens up for critique and even censure of its focal character and key motifs because, in itself, *Dekha* is a questioning of all that seems stable, a problematizing of what appears to be a given.

In relation to the broader issues under discussion in this study—how contemporary Bengali film directors juxtapose disintegrating forms of tradition with the more liberating aspects of an evolving culture—Sashibhushan, in *Dekha*, plays out the former, while, in their own discrete ways, the three female characters, Reba, Reema, and Sarama, embody the latter. Further, this chapter engages the irony embedded in the film in that as drawn in as Sashi is by ideas of radical Marxist-Leninist protest and revolution, and as committed as he is to humanitarian causes, he remains decidedly conservative and self-opinionated when it comes to interactions with the independent, progressive women characters. In this, he exemplifies most effectively the disjuncture between responses to resistance in the public and private domains. Although vis-à-vis Sashi, one of the female figures, Reema, continues to operate in and from the public sphere and thus faces minimum consequences because of his masculinist attitude, the other two, Reba and Sarama, are depicted by Ghose as negatively affected by his outdated reactions to women's autonomy.

Intersections of the maternal and the erotic

A persistent feature in the film, as realized in the character portrayal of Sashi, is not just the idealization of the mother, but the intersecting of the maternal and the erotic in his mind. Other than the obvious Oedipal implications here, Ghose repeatedly inserts such overlap to show where and how Sashi's understanding of women falls short.

When an aging Sashi visits the home of his professor from his college days, a home surrounded by forest, and hears of the possibility of seeing wild animals

74 *Representations of disjuncture*

during a planned trip into the very interior of the wilderness, he is overtaken by reverie. Ghose situates in this sequence of reverie what appears to be, at a distance, Sashi's beloved and wife from the past, Reba, dressed in elaborate costume, singing, dancing, and framed by nature. Through the words of her song, she entices him to enter the fullness of life with her. The indiscernible nature of Reba's features in this dance shot suggests the actual impossibility of such framing: Reba is a city girl who attended a prominent college in Kolkata and will not be easily "transplanted" into the wilderness.[3] Reba framed by nature is thus not just a spectacle "staged" by Ghose in his film, but a tactic he uses to show how Sashi "stages" women in his mind; they are frequently associated with the elemental and, more specifically, the primitive.

The next shot, also a part of this reverie sequence set in nature, shows Reba walking away from the camera, dressed now as a city girl would be, in a grey saree. She glances back, once, at an out-of-frame Sashi and smiles what could be seen as a smile suggesting both the erotic and derision. Although we continue to see from Sashi's perspective, his construction of the female beloved, with indistinguishable features dancing unrealistically in the midst of nature, is replaced by a Reba as she would most likely be in reality and one who is shown to walk away from him. Yet, Ghose fades this out too and fades in, in the same mist-shrouded milieu in which Reba was shown to be dancing and walking, a figure who slowly emerges from the mist, also dressed in a grey saree. It is not Reba but Sashi's mother. Through her song and measured hand movements, she entreats him not, as Reba did, to partake in the plenitude of life, but to get a hold of his "crazy" mind, a mind gone astray. We hear Sashi calling out, as one forsaken would, to his mother.

This reverie sequence cannot stop with a realistic Reba walking away from Sashi because Ghose wishes to underscore his protagonist's psychological aberrations, the distinctions that are blurred in his mind. Such sequences are a part of the directorial strategy that helps Ghose bring us Sashi as the central character of *Dekha* and also progressively empty out his significance. They prepare us, I believe, for the broader, culture-relevant message of the film, which the figure of Sashi helps Ghose deliver. By repeatedly attenuating the credibility of his focal character, Ghose suggests that dominant cultural beliefs that have taken root because of an adherence to tradition and that may seem irreversible are not necessarily so; they, too, may be questionable and are subject to revision.

Just as in the reverie sequence, another sequence earlier in the film also brings us such association between the object of desire and the mother. Reema works for the editor of a little magazine, and Sashi is intrigued by her youth and her forthrightness. His fingers have examined her unashamedly the first time she came to talk to him,[4] and he examines her again, without permission, when they run into each other accidentally in a bookstore, and she gets in a taxi with him. As a recluse, he is provoked by her insistence that he be chairperson of a gathering of poets she is organizing, and comments that in his heyday he would take her home and "devour this body of yours alive with salt and pepper."[5] In the course of this conversation, Sashi informs Reema that she talks in an unsparing manner, like his mother, and asks if she sings, for his mother sang beautifully. Ghose's insertion here, in this leisurely talk, of an unexpected shot of a traffic signal in which the light turns red concretizes the limitations of Sashi's mind and prepares us for an extended song sequence that brings us the intersection of the erotic and the maternal. Further, this sequence is noteworthy for Ghose's use of the "time-image," something not commonly seen in Bengali cinema, rather than the more conventional flashback.

Two-fold purpose of the motif of impermanence

In speaking of the "time-image" in his analysis of post-World War II cinema, Gilles Deleuze notes:

> But precisely what brings the cinema of action into question after the war is the very break-up of the sensory-motor schema: the rise of situations to which one can no longer react, of environments with which there are now only chance relations, of empty or disconnected any-space-whatevers replacing qualified extended space. It is here that situations no longer extend into action or reaction in accordance with the requirements of the movement-image. These are pure optical and sound situations, in which the character does not know how to respond, abandoned spaces in which he ceases to experience and to act so that he enters into flight, goes on a trip, comes and goes, vaguely indifferent to what happens to him, undecided as to what must be done. But he has gained in an ability to see what he has lost in action or reaction: he SEES so that the viewer's problem becomes "What is there to see in the image?" (and not now "What are we going to see in the next image?").
>
> (272)[6]

In Ghose's *Dekha*, the protagonist, Sashi, is not overtaken by post-war malaise, but by disillusionment that is two-pronged. He is anguished by aggressive materialism and corruption, evident in some in Bengal, such as his cousin, a disposition that suggests to him a fading of leftist revolutionary zeal that often marks the Bengali Communist.[7] Second, he is still in a state of shock from his wife's departure from their household, with their daughter, several years ago. I want to suggest that through presentation of this mindset, Ghose brings us a character fixated on the past, a figure for whom the present often has little significance. Deleuze argues that the "time-image" gives us "pure optical and sound situations," and the character's "ability to see" is enhanced even as he is rendered largely inactive. Sashi's "ability to see" remains mostly restricted to the past, however, and it is ironic that Ghose uses such "time-images" that unravel the magnitude of his character's investment in the past to also signal how he is out of step with the present.

What is complex about *Dekha* is that at the same time that it captures the fleeting, impermanent nature of the present and projects it as part of a

76   *Representations of disjuncture*

continuum, it also compels us to come face to face with the fact that we must live with it, dramatizing how sheer nostalgia and the intensity of memory, although beautiful, are ultimately inadequate. As I claim earlier in this chapter, Ghose deploys the notion of impermanence with a two-fold purpose in this film. Impermanence, associated with a sharply-felt sense of loss, brings home to the viewer the fragility of the present. However, it also suggests that like time, beliefs, in particular beliefs about women, are transitory. As entrenched as they may seem, they are not immutable. In this regard, *Dekha* uses the figure of Sashibhushan as cautionary, finally exposing how a myopic adherence to traditional views, particularly about women, renders his mental landscape as useless as untilled soil.[8]

I now return to my discussion of the song sequence that illustrates the intersection of the erotic and maternal; is rich in its use of the "time-image" as it underscores the tenuousness of the present; and that also concludes with a suggestion of how impoverished the immediate present is for the film's protagonist.

As Reema starts to sing at the piano, after her taxi-ride with Sashi and arrival at his house, Ghose prepares us for the transference to the past through a shot of Sashi breathing heavily. A dissolve is followed by a shot with his mother singing the same song at the same piano, but at a different point in time. One image directly replaces another here, suggesting the seamless movement in Sashi's mind and enabling Ghose to depict the present as a "fraction" and as part of a mental–emotional continuum. I cannot but quote here Deleuze's words as he discusses the "time-image" in post-World War II western cinema:

> How feeble the flashback seems beside explorations of time as powerful as this, such as the silent walk on the thick hotel carpet which each time puts the image into the past in *Last Year in Marienbad*. The tracking shots of Resnais and Visconti, and Welles's depth of field, carry out a temporalization of the image or form a direct time image.... "Rather than a physical movement, it is a question above all of a displacement in time."
>
> (39)[9]

And as he speaks of Henri Bergson's beliefs, Deleuze notes, "Time is not the interior in us, but just the opposite, the interiority in which we are, in which we move, live and change" (82).[10] Although it may be controversial to call Ghose's use of the image to shift back in time here a Deleuzian "time-image," it is useful to clarify that the technique Ghose uses here seems distinctly different from the conventional flashback. Rather than an image or set of images slowly fading into another set, the dissolve cleanly cuts the two time periods apart, and by focusing on the vividness of the image(s) from the past, Ghose establishes the immediacy of that temporality for the protagonist. It is not as if the present, which the character inhabits, makes way slowly for the past via a flashback. The past has no "secondary" status here for the character. Thus, while it is true that Deleuze is addressing cinematic temporality in relation to the effects of World War II, I draw on that part of his argument that highlights how the "time-image" evokes "pure optical and sound situations" and is more of a sharp, direct "displacement in time." As Ghose notes inside the cover of a DVD version of *Dekha*, "I have deliberately tried not to tell a story, but I created moments and intensified them." Further, as opposed to the traditional flashback in (Bengali) cinema where some agency is generally implied and time is presented as being more interior to the subject, in Ghose's treatment here, time becomes more of the Deleuzian "interiority in which we are" and over which we have little control. Thus, Ghose's cinematic technique in this sequence also underscores Sashibhushan's vulnerability. Ghose adds to this psycho-emotional vulnerability by focusing in, as in some other sequences of *Dekha*, on the frailty of Sashi's body as Reema's song commences. He is shown moving slowly and hesitantly, groping for a chair, and sinking into it.

As I mention earlier, if there is a temporal interiority Sashi inhabits, it his largely his past. As Ghose situates us in the past in this sequence, its visceral appeal for Sashi is conveyed to the viewer through the perfection of the mise-en-scène—the plush drapes and furniture, the remarkable beauty of the period costumes—and the haunting quality of the music, the playback singer for the mother's character different than the one for Reema.

The verses in the mother's section of the song invoke nature and the beloved simultaneously, reminding the viewer of Sashi's fondness for this association. A final shot of the mother gives way to a shot of Reema at the piano concluding the song, followed by a comment by Sashi's manservant that she has brought the old *jolshaghor* (music room) to life once again. Yet, precisely because of his use of the "time-image," which allows us to move between past and present without a mediating agent, what now strikes us are the windows without drapes that are closed and barred and the decrepit walls with paint peeling off them. What the mother's song offers to Sashi is what Kaja Silverman, in her discussion of the maternal voice in cinema, speaks of as a "choric enclosure" (86). Silverman connects this to the notion of the subject's "castration," claiming that castration

> refers in part to the differentiation of subject from object, and hence to the loss of imaginary plenitude.... In its fantasmatic guise as "pure" sonorousness, the maternal voice oscillates between two poles; it is either cherished as an *objet (a)*—as what can make good all lacks—or despised and jettisoned as what is most abject.
>
> (86)[11]

In the sequence discussed above, Ghose's "time-images" that unfold the past on the screen clearly bring us this "plenitude" and "'pure' sonorousness" through, as I state before, the mise-en-scène and music, but the pivot that holds everything together and "make[s] good all lacks" for Sashi is the figure of the mother. As the sequence brings us back to the present and to Reema, the absence of this maternal figure together with the markedly run-down appearance of the music room suggest again, as in the sequence in which the mother's song followed that of the wife, that the object of erotic attraction is never enough for Sashi and can never quite be the "*objet (a)*."

78 *Representations of disjuncture*

However, Ghose's focus on the impoverished condition of the music room also suggests, through association, the inadequacy of Sashi's responses to the present, and in particular, his responses to the contemporary Bengali woman. His fingering of Reema ceases to be a one-woman-specific reaction for the viewer and is more indicative of a protagonist who either finds unbounded pleasure when women, as in the space and time in which his mother sang, are inevitably coupled with a husband[12] or is aroused when he can treat woman as an object of sorts, often in the midst of wilderness. Thus, even as maternity is the crux of woman's identity for Sashi, yet to him, this maternity is not enough in and of itself unless framed and consolidated by a hetero-normative, patriarchal household. More than one sequence underscores such a mindset in *Dekha*'s protagonist.

In a particular shot in the film, an out-of-frame Sashi[13] watches his wife, Reba, groaning and giving birth. In a scene of a heated exchange in their bedroom, some years later, Reba informs him that despite his repeated efforts to stop her in the past, she has accepted a job offer and will pursue a career. In response to Sashi's query as to who will, then, raise their child, Reba says with confidence that she will be a professional and a mother at the same time. When Sashi realizes that Reba will leave him to accomplish her goals, his question to her is surprising and sounds archaic: "You will raise the only child of this family out of the house of the paternal ancestors?"[14] When, in the same sequence, Reba accuses him of being a "pervert" under the guise of a professor of literature and details his physical relationships with young girls, he does not hesitate to slap her face.

Dichotomous response to resistance in the public and private spheres

In contradistinction to such conformist and conservative tendencies towards women, Ghose presents Sashi as a character who is generally committed to Communist ideals, and at least one scene in *Dekha* suggests his faith in radical left-wing politics as a student in his youth. The Bengali viewer easily associates such politics with the CPML party (Communist Party of India Marxist-Leninist) in West Bengal, formed in 1969 shortly following the release from jail of key leaders of the well-known Naxalbari peasant uprising of 1967.

As I address in the following paragraphs, the Naxalbari revolt, subsequent peasant uprisings, and "the urban movement of the Communist revolutionary students and youth [1968 through the early 1970s] ... marked by demonstrations in Calcutta and other towns in defence of the peasants' armed struggle" (Banerjee 177)[15] showed a clean break with oppressive and exploitative power structures.

In his book *India's Simmering Revolution: The Naxalite Uprising*, Sumanta Banerjee addresses the peasant revolt which began in Naxalbari, in the Darjeeling district of West Bengal, in 1967:

> Peasants' committees were formed in every village and they were transformed into armed guards. They soon occupied land in the name of the peasants' committees, burnt all land records "which had been used to cheat

Impermanence in Dekha   79

them of their dues," cancelled all hypothecary debts, passed death sentences on oppressive landlords, formed armed bands by looting guns from their landlords, armed themselves with conventional weapons like bows, arrows and spears, and set up a parallel administration to look after the villages.

(87)[16]

Banerjee quotes one of the leading figures who inspired this movement, Charu Mazumdar:

"We shall always have to decide—on whose side or against which side we are. We are always on the side of poor and landless peasants. If there is a conflict of interest between the middle peasant on the one hand and the landless peasant on the other, we will certainly be on the side of the landless peasant".

(87)[17]

Banerjee also notes how Mazumdar "called upon the youth and students to … go to the workers and the poor and landless peasants to integrate themselves with these classes" (177–78).[18] A majority of these students, involved in the student uprisings of Kolkata from the late 1960s to early 1970s, came from the middle class. What I want to focus on here is not just the break with oppressive power structures mentioned earlier that was evident in these movements, but a continued identification with the underprivileged and less fortunate. The Bengali viewer of *Dekha*, as also others familiar with the history of these militant movements, thus understands easily what Sashi means in the sequence in which he tells his long-time friend that in their youth they dreamt of being "de-classed."

Also sadly resonant for the viewer is his speaking out the line "The father who is afraid to identify the corpse of his child" and shortly after, "This plain of death is not my country."[19] His friend remembers the latter as a line by a poet of the early 1970s, but the former brings to mind the relentless police brutality against the young revolutionaries in Kolkata. Banerjee notes, for instance:

With increasing help from the Centre [Central government of India] and imported paramilitary and military forces, police retaliation against the CPI (M-L) urban guerrillas began to gain momentum from the last quarter of 1970. No mercy was shown to any CPI (M-L) cadre or supporter if caught.

(186)[20]

Banerjee further notes:

Aided by … laws and a well-equipped military force, the police went about on the rampage in right earnest. In many cases, after beating senseless some political suspects, the police would take them outside the lockup, pump bullets into their bodies, and throw the bodies out in the streets.

(187)[21]

80 *Representations of disjuncture*

Ghose deploys Sashi's character, in the sequence mentioned above, to evoke not just the politically charged atmosphere of terror in the early 1970s Kolkata, but to indicate his emotional identification with a radical form of Communism. His recalling and mulling over the line "This plain of death is not my country" suggests his past hope for a better (and more egalitarian) India attained through and after revolutionary struggle and sacrifice.[22] I have addressed in my Introduction and in a note to this chapter another question Sashi raises in this sequence—his despondent question to his friend as to whether Communism will disappear from the country.

No less interesting is the scene in *Dekha* that situates Sashi and his "extortionist" cousin in the foreground with the hazy figures of slum-dwellers, bathing in the pond on Sashi's property, in the background. Even in the face of the cousin's aggressive materialism, as he encourages Sashi to dry out and fill up the pond and profit by having new property built on it, the latter expresses his desire to hold on to the pond that serves, in his words, as a "hamaam" or "public bath" for the surrounding slum-dwellers. Although his dreams of being "de-classed" may have ended with the dissolution of the radical youth movement in Kolkata, Ghose here continues to foreground Sashi's empathy for the less privileged and his perspective that is centered less on self than on others, at least in this particular instance.

Yet, as with a number of films under discussion in this study, *Dekha* effectively dramatizes a dichotomy in the response to resistance. This dichotomy, as mobilized through the portrayal of Sashi, brings us a faith in breaking from oppression and exploitation and an attempt to even out inequities in the social structure on the one hand. On the other, however, it reveals an antipathy to contemporary women's efforts to reject masculinist abuse or exploitation and erase the gender gap. Sashi is symptomatic of figures who unreservedly support revolution, for the right causes, in the public domain, but in the private domain, within their inner sanctum, remain rigid in preserving a gender hierarchy. Sashi's blindness then, other than suggesting his limited understanding of women, signifies beyond an individual as well. In my view, it points to blind spots within a cultural framework; these are areas where a "traditional" conceptualization, in this case of women, has taken root. They are areas marked by opacity and are difficult to remove.

Selected Bengali directors preceding Ghose had also effectively dramatized this dichotomy. In Satyajit Ray's *Pratidwandi* (*The Adversary*, 1970), Siddhartha Chowdhury, the protagonist, is enamored of the concept of revolution. In search of a job following his father's death, Siddhartha is shown at more than one interview. In the first one towards the beginning of the film, when asked what he would consider the most significant event of the last decade, he speaks about the resistance and courage of the Vietnamese peasant during the Vietnam War. He tries to convince his interviewers that this was more unexpected and impactful when they suggest the moonlanding.

More striking is a sequence with Siddhartha and his younger brother who Ray suggests is indeed a committed revolutionary against forms of social

Impermanence in Dekha 81

oppression.[23] In a memorable series of shots, the brother hands Siddhartha a book on Che Guevara, reminding him that it was Siddhartha who had given it to him once. Although the brother berates Siddhartha for having changed, presumably for having lost the force of his commitment to insurgence, this criticism spurs an interesting reaction.

Ray gives us a close-up frontal shot of Siddhartha with the suggestion of a mirror before him. As Siddhartha gazes at his own reflection and looks downward, his eyes transform and draw closer together in their fixed gaze. Superimposed on them are Che's eyes, both fierce and fearsome, and on his face, bearing a one-day stubble, that of Che Guevara with his close-cropped beard that the spectator saw a few shots prior on the cover of the book. Ray's background music that accompanies this transformation is fast, ceremonial, and both ominous and exciting. The imagined change is momentary, and Siddhartha is soon back to his everyday self, but not without the implication to the audience that he still connects deeply with the revolutionary who fights for human rights. Not surprisingly, towards the end of *Pratidwandi*, Siddhartha risks his own chances at a job as he storms into the room where the interviewers are and lashes out at them for their inhumane treatment of the candidates who have been kept waiting for hours in the outdoors heat of Kolkata with one fan working and few chairs on which to sit.

Yet, such identification with a revolutionary (i.e., Che) and exemplary power of protest as seen in Siddhartha seem at odds with his "traditional" attitude to women in the film. In one sequence, he implies to his friend that his sister, Topu, has landed a job because of her striking good looks. He follows this up with the comment that in these days, the "weaker sex" is the "stronger sex" and did not his friend notice how "confidently" the girls walked?[24]

Even more surprising is his response when the wife of his sister's boss comes to complain that his sister is ruining her marriage. Although Topu denies this charge, Siddhartha expresses disgust at a job that has her work late; and adopts a markedly paternalistic attitude towards her. It is worthy of note here that such instances of paternalism are often immediately followed in the film by flashbacks to childhood where Siddhartha sees his sister as a very young girl.

Although Topu clarifies that she goes places with her boss voluntarily after work, for instance to see his new house with other colleagues, Siddhartha considers this exploitation on the part of the boss. He takes it upon himself to visit her boss and reports to Topu, in a following sequence, that he has informed him that she will work for him no more. His sister laughs in his face, saying she will return to work the next morning. However, through Siddhartha's general comments about women and "traditionally" protective, masculinist attitude towards Topu, because of which he does not even consult her when he makes decisions about her life and career, Ray clearly foregrounds a dichotomy within him. Like Sashibhushan in *Dekha*, he is drawn to the concept of protest and revolution in the public sphere, but remains short-sighted and conservative in his views of women, their need and desire to progress in their careers,[25] and the gender hierarchy. That he keeps thinking of his sister as a young girl, via flashbacks,

82 *Representations of disjuncture*

following specific moments when he adopts a paternalistic attitude reinforces the fact that he cannot see women as adult, decision-making subjects.

As in the conversation sequence between Siddhartha and his brother in Ray's *Pratidwandi*, Che Guevara also figures in a dialogue between Neelkantha Bagchi, an alcoholic, intellectual, and the male lead in Ritwik Ghatak's *Jukti, Takko aar Gappo* (*Reason, Debate and a Story*, 1974),[26] and a young Naxalite revolutionary. In a night sequence in the woods, the camera focuses in on Bagchi/Ghatak and the revolutionary. The former classifies Marxism as "very much guided by dialectical and historical materialism"[27] and briefly addresses the evolution of Marx and Engels' scientific social theories through the work of Lenin, Stalin, Mao, and Che. He shows a clear understanding of the mission of each of these figures, even though the revolutionary dismisses his ideas as dated.[28]

Neelkantha Bagchi, i.e., Ghatak, continues that some of the brightest philosophical ideas were born in India, yet sections of society are now controlled by corrupt individuals. These elements will not disappear by themselves. It is necessary to comprehend their strengths and weaknesses, so they may be totally uprooted. Yet, Bagchi's comprehensive knowledge of world-wide revolutionary figures and movements as also his commitment, at least in theory, to radically eradicating corrupt, debilitating social forces in West Bengal and India in the early 1970s is not matched by a parallel understanding of women's needs and rights.

Although *Jukti, Takko aar Gappo* does not focus at length on this dichotomy within Neelkantha, it is evident in a sequence in which he is shown returning to his wife and son. His wife, Durga, has left him, because of his alcoholism and general lack of responsibility to family, and taken up a teaching job in rural West Bengal. As Neelkantha journeys, one of his traveling companions comments that although he seeks shelter with his wife, she will throw him out. Neelkantha disagrees with him, saying he knows his wife "has understood her mistake."[29]

Here, a Bengali intellectual aligned with radical Leftist forms of thinking implies that a wife who leaves her husband, despite his long-term shortcomings, and takes up a job is in the wrong. Like Sashibhushan in *Dekha* and Siddhartha in *Pratidwandi*, he exemplifies a stubbornly "traditional" mindset when it comes to women, but is committed to the process of revolution in society, in the public sphere.

The Bengali directors under analysis in this study, however, are not interested in situating these more "traditional" areas as the last word. Their endeavor, as evident in films made through the last 15 years, is to present culture as multifaceted and, more specifically, evolving and dynamic. Not only does Ghose undermine such "traditional" conceptualization discussed above by presenting all three major female characters in the film as negating one-on-one correspondences between woman and wife/mother, he suggestively links such blindness or cultural blind spots with sterility, regression, and a death-wish.[30] In this regard, in the course of a trip into the wilderness, Sashi pointedly inquires of Sarama, a woman who has separated from her abusive husband and whom Sashi lets stay

Impermanence in Dekha   83

at his house with her young son, if she hears the primitive love-making of the wild elephants. He asks to touch her as he hears this sound and does so despite her reluctance. As addressed earlier in this chapter, a proximity to the wilderness intensifies Sashi's desire for women, Ghose underscoring his inclination to associate women with the primal rather than the contemporary. The scene also helps reiterate his tendency to touch women, often without asking their permission, showcasing his sense of entitlement as he objectifies them.

But over and above representing his anachronistic attitude to women, the scene foregrounds Sashi's sterility, the uninhibited passion of the wild animals in the outdoors miniaturized and echoed feebly in Sashi's fingering of his professor's daughter, a woman whom he knew as a young girl and who previously called him "uncle." By outlining the limits of "passion" in his protagonist, Ghose suggests not so much a biological sterility as a mental-emotional one, also progressively taking away from Sashi's viability as "hero." As I mention at the beginning of this chapter, *Dekha* opens up for critique and censure its central character and some key motifs (such as associating woman/object of desire with the wilderness) in order to problematize and question certain "traditional" and seemingly entrenched perceptions in Bengali culture.

The failed poet and the passing of his "present"

What makes Sashi's character particularly complex, and his sterility tragic, is that Ghose also presents him as a poet in *Dekha*. Here, it is appropriate to refer to Maurice Blanchot's thoughts on the poet as addressed in *The Space of Literature*. Blanchot speaks of art and Rainer Maria Rilke and observes that Rilke

> refuses to "choose between the beautiful and the unbeautiful." Not to choose, not to refuse anything access to vision, and, in vision, to transmutation—to start from things, but from all things: this is a rule which always tormented him and which he learned perhaps from Hofmannsthal. The latter, in a 1907 essay, *The Poet and These Times*, said of the poet, "It is as if his eyes had no lids." He must not leave anything out of himself, he must not withhold himself from any being ...; he can reject no thought.
>
> $(152–3)$[31]

Soon after, Blanchot continues with this thought in the following words:

> if the poet must live at the intersection of infinite relations, in the place opened and as if void where foreign destinies cross—then he can well say joyfully that he takes his point of departure in things: what he calls "things" is no longer anything but the depth of the immediate and undetermined.
>
> (153)[32]

Hofmannsthal's mention of the lidless eyes of the poet and Blanchot's reference to the desired all-inclusive nature of poetic vision take me back, of course, to the

84 *Representations of disjuncture*

title of this Ghose film, *Dekha* (*Seeing*). Ghose progressively denudes the credibility of his protagonist by utilizing the notion of seeing both literally and metaphorically in this film. As addressed earlier, Sashi's near-total blindness suggests for me his myopic view of women and also, more broadly, a cultural obstinacy, that is, stubborn, deeply-entrenched ways of seeing that are difficult to erase or revise. Sadly, such blindness or limited vision is the precise opposite of Hofmannsthal's or Blanchot's conceptualization of poetic vision.

Tied to such limited, "traditional" perceptions of women, an individual or similarly disposed people of a culture cannot live, unlike the poet, "at the intersection of infinite relations, in the place opened and as if void where foreign destinies cross"; cannot appreciate "the depth of the immediate and undetermined" (Blanchot 153). Ghose dramatizes such inability by presenting Sashi's resistance to the extra-marital attraction Sarama feels for her lover, Gagan.[33] As he senses the growing passion between Sarama and Gagan, Sashi tells Sarama that he believes one day, she and her son will leave his house, the indication being that she will return to her husband. He prefaces this by saying that her son is growing up and misses his father. In this, Sashi overlooks Sarama's own needs and appeals to her maternal instincts.[34]

To use thoughts from Blanchot, a certain voiding or, at least, revision of previous perceptions is needed for one to be open to unexpected destinies coming together and, more importantly, to be receptive to the inherent but unknown possibilities of the present. Sashi's tragedy is rooted in his limited, outdated vision of women, but strikes deeper because of his failure as a poet to create such a mental-emotional space of openness. His own awareness of such failure is captured by Ghose as, in one of the final scenes of *Dekha*, he interrupts Reema as she reads from his earlier poetry and recites a late composition:

> Someday someone will come and say,
> The treasure-chest in your heart has not been opened a long time
> Give it some light
> I have brought a few shafts of lightning.
> Someday someone will come and say
> Your room has not been cleaned in a while
> I have brought a river.
> Someday, before descending into hell, someone will hold my hand.
> Someday people [will come] to people ...[35]

As he recites the poem, we see Sarama approaching, Sarama who stops as she hears it. It resonates for her, ironically signifying the newly-discovered passion in her life. She stands traumatized, caught in the cross-current of an expected commitment to tradition and the possibility of rejuvenation through a new relationship in the immediate future. Ghose's shot here is reminiscent of Tagore's prediction in *Religion of Man* addressed in my Introduction, "the continuous future is the domain of our millennium" (87). Tagore seems confident that the "mechanical spirit of tradition" (86) will be overtaken by the dynamism of the future. As Sarama stands, and Reema repeats the lines "Someday someone will come and say/Your room has not been cleaned in a while/I have brought a river," the camera pans to show Sarama framed by the green of trees, and the sound-track brings us the unmistakable reiteration of a moment of passion with her lover, Gagan. It is noteworthy that Ghose structures this scene to include the figures of both Sarama and Reema, women Sashibhushan felt entitled to touch in the past, objectifying their bodies because of his sterile, traditional perspective. Yet, it is one of these women who now voices (following his own recitation) the condition of his "room" or mental space, that which must be flooded and cleansed by the currents of the present and the oncoming future. The figure of the other woman in the scene conveys the choices open to women in this future.

Thus *Dekha* moves towards its close undermining, as in other sections but more poignantly now, the credibility of its male protagonist, who articulates an understanding of his own inner darkness and a mental-emotional space cluttered by the baggage of a "tradition" that works no more. Like his decrepit music-room, his reality, his "present" has fallen into disuse. In this closing section of the film, Ghose again signals clearly his affiliation with a more dynamic future by having Gagan's melodious song intrude unerringly into Sashi's recitation of his poem on unexplored potential and simmering regret. The camera cuts from the protagonist, and Reema, to Sarama's lover, Gagan, who in the penultimate scene of *Dekha* is shot sitting by slowly rippling water and framed, like Sarama in the previous sequence, by the green of trees as also fields. His song, categorical in its message, moves the audience beyond the tentative anticipatory mode of Sashi's late poem and foregrounds an explicit denunciation. The lines of this song, composed by Ramprosad Sen, used by Ghose are *mōn tumi krishi kaj janōna/mōn tumi krishi kaj janōna/tumi krishi kaj janōna/emōn manōb jōmeen rōilō pōtit/manōb jōmeen rōilō pōtit/abadh kōrle phōltō shōna/mōn tumi krishi kaj janōna.* The lines translate "oh mind, you do not know the work of cultivation/such human soil lies fallow [or untilled]/if you had sown, it would have yielded gold [alternatively, "a golden harvest"]."[36]

Whether Ghose intends these lines as a critical commentary on Sashi's waste of his own life and potential or his attitude towards women is less important here than the fact that his last words in the film are abruptly cut short by the force and beauty of this song. The final scene of *Dekha*, which follows, brings us Sashi's empty chair (although still rocking), the steady chiming of many clocks, and scattered papers flying about. Even if it is difficult to say whether the scene points to Sashi's passing, it clearly takes us back to Ghose's sustained focus on temporality in the film.

Beyond the individual and towards a "continuous future" in Bengali culture

Although it speaks the passing of time, the mood in this last scene, however, is not by any stretch of the imagination despondent. In fact, as discussed above, individual components of the scene are animated through movement, and the

86 *Representations of disjuncture*

chiming of one clock after another is marked by a strange ebullience, so that the room carries more of a dynamic charge in Sashi's absence than it did at any previous point in the film. Ghose strikes here a note of liberation, and that the reason for his protagonist's absence from the room is left unspecified might very well be a deliberate strategy, for the focus here is not the individual, but the addressing of a perspective and its passing. As my study has tried to show, this perspective is one embedded in forms of tradition that are problematic and often conflict-inducing in contemporary Bengal. Manifestations of such "traditional" perspectives and the conflicts they cause were discussed in Chapter 1, for instance, when I contrasted the masculinist power structure within one Bengali household represented in *Dahan* with the feminist actions of one of its lead female characters. Chapter 2 showed that to some extent, such a "traditional" perspective was encapsulated in the figure of the mother in *Utsab* who helped repress her daughter's incestuous romance, which led to the latter's outburst and upbraiding of the family after many years.

Like Rituparno Ghosh and Buddhadeb Dasgupta (discussed in greater detail in Chapter 6), Gautam Ghose, in *Dekha*, exposes the shortcomings of such forms of tradition. In this particular film, he does so chiefly by showcasing Sashi's archaic attitude and responses to progressive working women in the rapidly changing cultural climate of contemporary Bengal; by dramatizing the contradiction in his protagonist's responses to resistance in the public and private spheres; and ultimately, by implicitly critiquing a "traditional" perspective through a song sung by a character who, in his relationship with Sarama, stands outside what is considered normative. The final credits of *Dekha* are superimposed on the images of a shoreline with rippling water and some hints of green reminiscent of the scene of Gagan's song. The spectator knows it is ebbtide because of the visibility of rocks, stones, and tree branches. Yet, this very fact, and the camera's leisurely movement over exposed objects in the water, promises full-tide, when static things will be swept away by the force of a new current. It is no doubt a deliberate directorial gesture on Ghose's part that the milieu is somewhat different from that from which Gagan's song emanated and that both Gagan and Sarama are absent in these images. For again, here it is not specific individuals that the director is thinking about but the shifting terrain of Bengali culture in the twenty-first century and how this culture can be continuously invigorated by accommodating multiple and new perspectives.

Notes

1 Ghose's interview with me was conducted on August 20, 2007.
2 Deleuze, *Cinema 2.*
3 Such dancing to *Rabindrasangeets*—songs by Rabindranath Tagore—dressed in costume as Reba is, is typically an indoor and/or planned ceremonial event.
4 Reema comes with an installment for the printing press Sashi owns, where the little magazine she works for is being published.
5 My translation.
6 Deleuze, *Cinema 2.*

Impermanence in Dekha 87

7 Sashi observes, sadly, that the cousin's Communist parents had named him Biplab (Revolution) at birth, and today, he is an "extortionist." In *Dekha*, Sashi himself wonders if Communism will disappear from the country. It should be mentioned here that West Bengal has had an elected Communist (Communist Party of India Marxist-led Left Front) government for the last three decades. In 2011, after 34 years, the CPIM government was ousted by the United Allied Front led by Mamata Banerjee. It is also noteworthy that Goutam Ghose is a director known for his leftist sympathies.

8 Of relevance is the last song of the film, sung by Sarama's lover, which I will address towards the close of this chapter.

9 Deleuze, *Cinema 2*.

10 Ibid.

11 See Silverman, *The Acoustic Mirror: The Female Voice in Psychoanalysis and Cinema*. Bloomington: Indiana UP, 1988.

12 The male–female ratio is precisely one to one in the sequence segments that bring us the mother's song. In sharp contrast to this scenario from the past, Reema comes alone, that is, without her husband (although accompanied by her host), to Sashi's house and accepts a ride, late at night, from Sashi's cousin, a man she does not know, as she leaves.

13 The most likely reason for keeping the lead actor, Soumitro Chatterjee, out-of-frame for sequences situated in the past is his age at the time of the making of *Dekha*—65 to 66 years.

14 My translation.

15 Banerjee, *India's Simmering Revolution*.

16 Ibid.

17 Ibid. Banerjee explains middle peasants as poor peasants who had occupied land with legal help and subsequently changed into "complacent middle peasants" who "look[ed] down upon the vast majority of poor and landless, fighting outside the law to get land" (84).

18 Ibid.

19 Translations mine.

20 Banerjee, *India's Simmering Revolution*.

21 Ibid. The police violence against Naxalites is also addressed quite extensively in selected chapters of volume 1 in *Naxalbari and After*.

22 For a more detailed discussion of the impact of the Naxalite movement on the New Cinema in India, including Bengali films, see Ashish Rajadhyaksha, *Indian Cinema in the Time of Celluloid*. See especially pages 239–40.

23 Siddhartha asks him if he has a stock of hand grenades. The film is set in the time period when the Naxalite Movement was at its height in Kolkata.

24 The quoted words are from the film.

25 Prior to his visit to the boss's house, Topu had informed him that from the following month, she would be his personal assistant and get a 200-rupee salary "increment."

26 This role is played by director Ghatak himself. The film, his last, is an almost undisguised commentary on his own life, conveying also his disillusionment with society.

27 This comment is directly from the film.

28 Among other things, the young man is more interested to know if Bagchi has read contemporary publications such as *Deshabrati*, brought out by the Communist Party of India Marxist-Leninist.

29 Translation mine.

30 See my discussion of *Antarjali Jatra* in the Introduction, a film in which Goutam Ghose treats such cultural blind spots similarly.

31 See Blanchot, *The Space of Literature*. Trans., with an Introd. by Ann Smock. Lincoln: U of Nebraska P, 1982.

32 Ibid.

88 *Representations of disjuncture*

33 It is useful to note here that Gagan is also blind, chiefly to point out that Ghose does not use blindness merely with negative connotations in the film. Gagan reciprocates fully Sarama's love, as aware as he is of her marital status. He is shown to be attuned to nature and an excellent singer.
34 See my Introduction for a discussion of the traditional Bengali's idealization of the woman as mother over all other roles.
35 Translation mine.
36 Translation mine. In its entirety, this is a devotional lyric addressed to the Goddess Kali and one who has not yet learnt to be her worshipper.

References

Banerjee, Sumanta. *India's Simmering Revolution: The Naxalite Uprising*. London: Zed, 1980. Print.

Blanchot, Maurice. *The Space of Literature*. Trans., with an Introd. by Ann Smock. Lincoln: U of Nebraska P, 1982. Print.

Dahan (Crossfire). Dir. Rituparno Ghosh. Vijay Agarwal and Kalpana Agarwal. Gee Pee Films Pvt. Ltd., 1997. Film.

Dekha (Seeing). Dir. Goutam Ghose. Ramesh Gandhi, 2001. Film.

Deleuze, Gilles. *Cinema 2: The Time-Image*. Trans. Hugh Tomlinson and Robert Galeta. Minneapolis: U of Minnesota P, 1989. Print.

Ghose, Goutam. Director's Note. *Dekha*. By Ghose. Angel Video, 2004. DVD.

Ghose, Goutam. Personal interview. August 20, 2007.

Jukti, Takko aar Gappo (Reason, Debate and a Story). Dir. Ritwik Ghatak. Rita Productions and Ritwik Ghatak, 1974. Film.

Pratidwandi (The Adversary). Dir. Satyajit Ray. Nepal Dutta and Asim Dutta. Priya Films, 1970. Film.

Rajadhyaksha, Ashish. *Indian Cinema in the Time of Celluloid: From Bollywood to the Emergency*. Bloomington: Indiana UP, 2009. Print.

Sen, Samar, Debabrata Panda, and Ashish Lahiri, eds. *Naxalbari and After: A Frontier Anthology*. Vols. I and II. Calcutta: Kathashilpa, 1978. Print.

Silverman, Kaja. *The Acoustic Mirror: The Female Voice in Psychoanalysis and Cinema*. Bloomington: Indiana UP, 1988. Print.

Tagore, Rabindranath. *Religion of Man. Rabindranath Tagore Omnibus II.* New Delhi: Rupa, 2003. 1–175. Print.

Utsab (Festival). Dir. Rituparno Ghosh. Tapan Biswas and Sutapa Ghosh. Cinemawallah, 2000. Film.

Part II

Narratives of waste and rupturing the prohibitive

4 Woman as alienated commodity and surplus goods in *Bariwali*

Ghosh's *Bariwali* (*The Lady of the House*, 1999) unfolds the theme of the woman's body as alienated and a gratuitous commodity. This chapter addresses this notion of woman as redundant object by analyzing Ghosh's treatment of the idea of "waste," both metaphorically through dream and metonymically through representations of deteriorating property inhabited by his female protagonist.[1] Further, I argue that while *Bariwali* commences and closes with ideas of "leftover excess," the middle section of the film dramatizes a possibility of "transaction," whereby the lead female character attempts to use property, albeit deteriorating, in an effort to empower herself. Although this endeavor to move out of the stagnating conditions of her life is "unsuccessful," the fact that property alone cannot stand in for woman might precisely be Ghosh's point.

In the Introduction to this volume, I speak briefly of how selected contemporary Bengali directors expose a traditional impulse to make women substitutable or disposable. This chapter analyzes a film that exemplifies a woman's unfortunate internalization of her traditionally determined disposability once her wedding fails to materialize. In addressing the protagonist's attempts at "transaction," mentioned in the preceding paragraph, the chapter also engages the issue of unmaking and making in women, which is one of the foci of this book. However, the film seems to serve as a warning that long-term conditioning and a reduced sense of self can leave such processes of unmaking and making incomplete. The concluding section of this chapter thus posits that, for Ghosh, cinema itself, by embodying such incompletion or "failure" on the screen, can become a means for activating audiences to think beyond certain kinds of relegation and consider possibilities of liberation for women from restrictive social spaces.

Depleted remnants

Instead of plunging into the narrative proper, Ghosh begins with a segment that could seem apparently disconnected to the main storyline in *Bariwali*. The film opens with an officer from the Settlement Office visiting the sprawling home now inherited by Banalata, the female protagonist or *bariwali* of the film, so that he may write up a survey report to assess current taxes on the property. Prasanna, Banalata's old man-servant/retainer, comments that a Radha-Govinda

92 *Narratives of waste, rupturing the prohibitive*

statue[2] had been dug up by one of Banalata's ancestors and worshipped at the temple of the house. The officer responds that according to the Archaeological Survey of India, some remnants of the Pala dynasty[3] were known to exist in the area. Ghosh inserts in this sequence what is to become a major motif in the film, that of depleted remnants when Prasanna informs the officer that the Radha (read "female" or "archetype of the beloved") section of this statue had been stolen and the stone image of Radha replaced by a metal version for the purposes of worship. The officer asks for the deed of the temple and house to ascertain if, indeed, the excavated images were remnants from the Pala period.

This sequence is followed shortly by one in which Prasanna and Banalata debate how to bribe or appease the officer if he should assess high taxes on the property. Prasanna suggests giving to him the painting of a woman draped in wet clothes, something he had admired in the house as an original by the artist Hemen Mazumdar.[4]

After Ghosh establishes here for the audience the possible items for trans-action, i.e., woman's corporeality for reduced taxes, he introduces the main sto-ryline—renting Banalata's premises for the shooting of a film based on Rabindranath Tagore's novel *Chokher Bali*. The director, Dipankar Sengupta, is ready to pay a substantial amount each day for Banalata's property. Prasanna reminds Banalata that this may help her pay off the officer from the Settlement Office if he should prove difficult about assessing reasonable taxes on the house.

But it is not without purpose that Ghosh has already introduced in the mind of the viewer the notion of depleted remnants or relics and the concept of property somewhat difficult to maintain. He genders, more explicitly, the theme of depleted or even gratuitous property through the figure of the middle-aged, bloated, ailing, and single woman—Banalata. Not just the *bariwali* or owner of the house, Banalata embodies traits of the house itself, which is something of a white elephant and now in a state of dereliction. Ghosh adds to this the theme of property tainted by a generational curse (as Marx, reversely, sees poverty).[5]

Banalata is not only inheritor of the house, but bears the burden of a curse which, as we are told in the scenes with the officer and Prasanna, has taken early the lives of some of her male ancestors in the house as also that of her mother three years after her birth. Further, although Banalata lives on, her husband-to-be dies of snake-bite two days before their arranged wedding. Thus, particularly as contrasted with her youthful maid, who is engaged in a passionate affair with her lover,[6] Banalata is presented as an alienated, degenerating body, as surplus goods or property that cannot be *put to use*.

The metaphor of waste

Ghosh underscores this notion of excess or waste through a remarkably executed dream sequence in which Banalata envisions the never-to-materialize events of her own wedding. In this first dream sequence in the film, Malati, the maid, informs Banalata that the members of the groom's party will not eat the food served them because this has been eaten first by a cat. This, of course, is

Woman as alienated commodity and surplus goods 93

transferred over into Banalata's dream from an actual event earlier in the day when Malati reported that a cat had mouthed the food left uneaten by the officer from the Settlement Office. As Sigmund Freud explains for us in *An Outline of Psycho-Analysis*:

> It is best to begin by pointing out that the formation of a dream can be provoked in two different ways. Either, on the one hand, an instinctual impulse which is ordinarily suppressed (an unconscious wish) finds enough strength during sleep to make itself felt by the ego, or, on the other hand, an urge left over from waking life, a preconscious train of thought with all the conflicting impulses attached to it, finds reinforcement during sleep from an unconscious element.
>
> (166)[7]

Banalata's "preconscious train of thought" on the food offered to but not eaten by the officer finds expression in the "*manifest* content" (Freud 165)[8] of her dream as food rejected by members of the groom's party.

However, the larger part of the "manifest content" of Banalata's dream seems to be "provoked" by an "instinctual impulse" for marriage or companionship. Thus, next in the dream, Banalata, dressed as a Bengali bride would be on the morning of her wedding and marked by turmeric paste on her face,[9] walks up to a window decorated above with colored glass and through which we can view the wedding *pandal*.[10] We can also see, through Banalata's perspective from an upper story window, a handful of married women circling that which is hidden. In a Bengali wedding ceremony, this is one of the first rituals—the *boron*, in which married women circle the newly-arrived groom to welcome him into the bride's family. The invisibility of the groom in this case, however, suggests the emptiness of the ritual. Banalata calls out to Prasanna, from the window, to lay out the banana/plantain leaves—leaves on which food is traditionally served at a Bengali ceremony. Even if we assume that Banalata asks Prasanna to put out the leaves for the groom's party and not the general guests at the wedding,[11] in spite of the fact that earlier in the dream she hears of their rejection of the food, this coheres well with Freud's analysis of what he calls the "dream-work," "the way in which unconscious material from the id (originally unconscious and repressed unconscious alike) forces its way into the ego, becomes preconscious and, as a result of the ego's opposition, undergoes the changes which we know as *dream-distortion*" (165).[12]

In reference to his study of the "dream-work," Freud notes that:

> The governing rules of logic carry no weight in the unconscious; it might be called the Realm of the Illogical. Urges with contrary aims exist side by side in the unconscious without any need arising for an adjustment between them. Either they have no influence whatever on each other, or, if they have, no decision is reached, but a compromise comes about which is nonsensical since it embraces mutually incompatible details. With this is connected the

94 *Narratives of waste, rupturing the prohibitive*

fact that contraries are not kept apart but treated as though they were identical, so that in the manifest dream any element may also have the meaning of its opposite.

(168–9)[13]

Thus, it is possible that Banalata's urge to feed a guest who arrives at her house, in this case the officer, and her urge for marriage co-exist "in the unconscious" and constitute "mutually incompatible details." A "nonsensical" "compromise" does come about, so that in her "manifest dream," these two "contraries" are brought together in her enjoinder to Prasanna to serve food at her own wedding, but what we also see are two other "contraries" that are brought together, two elements, in fact, that have precisely the "opposite" meanings of each other, and these are Malati, the maid's mention of the rejection of the food and Banalata's insistence, nevertheless, that the leaves be laid out so the food may be served.

After she calls out from the window, one of the married women circling the void looks up, askance, at her. It is Prasanna, the male retainer, draped in a red sari, wearing the bright red powder in his parting and on his forehead,[14] and with a face now horrifically transformed into that of a *hijra*.[15] He tells Banalata that the banana leaves cannot be used for food, for they are needed to build a float in which to put the snake-bitten corpse to send it down the river.

In having the old manservant of the film transform into a married woman, a servant who also, because of the occasional association of castration with the *hijra* in India, represents the site of the possible absence of sexuality, Ghosh signals the complete negation of sexual intimacy and gratification that marriage could have brought Banalata. Prasanna, here, signifies both what could have been and what never will be for Banalata. In my reading, Ghosh's depiction of him as *hijra* foregrounds not so much the grotesqueness of otherness, but the marginalization that marks Banalata's life.

For the Bengali viewer, this first dream sequence further reverberates with echoes from the Bengali epic *Manashamangal*, written somewhere between the thirteenth and eighteenth centuries. The epic recounts the Behula-Lakhindar legend, in which Chand Saudagar's refusal to worship the snake-goddess, Manasha, results in his son, Lakhindar, dying from snake-bite on the night of his wedding, despite an iron chamber that had been built to protect the married couple, Lakhindar and Behula. Behula then carries her husband's corpse in a banana boat down a river and pleases the gods through her prowess in dancing, successfully persuading them to plead with Manasha. Her husband's life is consequently restored.

In the theme song of *Bariwali*, a song about marriage and the rituals of marriage, and a song heard in the background in the three dream sequences of the film, the groom's father is referred to as Chand, reminding the viewer of the father-in-law in the Behula-Lakhindar legend. However, in an early flashback in the film, Banalata's wedding invitation card, read out aloud obviously for the benefit of the audience by an ancestor now long dead, gives us Manashacharan (one who is the feet of or worships at the feet of Manasha) as the actual name of the father-in-law to be. However, in spite of the fact that the initially intransigent father-in-law of the Bengali epic *Manashamangal* is suggestively replaced here by a more compliant one, that is, one who is ready to be a devotee, Banalata's destiny cannot be reversed. And Ghosh implies the waste that is a corollary of this fate through mention of tainted food that is rejected by the groom's party and banana leaves that instead of satiating eaters with a feast will now drift away, bearing the corpse of the groom who did not even arrive to be received into the bride's family.[16]

The non-happening of this wedding also, of course, as suggested metaphorically in the dream sequence, marks Banalata as isolated property and wasted goods—concepts she internalizes about herself, particularly as she ages, and concepts she plays out in her own life, alienating herself from social interaction and seeing herself often as ailing and non-functional.

Dream as explosion of desire

The renting out of her property to director Dipankar Sengupta for the shooting of an art film, thus, signifies on two levels: first, it is the profitable *putting to use* of Banalata's run-down premises, and second, it is the opening up of herself, although tentatively at first, for social interaction. The fact, however, that the shooting is scheduled to commence on February 17, a few days before Banalata's wedding date several years ago, also suggests a quasi-shadowy penumbra zone. It evokes a time from the past when Banalata awaited the arrival of a much-anticipated wedding day that promised the fulfillment of desire, a promise negated because of the groom's death from poisonous snake-bite.

If we can conceptualize the shooting of this film within a film, in its entirety, as a second, and therefore reiterated, unfolding of that time in Banalata's life—a time in which the reality of the poison-ridden body cancels out the possibility of romantic and sexual gratification—, then we can understand the significance of February 17 and the fact that Ghosh juxtaposes here (in the shooting sequences) the forces of negation and desire. I will return, later in this chapter, to this notion of a film within a film to discuss in more detail the kinds of contrast it arguably mobilizes.

The third dream sequence of *Bariwali* resonates with Banalata's growing romantic and erotic desire for the director, Dipankar Sengupta. Ghosh conveys that Banalata's craving for marriage has not dissipated through visual and auditory cues, such as a framed wedding photograph of her ancestors in the background and the soundtrack playing the film's theme song about wedding rituals. As Banalata lies on her bed, her movements suggest erotic interactions, and an elaborately hand-embroidered quilt is progressively pulled off her body. In a separate shot, we see the director, Dipankar, apparently standing at the foot of the bed, gazing down at Banalata's quilt, fingering it, putting his face in it, and commending her for her work in embroidery. It should be mentioned here that in actuality, as the film's crew sought around for items they needed on the sets and borrowed a few such from Banalata, Dipankar chose and admired a piece of fabric, secured tightly in a frame, that Banalata was then embroidering.[17]

96 *Narratives of waste, rupturing the prohibitive*

Having this fabric come loose and take on the form of an enveloping quilt, in this third dream sequence, enables Ghosh to begin unpacking for his audience the totality of repression in Banalata's desires. When Banalata says that the quilt is made not just by her, but passed down and added on to through three generations, we are reminded of the generational curse that haunts this family. It is as if the curse is concretized now in a material item, an item owned presently by Banalata, just as she owns the sprawling and deteriorating premises on which she must accommodate the film's crew. But of course, the notion of adding on also brings to mind the accretion of repression, in Banalata's body and psyche, as the years pass.

In contrast to the reality of this repression, Ghosh presents the explosion of desire in dream, as it is revealed that beneath the quilt, Banalata wears the fashionable undergarments worn by the beautiful actress cast as the heroine of Dipankar's film rather than her traditional garb that drapes over and covers her body.

It is necessary to digress here, from the dream, to explain the impact of the heroine, Sudeshna, on Banalata, especially because of how this impact leads to the unfolding of desire in this third dream sequence of *Bariwali*. In a terrace scene in the film, as Banalata and Dipankar walk, they are acutely embarrassed by the sight of a woman's (most likely Sudeshna's) undergarments drying in the sun, draped over the body of a nude, female, and European-looking statue. Dipankar orders that his cast dry their clothes on a different section of the terrace, obviously one not frequented by Banalata. Towards the beginning of this sequence, as Dipankar and Banalata proceed together, Sudeshna appears and points to a grayish shawl that she is wearing and that has been designated as part of her costume for an upcoming shot, asking Dipankar if she could borrow his black one instead. Earlier in the course of the film, the audience has come to know that Sudeshna and Dipankar shared a romantic relationship at one time, and this information is conveyed to Banalata by her maid, Malati, who is inordinately interested in film-related gossip. Another fact that Malati reveals to Banalata is that Sudeshna wears exquisite nylon petticoats edged with lace embroidery, beneath her saris, rather than the more common cotton ones.

As the quilt is pulled down from Banalata's body in the third dream sequence, we see, other than the fashionable bra, which Banalata does not wear in actuality, a nylon petticoat lined with lace embroidery covering her legs. In a film distinctly about concepts of property, ownership, and material possessions, Ghosh strategically uses material items to show the build-up of desire and Banalata's need to become Sudeshna. In this dream, Banalata fulfills that need by discarding material items she dons in her everyday life or visualizing *her* material possessions being pulled off her body and putting on articles of clothing owned by the woman who had once been the object of Dipankar's desire. A further transference is played out as Banalata asks Dipankar for his black shawl in order to cover her undergarments and conceal them (it is unclear whether she means undergarments on her body or hanging on the terrace), thus taking Sudeshna's earlier intimacy-based request to him one step further.

Property and the romantic circuit of exchange

Yet, in reality, Banalata is represented as having not much to offer Dipankar either in terms of physical beauty or talent. The sub-text of the Behula-Lakhindar legend, used by Ghosh in this film, reminds the viewer of how Behula uses her prowess in dancing to bring her husband back to life. Similarly, Sudeshna, the heroine of Dipankar's film, is shown to be an expert exponent of Tagore's songs, songs that she sings spontaneously and beautifully when there are breaks from the shooting. In the absence of youth, or beauty, or talent, and in the face of her characteristic reserve, what does Banalata use to begin a process of exchange, even if this is a process of romantic exchange, with Dipankar?

If the audience understands that Behula, in the midst of grief, barters her dancing to regain life for her husband, and Sudeshna, also marked by sorrow because of the end of the affair with Dipankar, attempts to lure him again with her singing and the authenticity she brings to her acting, then they also see that Rituparno Ghosh has already indicated that Banalata is interested in such processes of exchange. This brings me back to my previous points on depleted remnants, redundant property, and woman as gratuitous commodity. Early in *Bariwali*, Ghosh suggestively conflates property and woman. As Banalata opens up her premises for the shooting of the film or finds items for the sets, Ghosh implies that she is ready to *put herself to use* once again. Other than her romantic interest in Dipankar, her growing friendship with another member of the film's crew, the art director, Debashish, further corroborates this fact.

Banalata understands that the process of a romantic transaction with Dipankar is a difficult one, as stripped as she is of youth and glamour and without any striking talents with which to captivate him. She attempts to compensate by cooking an elaborate meal for him on his birthday and asking him *not to pay her anything* for the use of her property for the shooting of his film. At this point, because of an altercation between the hero of Dipankar's film and the art director, the hero has departed from the sets, and the shooting is stalled. So, apparently it seems Banalata wants to help reduce Dipankar's financial losses. However, it can be argued that this offer of her property gratis stands in for things she is unable to offer him herself. In the early sequences of the film, Ghosh focused on showing the parallels in the decrepitude that was in evidence in both the woman and her property. In subsequent sections of *Bariwali*, however, he shows us how the woman attempts to *use* her property precisely because she is aware of the decrepitude and dearth within herself.

Thus, I prefer translating the title of this Ghosh film not as he does, *Lady of the House*, but more literally as *Owner of the House*. As I discussed earlier, Banalata's servant, Prasanna, mentioned giving to the officer from the Settlement Office the painting of a scantily-clad woman in the hopes of him assessing reduced taxes on the property. In the absence of such alluring corporeality with which to entice Dipankar, Banalata has her house stand in for herself. She makes the decision to forego the profit she could make from renting out her premises, a profit that Prasanna told her would help pay the officer if he should assess high

98   *Narratives of waste, rupturing the prohibitive*

taxes on the house. Not only is her inherited property no longer a white elephant, now replete with the possibility of profit, but Banalata herself cancels out that possibility of economic profit in order to *use* the house, in a final attempt to convert the waste of her life to meaningful gain. And so, if we translate *Bariwali* as *Owner of the House*, it follows that not only can Banalata rent out the house if she pleases, but she can retract from that position and put the house to *use* in any other way more profitable to herself.

In *Capital*, Karl Marx writes of the owner of a commodity who is ready to introduce it into the circuit of exchange:

> His commodity possesses for himself no immediate use-value. Otherwise, he would not bring it to the market. It has use-value for others; but for himself its only direct use-value is that of being a depository of exchange value, and consequently, a means of exchange. Therefore, he makes up his mind to part with it for commodities whose value in use is of service to him. (97)[18]

Further, he says, "The first step made by an object of utility towards acquiring exchange-value is when it forms a non-use-value for its owner, and that happens when it forms a superfluous portion of some article required for his immediate wants" (99).[19]

The terms from Marx most relevant to my argument here are "a depository of exchange value" and "a superfluous portion of some article required for his immediate wants." In *Bariwali*, Banalata rents out that portion of her property that she does not use herself, that is, in fact, "superfluous" or a surplus. As per Prasanna's advice, this portion becomes for her "a depository of [possible] exchange value." And quite clearly, this portion of her house "has use-value for others," namely the film's crew. But since, from the very beginning of his film, Ghosh has conflated property and woman, merely getting monetary value for her premises is not going to help in the closing of the narrative in *Bariwali*.

What Banalata comes to understand then, in the unfolding of this narrative, is that it is the "superfluous portion" of herself, no matter how depleted, that portion which is more than her needs of consumption for survival, that she desires to become "a depository of [possible] exchange value." It is this "portion" or part of herself whose worth she wants affirmed. Yet, as I discussed above, in the absence of striking beauty or explicit talents, Banalata understands it is difficult for Dipankar, in the short time he is there to complete the shooting of his film, to affirm her worth, to reciprocate the desire she begins to feel for him.

If we go back to Marx's terminology, we know that the owner of a commodity "makes up his mind to part with it for commodities whose value in use is of service to him" (97).[20] Initially, Banalata parts with a section of her property, temporarily, for a monetary gain. Yet, progressively, what she wants in exchange for her property or commodity is not money, but some form of romantic reciprocity from Dipankar. Thus, she offers up her house to him for free, not only to

Woman as alienated commodity and surplus goods   99

make up for the perceived lack in herself, but in hopes that he will close the circuit of exchange by affirming her value as someone meaningful to him personally. There is a brief suggestion that this is a possibility when, at the end of the birthday sequence, Dipankar admits to Banalata that no one has ever given him such a good birthday present, and is about to join hands with her in what we could read as a closing of this "transaction" between them.

Mark Osteen's comments, in his essay "Female Property: Women and Gift Exchange in *Ulysses*," are relevant here. Osteen provides key points from Lewis Hyde's argument in *The Gift: Imagination and the Erotic Life of Property* to show how gift-giving undermines the material value of objects/property, promoting instead an "erotic" system of exchange that induces "kinship." He notes:

> gifts are "anarchist property" because they must always move: to retain a gift is to deny the very social relation that engenders its meaning.... As property, then, gifts always perish.... Because of this kinetic pattern and their theoretically infinite circulation, gift exchanges blur or transcend interpersonal boundaries and knit together donor and receiver. Moreover, the gift economy flouts the market economy of commodified exchanges designed to create balance, instead offering a fluid economy in which persons are not alienated from goods. Perhaps because of this subversion of market exchange, Hyde describes gifts as "female property."... Furthermore, he maintains that the process is itself feminine, because gift exchange embraces fluidity and promotes the establishment of kinship and communal ties.... The feminine gift economy is thus an erotic economy—one associated with *Eros*—in contrast to the male, logocentric economy of profit and commerce.
>
> (29)[21]

Osteen adds, "The gift economy is thus 'improper,' in that it subverts the idea of '*proper*'-ty" (41).[22]

I would like to reiterate here, however, that Banalata attempts not only to initiate what she hopes will be a romantic circuit of exchange, but uses property to empower herself. Thus, the birthday sequence in *Bariwali* captures not just the fluidity of the gift-giving economy, but how in Banalata's case, this system of exchange also indicates a movement towards self-empowerment, a movement away from the sense of waste and alienation that has dominated her life.

Perhaps it is to underscore this incipient power in his female protagonist that Ghosh follows up the birthday sequence, in which Banalata makes Dipankar this offer, with one in which Sudeshna, the heroine of Dipankar's film, is left to feel totally inadequate before her. In this latter sequence, Sudeshna sits on the steps of Banalata's house at dusk and sings a song by Tagore, "*Tumi kōn bhangōner pothé elé, shuptō raté*" ("Down what path of destruction have you come, in the sleeping night?").[23] Although it might seem that she has Dipankar in mind, because she continues to feel drawn to him in spite of the fact that their relationship did not work out and his love of alcohol is openly discussed by his crew, the sequence actually shows us Banalata approaching and sitting down by

100 *Narratives of waste, rupturing the prohibitive*

Sudeshna. If Ghosh intends to show a degree of empowerment in Banalata by the way in which she uses her property, he complicates that in this sequence with Sudeshna, in which Banalata's approach, if analyzed in conjunction with the first line of Tagore's song, can be read as the arrival of destruction.

This destructive potential in Banalata, foregrounded briefly by Ghosh to suggest that she can wipe out the last vestiges of romance between Sudeshna and Dipankar, takes on overtones of an ominous need to control and contain when Banalata asks Prasanna three times to lock the gates to the house. She then reminds Sudeshna that it is Dipankar's birthday and not only has she given him food offered up during worship, that morning, at the temple of her house, but herself prepared and served him a meal appropriate to the occasion. When Sudeshna requests that the gates be unlocked, so she may go and wish Dipankar,[24] Banalata refuses gently but firmly, elaborating that the process of locking the gates is a complex one and not easy to undo.

In this sequence, not only does Banalata contain the rival claimant to Dipankar's attention, but once again, Ghosh demonstrates how, as *bariwali*, she manipulates her rights to her property in ways most suitable to herself. The destructive and the ominous forces that marked her early life with tragedy and later unmitigated sterility are now shown to exist as submerged forces in her own personality, forces she ironically brings into play with the help of inherited property.

Disposability in life and art

Ultimately, however, Ghosh is not focused on showing how inherited wealth enables empowerment. Consequently, the end of the film dramatizes the process of a second negation and disillusionment for Banalata. In this instance, though, it is not an accidental death, but the incisive professionalism of Dipankar's personality, that forecloses the possibility of gratification for Banalata.

When an actress designated to play a minor role in his film fails to show up for location shooting, Dipankar goes to Banalata. Uncomprehending, she says to him that ultimately, he has to depend (for a solution) on the benevolence of her household deities, Radha-Govinda, this, of course, reminding the audience of the statue of the twosome that was once depleted. Dipankar, however, informs her that it is Banalata whom he depends on, she who must now enact this role in the film, the role of a married woman who, in one scene, acts as foil to the widow played by Sudeshna.

In dramatizing beautifully for us Banalata's initial outright refusal and then, her continued tremulousness and hesitance in playing this role, Rituparno Ghosh connects her back to the depleted relics that serve as her household gods, obviously underscoring her undermined sense of self. But this reluctance also brings to mind significant passages from Freud's *Mourning and Melancholia*. Although Banalata does not evince all the characteristics of Freud's full-fledged melancholic, certainly applicable to her is the following observation, "The melancholic displays something else besides which is lacking in mourning—an extraordinary

Woman as alienated commodity and surplus goods 101

diminution in his self-regard, an impoverishment of his ego on a grand scale" (*Mourning* 246).[25]

More significant to my discussion, however, is another passage from Freud's text:

> There is one observation not at all difficult to make.... If one listens patiently to a melancholic's many and various self-accusations, one can not in the end avoid the impression that often the most violent of them are hardly at all applicable to the patient himself, but that with insignificant modifications, they do fit someone else, someone whom the patient loves or has loved or should love. Every time one examines the facts this conjecture is confirmed. So we find the key to the clinical picture: we perceive that the self-reproaches are reproaches against a loved object which have been shifted away from it on to the patient's own ego.
>
> (*Mourning* 248)[26]

In the case of *Bariwali*, the "someone" whom Banalata feels she "should love" is, as suggested in all three dream sequences of the film, a husband. This husband or, in her life, husband-to-be dies, thus not just denoting absence, but connoting incapacity, the inability to bring to her all that marriage signifies for a traditional Bengali woman.

It is most likely this inability, this *not being able to perform* that angers Banalata about the "husband" she "should love." If anything, it is this aspect about his absence that she wants to subject to reproach.[27] However, Banalata shifts the reproach away from the husband she should have loved to herself, recounting to Dipankar how, even in her childhood, she could never perform the right action at the right time. As Freud notes of the melancholic, "He is not of the opinion that a change has taken place in him, but extends his self-criticism back over the past; he declares that he was never any better" (*Mourning* 246).[28] As I mentioned earlier, although Banalata is not quite the melancholic that Freud describes, because she *is* able to transfer her love to other objects/persons than the one lost,[29] she clearly demonstrates a "diminution in ... self-regard" (Freud, *Mourning* 246),[30] both in addressing her inadequacy in her childhood and in her belief that she will be unable to perform the role offered her. It can also be argued, following Freud's line of thought in *Mourning*, that she attacks this inability not so much in herself, but in the dead husband-to-be whose failure to arrive affects her life and thinking so significantly.

Eventually, Banalata does perform in the scene in Dipankar's film, dressed elaborately as a married woman, but the last heavy blow in *Bariwali* is dealt her when she is informed that during editing Dipankar has cut the scene from his film, which was getting too long and unwieldy. This signifies at least two things for Ghosh's viewing audience. First, even Banalata's attempts to *impersonate* a married woman, in the realm of art, are brought to naught, forcefully re-invoking the sense of waste with which *Bariwali* opened. As in life before Dipankar's crew arrived at her house, so also in the world of Dipankar's film, Banalata is

102 *Narratives of waste, rupturing the prohibitive*

nothing but a redundant, and in the latter case disposable, commodity. Second, it points to Dipankar's expediency, clarifying for us that Banalata has no emotional value for him[31] and that, in fact, he was never seriously interested in a process of romantic transaction with her.

This leaning towards what is most expedient is foregrounded as a not very attractive aspect of Dipankar's character somewhat earlier in Ghosh's film. For instance, towards the end of *Bariwali*, when the shooting on Banalata's premises is still in progress, the officer from the Settlement Office returns, but instead of being interested in assessing Banalata's property, he attempts to provide Dipankar with published materials about the status of women, particularly widows, in Bengal in order to help enhance the authenticity of representation in his film. The film Dipankar is shooting, *Chokher Bali*, focuses primarily on the trials and tribulations faced by widows in late nineteenth-century Bengal.

At first, the officer mentions serialized compositions by Kanaklata Devi, a Bengali woman, published between 1953 and 1955 in a weekly journal, *Amrita*. Although from a different time period than the context of Dipankar's film, he says that these are recorded facts that capture contemporary society from a woman's perspective; that he has the cut-outs of the articles; and would be willing to give them to Dipankar. He also produces a list of books on related issues. As director, however, Dipankar is uninterested in his first offer and turns the list over, without glancing at it, to one of his production assistants. Finally, the officer says that he has forgotten to include one engaging article in the list, an article on widows following certain rules, but Dipankar cuts into his talk, claiming that film is not all about conveying information, but about "visual appeal" and "mood."

This is also the time when the crew is disturbed by the failure of the actress to show up and before Dipankar asks Banalata to play the role. Not only does Dipankar interrupt the officer, he virtually dismisses his presence as he shifts his attention to his assistant, asking him to go to the club in the area and inquire if the members could suggest a local actress for the part.[32] For him, authenticity of representation is far less important than completing the shooting as quickly as possible.

Cinematic illusion and the ideal spectator

Dipankar's immediately preceding comments on film being about "visual appeal" and "mood" are, of course, highly debatable, but they also bring to mind well-known concepts from Christian Metz's *The Imaginary Signifier: Psycho-analysis and the Cinema*, concepts which juxtapose the "perceptual wealth" offered by film with the very absence at its heart. As Metz notes:

> Thus the cinema, "more perceptual" than certain arts according to the list of its sensory registers, is also "less perceptual" than others once the status of these perceptions is envisaged rather than their number or diversity; for its perceptions are all in a sense "false." Or rather, the activity of perception

Woman as alienated commodity and surplus goods 103

which it involves is real (the cinema is not a phantasy), but the perceived is not really the object, it is its shade, its phantom, its double, its *replica* in a new kind of mirror.... The unique position of the cinema lies in this dual character of its signifier: unaccustomed perceptual wealth, but at the same time stamped with unreality to an unusual degree, and from the very outset.

(44–5)[33]

Metz draws on Freudian and Lacanian notions of the ego and ego formation to argue that:

The imaginary of the cinema presupposes the symbolic, for the spectator must first of all have known the primordial mirror. But as the latter instituted the ego very largely in the imaginary, the second mirror of the screen, a symbolic apparatus, itself in turn depends on reflection and lack.

(57)[34]

Metz goes on to note that "the specific affinity between the cinematic signifier and the imaginary persists when film is compared with arts such as the theatre" (61). Whereas in theater, the "audio-visual given" "is physically present, in the same space as the spectator," the

cinema only gives it in effigy, inaccessible from the outset, in a primordial *elsewhere*, infinitely desirable (= never possessible), on another scene which is that of absence and which nonetheless represents the absent in detail, thus making it very present, but by a different itinerary.

(Metz 61)[35]

Of course, it can be argued very easily that in *Bariwali*, Ghosh uses the making of a film within a film to indicate that Dipankar and his crew's arrival on Banalata's premises is, indeed, an adumbration of what will constitute a deeper and more devastating awareness of lack for Banalata; that the making of a film within a film juxtaposes, as I claim earlier in this chapter, the forces of desire and negation in a modified reiteration of the earlier tragedy in Banalata's life; that it only "gives" what is "inaccessible from the outset, in a primordial *elsewhere*, infinitely desirable (= never possessible)" (Metz 61).[36] In other words, Ghosh's insertion of film-making within *Bariwali*, with Banalata largely a spectator of this process, places at center something "stamped with unreality" (Metz 45)[37] to prepare us for the absence(s) that will continue to mark Banalata's life. While Metz addresses the *apparatus* of cinema in his argument, I draw here on his ideas to show how the "unreality" and the non-possessible that he associates with cinema work metaphorically in Ghosh's film.

Yet, I will launch here a somewhat different argument as regards the role of cinema in *Bariwali*. This is perhaps the only one of his four films under extended discussion in my study in which Ghosh does not show his female protagonist empowered in some form or other at the close of the diegesis.[38] Thus, we are left

104 *Narratives of waste, rupturing the prohibitive*

with Banalata with her expectations negated, disillusioned, and "broken" a second time. Yet, this "double denial" that seems to enclose the narrative about Banalata within the diegetic material of the film could, other than pointing to a sense of waste and vulnerability, suggest that it is timely and necessary to move beyond cultural constructs that induce such feelings in women.

In a discussion of Tsai Ming-liang's *The River*, in *Sentimental Fabulations, Contemporary Chinese Films*, Rey Chow addresses a scene in which father and son unintentionally engage in sex in the darkness of a gay men's bathhouse. Despite drawing our attention to the "public facility" in which this act happens, its "seedy-looking interiors," the "transient" nature of the relationships there, Chow yet locates in this scene a "rare instant of connectivity" and "a reciprocal tenderness" (189).[39] She goes even further to note:

> In this scene, the allegorical nature of Tsai's work can be clearly detected, in the enigmatic manner in which a utopian aperture unveils itself under the most oppressive and censorious of social conditions.... I am tempted to add that herein lies, perhaps, the uniqueness of Tsai's cinematic discursivity. Whereas in the hands of some other directors, the obvious destitution and deviance of his characters—lonesome, inarticulate, mysteriously ill, sexually perverse, morally anarchic—might have simply stopped at being stark portrayals of existential angst, in Tsai's works, such destitution and deviance, collected from an archaeology of contemporary urban human types—psychically defective and disabled, to be sure—become elements of a different sensorium and sociality, whereby it is precisely the limits, thresholds, prohibitions, and repressed intensities that are tracked, taken apart, and remolded into potentialities for remaking the world.
>
> (Chow 190)[40]

In her discussion of *The River*, then, Chow is interested in looking at the other side of "destitution and deviance" (190),[41] in examining how, for Tsai, possibilities for re-thinking socio-cultural constructs exist within figures and relationships that are on the margins of what is considered normative. I believe that similarly in *Bariwali*, Ghosh does not give his audience a reprieve from the intensity of the (second) rejection and consequent grief felt by Banalata *because* he wants us to assess the limits of her situation. After the accidental death of her husband-to-be, she leads, for years, a life of isolation, (self) confinement, and general immobility. One could speculate that she has internalized the cultural stigma that sometimes attaches, in India, to women whose grooms fail to arrive on the wedding day.[42] It is as if these women are inadequate even though they may have had nothing to do with the non-arrival of the groom. Indeed, it is not uncommon to view them as "surplus goods" since it is supposedly difficult to find another husband for them. When Banalata is attracted to another man, who happens to arrive at her house, she attempts to empower herself through the use of inherited property rather than through traits that she possesses and believes in. This general lack of conviction in herself and her chosen life of alienation and inactivity prior to Dipankar's arrival show her acquiescence to one way of thinking within the culture, a way of thinking that relegates such women to the margins as "commodities" without much use.

I like to think that at the end of *Bariwali*, Ghosh wishes the cinematic signifier, its "unaccustomed perceptual wealth" (Metz 45)[43] to resonate for his audience beyond the dimensions of the screen. In *The Imaginary Signifier*, Metz argues that the spectator of cinema understands himself as "a kind of transcendental subject," as "the condition of possibility of the perceived" (49).[44] He says of the spectator, "I ... know that it is I who am perceiving all this, that this perceived-imaginary material is deposited in me as if on a second screen, that it is in me that it forms up into an organized sequence" (Metz 48).[45] Beyond the "perceptual wealth" that unfolds on the screen, beyond what Dipankar calls "visual appeal" and "mood," and after the viewing time of the film itself, there still remains the spectator, whose presence not only brings meaning to the events on the screen, but whose presence can continue to ensure the presence of the ideas the film puts into circulation.

Thus, although both the film within the film in *Bariwali* and *Bariwali* itself can be seen, in Metz's words, as a "shade," a "phantom," a "double" (45)[46] of the real, I will argue that it is this "unreality," this absence that Ghosh wishes to situate as continuing presence in the minds of his viewers. To put it differently, although the abundance and immediacy of the perceptual are forms of illusion in film and lost with the end of the viewing, their initial force and residual impact translate into gain, with the audience assessing and disseminating the ideas generated by the film.

It is unfortunate that as spectator even of the *process* of film-making itself, a process that with its setting up of scenes, cuts, and so forth, should have alerted Banalata to its inherent constructed nature, she is devastated by the cutting that deletes her from a world already always marked with unreality. She focuses on this deletion, an act which removes her (or her performance/contribution) and in which she had no part. Thus, she refuses to see the film when it is released, a film that with its exploration of the restrictions in a widow's life could very well have made her think anew about her own.

What I wish to conclude with here is that Ghosh gives us Banalata as an incomplete or inadequate spectator, that is the spectator so seduced by the "perceptual wealth"[47] that helps construct a set or unfolds on the screen[48] that she is unable to move beyond this "fullness," the reverse of which is emptiness. Thus, the process of film-making within *Bariwali* foreshadows not just further deprivation in Banalata's life, but suggestively foregrounds Ghosh's notions of the ideal spectator. For this spectator, the screen cannot and must not be the last word of cinema. The lack or absence that lurks behind the fullness temporarily embodied on the screen is less significant to this viewer than how cinematic plenitude can transform to a different kind of fullness: an assessing of the ideas generated by the film.

In Jean-Luc Godard's *La Chinoise*, the character of Kirilov says that art or "the imaginary doesn't reflect reality. It's the reality of the reflection."[49] Through

106 *Narratives of waste, rupturing the prohibitive*

his representation of the character of Banalata in *Bariwali*, Rituparno Ghosh brings for us a cultural reality to reflect on—a reality in which certain women involuntarily become excess and are relegated to the fringes of society. Yet, it is also *his* version of this reality—an entire film devoted to such an existence—not the least because his protagonist is complicit in such social marginalization. His protagonist absorbs, without questioning, what society or cinema (within cinema) constructs for her and breaks down when she can absorb no more. When we have left behind the plenitude of the diegesis in *Bariwali* and have been unsettled by the shock of Banalata's "second exclusion," the last thing Ghosh wants us to be is an uncritical spectator whose cinematic experience stops with absorbing his representation of a social reality on the screen. Rather, I believe Ghosh wishes us to continue to ponder, in our individual ways, the issue of waste—both the waste that happens when women are culturally marked as "surplus goods" and play into such marking and the waste that could happen if we relegate a cultural text such as *Bariwali* to the screen and fail to evaluate or mobilize discussion about the ideas it brings into play as its audience.

Notes

1 Here, I draw on Christian Metz's use of the terms "metaphor" and "metonymy" in his discussion of film in *The Imaginary Signifier: Psychoanalysis and the Cinema.* Trans. Celia Britton, Annwyl Williams, Ben Brewster and Alfred Guzzetti. Bloomington: Indiana UP, 1982.
2 Govinda is one of Lord Krishna's many names. Krishna, the most famous incarnation of Vishnu, the Preserver in the Hindu Trinity, is also, perhaps, the most secularized of the Hindu gods in that myth, literature, and song have detailed his amorous play with his beloved, Radha.
3 The Pala dynasty ruled over Bengal and Bihar from the eighth to the twelfth century AD. The Palas were Buddhists, so, if indeed, as the officer says, the Radha-Govinda statue is a remnant from the Pala period, this statue would have been worshipped by a Hindu household or population in the region. Of course, it is possible that this is not an archaeological remain from the Pala period.
4 Originally from what is now Bangladesh, Hemen Mazumdar was a renowned Bengali artist who lived and worked in prominent Indian cities, such as Kolkata and Mumbai, in the first half of the twentieth century.
5 For instance, in *Capital: A Critique of Political Economy*, Karl Marx notes:

> The folly is now patent of the economic wisdom that preaches to the labourers the accommodation of their numbers to the requirements of capital.... The first word of this adaptation is the creation of a relative surplus-population, or industrial reserve-army. Its last word is the misery of constantly extending strata of the active army of labour, and the dead weight of pauperism.
>
> (707)

See *Capital.* Vol. I. Ed. Frederick Engels. Trans. Samuel Moore and Edward Aveling from 3rd German ed. Rev. Ernest Untermann according to 4th German ed. Chicago: Kerr, 1906. In Ghosh's film, it is not wealth, per se, which is the generational curse, but things associated with wealth. Prasanna tells the officer, for instance, that one of Banalata's uncles died of a "wealth-related illness." One can assume that this could be excessive drinking or contracting a disease from visiting prostitutes. Banalata, herself, suffers not because she is rich, but because she has to

Woman as alienated commodity and surplus goods 107

maintain, at least to some extent as through paying taxes, the considerable property that she has inherited. Other than these, there is also some sense of a curse on the property itself.

6 In a 2007 interview with me, Ghosh discussed how Banalata sees her maid, Malati, as a threat because of her youth. In contrast to this, she feels more comfortable with her aging manservant, Prasanna. Further, in the second dream sequence of the film, although Banalata is beautifully dressed and engaged in an intimate conversation with the director, Dipankar, the figure that is dressed as a Bengali bride and intervenes between them is that of the maid.

7 In *The Standard Edition of the Complete Psychological Works of Sigmund Freud.* Vol. XXIII. Trans. and Gen. Ed. James Strachey. London: Hogarth and the Institute of Psycho-Analysis, 1964. 141–207.

8 Freud, *An Outline of Psycho-Analysis.*

9 An important ceremony on the morning of a Bengali wedding is *gayé hōlud*, in which turmeric, which has arrived from the groom's house (first having been touched to the body of the groom), is put on the face and body of the bride.

10 A *pandal* is a structure built of bamboo and decorated with cloth of different colors (specific to the occasion, such as red and white for a wedding) and lights for ceremonies in Bengal.

11 In a Bengali wedding, it is a courtesy to serve food first to the members of the groom's party.

12 Freud, *An Outline of Psycho-Analysis.*

13 Ibid.

14 The bright red powder is *sindoor*, worn on the parting and as a circular mark on the forehead by Hindu married women in India.

15 The *Hijra*, a figure seen occasionally in public places on the Indian sub-continent, is neither quite man nor woman. Apparently or physically male or with ambiguous sexual organs, *Hijra*s generally dress as female. They are severely marginalized in Indian society, live in their own communities, and one way in which they make a living is by arriving in a small group when a baby is born and demanding to bless the baby. They then have to be paid for this.

16 In the West (or specifically in American literature), one story that brilliantly brings us this notion of waste connected with the non-happening of a wedding is Katherine Anne Porter's "The Jilting of Granny Weatherall." See Katherine Anne Porter. "The Jilting of Granny Weatherall." *The Collected Stories of Katherine Anne Porter.* New York: Harcourt, 1965. 80–9.

17 Further, during the shooting of the film on her premises, as Banalata looks in a chest for silver utensils that will be useful for the film's crew, the title deed of her house finally emerges. The fact that she finds this document, which will determine the current value of her property, in the same chest in which she finds items that will be suitable for the sets of Dipankar's film suggests that, somehow, the assessment of her own worth is tied up with the shooting of this film.

18 Marx, *Capital.*

19 Ibid.

20 Ibid.

21 In *Gender in Joyce*. Eds. Jolanta W. Wawrzycka and Marlena G. Corcoran. Gainesville: UP of Florida, 1997. 29–46.

22 Mark Osteen, "Female Property: Women and Gift Exchange in *Ulysses*." *Gender in Joyce*. Eds. Jolanta W. Wawrzycka and Marlena G. Corcoran. Gainesville: UP of Florida, 1997. 29–46. Print.

23 Translation mine.

24 During the shooting of Dipankar's film, he and the rest of his crew members live in rented bungalows outside of Banalata's property, while Sudeshna stays in a room in Banalata's house.

108   *Narratives of waste, rupturing the prohibitive*

25 Sigmund Freud, *Mourning and Melancholia. The Standard Edition of the Complete Psychological Works of Sigmund Freud.* Vol. XIV. Trans. and Gen. Ed. James Strachey. London: Hogarth and the Institute of Psycho-Analysis, 1957. 237–58.

26 Ibid.

27 The second dream sequence of the film, a sequence I have not discussed at length in this chapter, illustrates the importance of "successful" performance in Banalata's psyche. In this dream, Banalata brings Dipankar a book, the novel by Tagore that his film is based on, and asks him to "unlock" it. Dipankar does so with a pen-knife, an obvious phallic symbol in the sequence, and as he "unlocks" it, blood splatters onto Banalata's face, a clear indication of the taking of her virginity.

28 Freud, *Mourning and Melancholia.*

29 In this regard, Banalata is closer to the mourner than the melancholic. See *Mourning and Melancholia*, especially pages 249 and 255. We also, of course, understand that Banalata transfers not so much her love, as the husband-to-be dies before she ever sees him, but her readiness to love.

30 Freud, *Mourning and Melancholia.*

31 Of course, it can be argued that the production of good art should not be tangled up with emotional investments, but Dipankar is well aware that this is the one scene Banalata performed in and also cognizant of the difficulties she surmounted in order to be able to do so. The prioritizing of art over the possible emotional consequences for her, because of this excising, shows his lack of engagement with the human dimension. It should also be mentioned briefly here that Dipankar is, officially, married although he has hardly any contact with his wife, and they live and work separately.

32 In Bengal, sub-groups of local clubs are often engaged in rehearsing for and putting up amateur plays. Thus, they have fairly seasoned actors and actresses. This is what Dipankar is thinking of when he talks to his assistant.

33 Metz, *The Imaginary Signifier.*

34 Ibid.

35 Ibid.

36 Ibid.

37 Ibid.

38 Towards the very end of *Bariwali*, Banalata is able to fix an electrical fuse by herself, something Dipankar had done for her, during an early visit to the house, when it had occurred before. Some viewers may see this as a form of empowerment.

39 See *Sentimental Fabulations, Contemporary Chinese Films: Attachment in the Age of Global Visibility.* New York: Columbia UP, 2007.

40 Ibid.

41 Ibid.

42 In Satyajit Ray's *Apur Sansar* (*The World of Apu*), for instance, the heroine Aparna is about to be left without a husband on her wedding night when it is discovered that the groom is mentally unbalanced. Her cousin requests his friend, Apu, the hero of the film, to marry her so she can escape such cultural stigmatizing.

43 Metz, *The Imaginary Signifier.*

44 Ibid.

45 Ibid.

46 Ibid.

47 Ibid.

48 In *Bariwali*, Ghosh also depicts Banalata as an avid viewer of television.

49 I am quoting from the English subtitles provided for the film.

References

Apur Sansar (*The World of Apu*). Dir. Satyajit Ray. Satyajit Ray Productions, 1959. Film.

Bariwali (*The Lady of the House*). Dir. Rituparno Ghosh. Anupam Kher, 1999. Film.

La Chinoise. Dir. Jean-Luc Godard. Anouchka Films. Athos Films, 1967. Film.

Chow, Rey. *Sentimental Fabulations, Contemporary Chinese Films: Attachment in the Age of Global Visibility*. New York: Columbia UP, 2007. Print.

Freud, Sigmund. *Mourning and Melancholia. The Standard Edition of the Complete Psychological Works of Sigmund Freud*. Vol. XIV. Trans. and Gen. Ed. James Strachey. London: Hogarth and the Institute of Psycho-Analysis, 1957. 237–58. Print.

Freud, Sigmund. *An Outline of Psycho-Analysis. The Standard Edition of the Complete Psychological Works of Sigmund Freud*. Vol. XXIII. Trans. and Gen. Ed. James Strachey. London: Hogarth and the Institute of Psycho-Analysis, 1964. 141–207. Print.

Ghosh, Rituparno. Telephone interview. 16 Aug. 2007.

Marx, Karl. *Capital: A Critique of Political Economy*. Vol. I. Ed. Frederick Engels. Trans. Samuel Moore and Edward Aveling from 3rd German ed. Rev. Ernest Untermann according to 4th German ed. Chicago: Kerr, 1906. Print.

Metz, Christian. *The Imaginary Signifier: Psychoanalysis and the Cinema*. Trans. Celia Britton, Annwyl Williams, Ben Brewster and Alfred Guzzetti. Bloomington: Indiana UP, 1982. Print.

Osteen, Mark. "Female Property: Women and Gift Exchange in *Ulysses*." *Gender in Joyce*. Eds. Jolanta W. Wawrzycka and Marlena G. Corcoran. Gainesville: UP of Florida, 1997. 29–46. Print.

Porter, Katherine Anne. "The Jilting of Granny Weatherall." *The Collected Stories of Katherine Anne Porter*. New York: Harcourt, 1965. 80–9. Print.

5 *Chokher Bali*

A historico-cultural *translation* of Tagore

In his renowned 1936 essay "The Work of Art in the Age of Its Technological Reproducibility," Walter Benjamin says:

> what withers in the age of the technological reproducibility of the work of art is the latter's aura.... *It might be stated as a general formula that the technology of reproduction detaches the reproduced object from the sphere of tradition.... And in permitting the reproduction to reach the recipient in his or her own situation, it actualizes that which is reproduced.* These two processes lead to a massive upheaval in the domain of objects handed down from the past—a shattering of tradition which is the reverse side of the present crisis and renewal of humanity.... Their most powerful agent is film. The social significance of film, even—and especially—in its most positive form, is inconceivable without its destructive, cathartic side: the liquidation of the value of tradition in the cultural heritage.
>
> $(22)^1$

Benjamin, of course, speaks of the reduction in the "aura" of the original artwork as "reproducibility" "substitutes a mass existence" for "the unique existence" of the original (22). Further, he focuses on the reproduction being able to *travel* in *space* and the spectator being able to interact with it in her/his individual context. The reproduction(s) thus elicits myriad responses in different individualized contexts.[2]

In transferring to screen Rabindranath Tagore's novel *Chokher Bali*, Rituparno Ghosh brings us the story of a newly-married couple, Mahendra and Ashalata, who are passionately in love, until this love is temporarily tarnished by the arrival into their extended family of a young, intelligent, and educated widow, Binodini. While in line with Benjamin's thought, it is certainly true that many copies of Ghosh's *Chokher Bali* (*Sand in the Eye*, 2003) are available and, in some cases, these travel globally and evoke a range of reactions, I would like to focus, more specifically, on Benjamin's notions of the "shattering of tradition," the "destructive, cathartic side" of film, and his concept of reactivation or actualization. What is also more important to my discussion is the passage of *time*, between the publication of Tagore's text, *Chokher Bali*, and the predicament of widows in late nineteenth- and early twentieth-century Bengal on the

Chokher Bali 111

one hand and the making of Ghosh's film in the early twenty-first century on the other, rather than the ability of the reproduction(s) to travel through *space*.

Rupturing "tradition" and reactivating the subject

While it is undeniable that even in a novel published in 1901–02,[3] Tagore depicts Binodini not as a widow accepting of her fate, but as an intermittently angry, resentful one who interrogates all the injustices that mar her life, Ghosh clearly adds more to his cinematic representation of Binodini's character. Some features of this representation that stand out prominently, particularly for a Bengali audience familiar with Tagore's *Chokher Bali*, are her receptivity to physical passion; her willingness to help other widows partake of pleasures that are taboo (such as drinking tea); and her unhesitating use of her widowhood to further her own ends. Thus, it can be argued that in his "technological reproduction," Ghosh deliberately "destroys" the authenticity of Tagore's "original," but also more broadly "detaches the reproduced object from the sphere of tradition."

In reactivating Binodini's character, not only in ways divergent from Tagore's novel, but with elements of agency that, hopefully, are more acceptable to an early twenty-first-century global audience familiar with struggles for women's rights, Ghosh participates in the "liquidation of the value of tradition in the cultural heritage." As artist and film director, he challenges the moribund aspects of Bengali (or Indian) cultural tradition, drawing us into the "fixed" space of the widow as defined by this tradition and showing how mobilization in and out of this space is possible.[4] Ghosh's *Chokher Bali* permits us to "meet" the "reproduction" of Binodini in our "own situation," that of the early twenty-first century, and makes us ponder how entrenched the "aura" of tradition is and what role film plays in disrupting this "aura."

A brief discussion of Tagore's novel is relevant here. Tagore's *Chokher Bali* addresses the numerous restrictions in the life of a Bengali Hindu widow, Binodini, and is distinctly Modernist in its exploration of psychological motivations of characters. In the novel, Binodini, who comes to live temporarily in Mahendra and Asha's family, as discussed above, attempts at first to vicariously satisfy her (repressed) desire for love by composing love letters for her friend, the little-educated Asha to send to her husband, Mahendra. Shortly after, during Asha's absence from home, Binodini is portrayed as not averse to receiving romantic attention from Mahendra and creates possibilities for romantic moments as well. However, in the second half of the novel, Tagore depicts her as rejecting Mahendra's advances, contemptuous of him, and steadfastly in love with his friend Bihari. Following the family's discovery of Mahendra's growing attraction for her, she is compelled to leave his household and, because of a combination of difficult circumstances, is obliged to take shelter and travel with him. However, she remains committed to Bihari, and when he finally encounters her in her travels and proposes marriage, she accepts his love and respect, but spares him the social censure of marrying a widow and offers to engage herself in one of his philanthropic missions instead.

112   *Narratives of waste, rupturing the prohibitive*

In his film, similar to Tagore's depiction, Ghosh represents Binodini as quite the opposite of the generally voiceless and acquiescent traditional Bengali widow. In an early scene of *Chokher Bali*, she comes across as almost malevolent as she refrains from pouring the water that will help her *sōi*,[5] Ashalata, wash off the soap and excess *sindoor*—the red powder, worn on the parting, that is the most explicit traditional marker of marriage for Hindus in India—from her face. As the bewildered Ashalata pleads for the water with eyes closed, the audience sees an apparently wicked smile flicker over Binodini's face, but this, of course, could be more than pleasure that Binodini derives from her friend's pain. Inhabiting a space where all things desirable are withheld from her, despite her youth and remarkable beauty, this gesture could be read as one of Binodini's first attempts to draw the pampered wife into that unredeemed zone of denial that was the reality for the widow.[6]

Ghosh has Asha occupy the center of the frame, while Binod is positioned to her side. The scene has us focus on the easy mobility of Asha's fingers as she quickly soaps and rinses her face while Binod's gestures are deliberately presented as slow and meditative, drawing the spectator's gaze towards her face and its expressions. It is also noteworthy that Asha's face is often covered in this scene while we are never allowed to lose sight of Binod's. Thus even as the framing of the scene situates the privileged wife at the center, it is Binodini, one of the peripheral figures in the scene, who ultimately commands our attention through her expressions and temporary act of denial.

Foreshadowing transgression with echoes from Ray

There are, however, other instances in which if not Binodini, then the director himself calls for a crossover into the space of the widow. In this regard, it is important to mention that Rituparno Ghosh is one director who is unhesitating in using key motifs and echoes from Satyajit Ray's films to help unfold themes in his own.[7] Thus, the picnic scenes in *Chokher Bali*, in which Binodini swings and Ashalata pushes the swing, cannot fail to remind the viewer of Charu, the female lead and neglected wife of Ray's film *Charulata* (based on a short story, "Noshtōneer," also by Tagore), whose feet rise progressively farther from the ground as she swings. Soon after, she begins to feel the illicit love for her husband's cousin, Amal. In a relationship in which there will be no physical consummation, Ray foreshadows for the audience Charu's emotional and imaginative transgression through the shot of her feet leaving the solid realm of the real.

A quick contextualization of Ray's *Charulata* is helpful here. *Charulata* is generally regarded as a Ray classic. It illustrates Ray's superbly sensitive treatment of a wife's initial isolation and consequent emotional "betrayal" of her husband as she develops a romantic interest for his cousin. Charu's husband, Bhupati, who belongs to the privileged upper class, is preoccupied with a newspaper he publishes and with political issues during British colonial rule in late nineteenth-century Kolkata. His cousin, Amal, who arrives as a guest at his house,

Chokher Bali   113

shares with Charu a deep interest in literature. Their bond deepens with their discussions about literature and about each other's writing. The swing sequence captures one such discussion and the beginning of Charu's romantic interest in Amal. With the publication of her first piece, however, Charu implies to Amal that her writing is of little significance compared to her feelings for him. Amal leaves, terrified of betraying his cousin. Charu is devastated and able to effect no more than a partial compromise with her husband and hence the significance of Tagore's title for his story "Noshtōneer"/"The Broken (or Defiled) Nest."

Although in later scenes involving Binodini and Mahendra, Ghosh's film clearly takes the viewer into the area of physical passion (interestingly, the subtitle of *Chokher Bali* is *A Passion Play*), the swing scene, as it reverberates with echoes from *Charulata*, is an early indication that the characters will move beyond the prescriptive boundaries of a socially-sanctioned love or existence.

Yet, if I go back to my earlier point, how exactly do the picnic scenes encourage a crossover into the space inhabited by the widow, Binodini? The song, written by Tagore (*Rabindrasangeet*), that Ghosh uses in this scene, a song that Binodini and Ashalata sing with ease together in the swing sequence is one that could, nonetheless, point to the sharp difficulties in communication between a wife and a widow. The song, easily recognizable and much loved by a Bengali audience, is in its first four lines:

> *Puranō shei diner kotha*
> *Bhulbi kire hayē*
> *Ō shei chōkher dekha, praner kotha*
> *Sheō ki bhōla jaye.*

The above lines are broadly translatable as "O, will you forget/those old times;/ is it possible to forget/how we saw each other, how we exchanged intimate talk?"[8]

The middle verses of the song, those heard most distinctly in one of the picnic scenes of the film, are as follows:

> *Mōra bhōrer belaye*
> *Phool tulechi dulechi dōlaye*
> *Bajiyé bashi gan geyechi*
> *Bōkuler tolaye.*

> *Haye majhe hōlo chhara chhari*
> *Gelem ke kōthaye*
> *Abar dekha jōdi hōlō shokha*
> *Praner majhe aye.*

Translated, the above lines are "We have picked flowers at dawn/swung on the swing/played the flute and sung/under the *bokul* tree./Somewhere in between, there was separation/and no knowing where we went./If we have met again, my friend,/come in the midst of the heart."

114 *Narratives of waste, rupturing the prohibitive*

Ghosh's film dramatizes on screen the action embedded in the song in that the friends gather flowers, swing, and sing. But of course, Binodini and Ashalata did not know each other before (so there is no question of a separation), and Ghosh's insertion of this song in a scene very reminiscent of *Charulata* seems to move it beyond its simple meaning of longing for union between friends (or lovers) temporarily separated. The earlier film focused on Charu's desire that remains largely unspoken and unrealized due to the constraints of her household; because of Amal's hasty departure without letting Charu know; and because of Charu's own sense of commitment to her husband, Bhupati. Just as Ghosh uses the swing to bring together the transgressive desires of Charu and Binodini, so also he uses the song to evoke possibilities of communication between women (such as Charu and Binodini) who are thwarted and repressed in a normative culture. In addressing intertextuality in Ray and Ghosh's canons, Mandakranta Bose observes that *Chokher Bali* takes its place in a "line of cinema set by Satyajit Ray when he made *Charulata*." She continues that it is reasonable to assume that in making *Chokher Bali*, "Ghosh has deliberately tried to follow Ray ... by choosing a story about a woman's gradual recognition of autonomy denied" (Bose 196).[9]

If contextualized within the specific concerns of *Chokher Bali* itself, the song calls for fullness of dialogue between the wife and the widow; between Bengali women who occupy two distinctly different spaces within the socio-cultural matrix, one replete with privileges while the other is merely about deprivation.

And yet, through its third verse, quoted and translated above, the song also adumbrates the rift between Binodini and Ashalata once the former becomes the object of Ashalata's husband, Mahendra's erotic desire. Further, instead of just expressing a wish for re-union of friends parted for unspecified reasons, in this film, the song looks ahead to the last scenes in which Ashalata, despite clear knowledge of what can be seen as Binodini's betrayal, asks if she has left any address behind.

The song ends with the verse:

> *Aye arektibar aye re shokha*
> *Praner majhé aye*
> *Mōra shukher dukher kotha kobō*
> *Pran jurabe taye.*

And the above lines can be translated as, "Come one more time, come my friend/ in the midst of my heart/we will talk of happiness, we will talk of pain/and the heart will be filled." Within the parameters of *Chokher Bali*, Ashalata and Binodini never meet again, but if the use of Tagore's song is Ghosh's mediated wish for communication between these two women, then it certainly foreshadows Ashalata's openness to that possibility at the end of the film.

Moreover, because Ghosh persistently makes so evident the inter-textual connections between his films and Ray's, such lines of the song as "*Aye arektibar aye re shokha/praner majhé aye*" (Come one more time, come my friend/in the midst of my heart") can be read as the younger director's invocation or expression of indebtedness to a director who brought to Bengali cinema a tenor of seriousness not seen hitherto and simultaneously helped to internationalize it on a generally significant scale. In this regard, the word "shokha" is particularly relevant, as in Bengali it means "male friend," although within the context of Ghosh's film, the word signifies in a non-gendered way. What I read, on one level, as Ghosh's invoking of Ray assumes added importance as he continued to direct film after film centered on women's issues, an endeavor seen in several Ray films such as *Mahanagar, Nayak, Aranyer Din Ratri*, and *Pratidwandi*.[10]

Within the picnic scenes of *Chokher Bali* itself, Binodini's vocalized interest in attending meetings of nationalist protest; her mention of the radical Bengali activist Ram Mohan Roy finally stopping *satidaha*;[11] and Mahendra's, albeit sarcastic, reference to both the cessation of *satidaha* and introduction of widow remarriage solidify for the audience Ghosh's concerns about charting through cinema the progressive increase in women's rights in early twentieth-century Bengal.[12] The above also substantiate my reading that the use of Tagore's song in this sequence connotes more than just a parting and re-union between any two people and is one of Ghosh's endeavors to have us re-think the traditional space of the widow in Bengali (Indian) culture.

Desire and the specters of orthodoxy

Although resonant with echoes from *Charulata*, a specific way in which *Chokher Bali* diverges from the former film is in its unreserved exploration of sexuality. Thus, Ghosh uses the binoculars (field glasses), a device that Charu in an early scene of *Charulata* used in her alienation and frustration to gaze on the streets of Kolkata,[13] but empties them of their particular significance of providing sporadic visual pleasure to the housewife. In having Binodini, at her window, use binoculars to frantically search for signs of sexual intimacy in Ashalata and Mahendra's room, Ghosh recharges this sign to not only underscore the severe limitations in the widow's existence, but to also make clear that Bengali film has moved to a point where a serious and unreserved addressing of her (repressed) sexuality is in order.[14]

In several sequences of *Chokher Bali*, two elements that Ghosh reiteratively yokes together are the force of desire and the spectral presence of the dead husband. Even in the first scene of passion between Binodini and Mahendra, Binodini makes pointed and what appears perverse reference to her dead spouse. "My husband died of tuberculosis,"[15] she tells Mahendra, who draws back immediately from caressing and kissing her. However, it is more than his courage about contagion that she tests as she laughs in his face. Throughout *Chokher Bali*, Ghosh clearly presents Binodini as supremely skeptical of Mahendra's ability to break with tradition and do what is daring or unconventional. Further, by repeatedly bringing the dead into the realm of the erotic, Binodini mocks and yet underlines the stubborn persistence of specters that defines the widow's existence. The dead husband is, of course, also the innumerable restrictive

116 *Narratives of waste, rupturing the prohibitive*

stipulations of orthodox Hinduism that will not be put to rest and which vitiate or obstruct the erotic in the life of a widow. This haunting of *eros* by *thanatos* seems an endless one to Binodini.

In a carriage scene in which Ghosh's representation of passion between the two characters is explicit, Binodini again drags her dead husband into her conversation with Mahendra. As she deliberately smears his shirt with the *sindoor* from *Kalighat*[16] that he has accidentally got on her forehead during an embrace, he chides her affectionately because it will be difficult to erase the red powder. In response, Binodini says undeterred, "Is it possible that you will meet with me" (the Bengali word *songō*—"meet" is not an exact equivalent for this—is alternately translatable as "keep company with me"), "but leave no sign? Don't you see, so long ago, I kept company with" (or "was united with") "[my husband] who is dead and a ghost, and yet, for all these years, I bear with me that sign" (or "mark")?

But of course, within the context of the masculinist culture that early twentieth-century Bengal was, the two predicaments are not comparable. In general, the agents,[17] or even more passive elements, of such a culture would facilitate Mahendra's erasing of the "sign" of his illicit involvement with Binodini, but would unrelentingly uphold the necessity of the austere existence that signified Binodini's widowhood until her death. Even as she determinedly "marks" Mahendra with the "sign" of their passion, Binodini is aware that this passion cannot compete with the force of the "sign" that makes her captive to her spectral husband. Her widowhood, in the cultural context of late nineteenth- and early twentieth-century Bengal, has always already won over any *eros* that might enter her present or future life.

In one of the later scenes of *Chokher Bali*, when Mahendra leaves home to come to Binodini who has moved to her native village, en route to *Kashi*, she says to him as he is about to sit on the bed, "That is my marriage bed. It is on that bed that he [my husband] died." Once again, she deliberately introduces the dead husband into a context charged with intimacy. However, what is more interesting is that through this act, she seems to forestall the possibility of passion between herself and Mahendra, almost instinctively guarding against any future disillusionment when Hindu society itself would stand against it.

The corpse of the widow and film as "historically situated" dialogue

Other than through the character of Binodini, as director, Ghosh uses different strategies to juxtapose romance/passion in the widow's life with death. Once they are in *Kashi*, for instance, talk about a child between Binodini and Mahendra (even though the two are talking at cross purposes: she about his child that Ashalata carries and he about a child with her) is followed by a sequence in which Binodini is visibly agitated by the death of a widow on the banks of the Ganges. Furthermore, the doctor who confirms this death is Behari, who Binodini believes has a romantic interest in her.[18] As the two stare at each other

Chokher Bali 117

across the widow's dead body, Behari inquires where Mahendra is. Binodini asks with a smile of anticipation, "Haven't you come to me?" Behari informs her that Mahendra's mother (another widow in the film) has passed away (in Kolkata) and reiterates his query about Mahendra.

Ghosh's cinematization of this sequence is telling. The shot-reverse shots bring us both Behari and Binodini, but help accentuate for the spectator the sheer pleasure on Binod's face as she seems to block out the signifiers of death all around her on this burning *ghat* (a bank of the Ganges where bodies are cremated). In quick contrast, the shots of Behari's face convey beautifully the duality of his experience of bringing grave news and the unexpected pleasure of seeing Binodini. What is also noteworthy about this sequence is that although Behari sits very close to the corpse as he stares at Binod, the body of the dead widow is always kept out of frame during the exchange of glances. This invisibility yet proximity of death in a late sequence of *Chokher Bali* underscores once again for the audience that the possibility of romance in a widow's life is framed by obstacles that are not always explicit.

When Behari finally proposes marriage to Binodini, the background of the scene is intermittently lit up by funeral pyres, one of which happens to be that of the widow whose death Binodini has recently witnessed. This is evident to the viewer because the red shawl that had covered the body of the dying widow is now worn by another widow who limps around the funeral pyre, possibly in hopes of getting exactly such discarded items before the body is set on fire. The Indian viewer understands that the red shawl is used in both cases only for purposes of providing warmth and is not appropriate attire for the Hindu widow. It is supremely ironic that Binodini had previously, in *Kashi*, asked Mahendra if he would buy her a red shawl that she liked, and Mahendra had expressed his disapproval (red being associated with brides in the Hindu context and white with widows). Ghosh signifies the utter futility of such desire as Binodini's by using a red shawl to cover the body of an unconscious widow about to exit life or by transferring it to the body of another aged widow whose existence seems to be seeking disposable goods around funeral pyres. No longer an object of desire, the red shawl figures now as shroud for bodies marked by deprivation.[19]

As *Chokher Bali* draws to its close then, it is no longer the specter of the long-dead husband that Binodini drags into moments marked by passion or the possibility of passion. In these last sequences of the film, Rituparno Ghosh focuses squarely on the corpse of the widow itself, the raw reality of the female body that has lived and died in deprivation, and that Binodini must look at up close, as ominous as that may be to her. For it is not so much her understanding of the *cause* (i.e., the dead masculine that lives to haunt), but her confrontation of the female body that bears the *effects* (i.e., herself and others similar to herself) that moves her towards validating passion almost all through the film, and at its end, enables her to reject the confines of the domestic realm in which she had largely been situated.

Thus, even as he portrays her as fully cognizant of the odds stacked against her, in transferring Binodini's story to screen in the early twenty-first century,

118 *Narratives of waste, rupturing the prohibitive*

when feminist struggles have left and leave their mark in most world cultures, Ghosh presents her as willing and able to manipulate the "immobility" of the "mark" that is her widowhood. In this regard, as they comment on the contextualized nature of film in *Unthinking Eurocentrism: Multiculturalism and the Media*, Ella Shohat and Robert Stam note:

> Indeed, for Bakhtin art is incontrovertibly social, not because it represents the real but because it constitutes a historically situated "utterance"—a complex of signs addressed by one socially constituted subject or subjects to other socially constituted subjects, all of whom are deeply immersed in historical circumstance and social contingency.
>
> (180)[20]

Further, in the same book, Shohat and Stam claim:

> The issue, then, is less one of fidelity to a preexisting truth or reality than one of a specific orchestration of ideological discourses and communitarian perspectives. While on one level film is mimesis, representation, it is also utterance, an act of contextualized interlocution between socially situated producers and listeners.
>
> (180)[21]

In more than one film, Ghosh focuses on this notion of art as "a historically situated 'utterance'" rather than "fidelity to a preexisting truth or reality."[22]

In the same carriage scene that I discussed earlier, for instance (long before their arrival in *Kashi*), Binodini tells Mahendra that she left home for *Kalighat* saying, "[Today] is my husband's death day.[23] For the first time, I have been able to take advantage of my widowhood." That Ghosh makes Binodini "use" her widowhood to gain erotic pleasure may very well take us back to Benjamin's notion of "a shattering of tradition." In their discussion of Third Worldist film in *Unthinking Eurocentrism*, Shohat and Stam note that simply "the exaltation of 'the national' provides no criteria for distinguishing what is worth retaining in the 'national tradition.' A sentimental defense of patriarchal social institutions simply because they are 'ours' can hardly be seen as emancipatory" (286).[24] Ghosh is clearly not interested in upholding (the value of) patriarchal constructs that prove to be generally constrictive or detrimental to women.[25]

However, it is more than an aspect of Bengali and Hindu cultural tradition that Ghosh challenges by giving Binodini this kind of subversive agency in his film. It is quite likely that he also attempts to reverse broad global perceptions of the Indian widow, as I mentioned earlier. In *Primitive Passions*, Rey Chow notes:

> What is needed, after the ethical polemic of Said's *Orientalism* is understood, is the much more difficult task of investigating how visuality operates in the postcolonial politics of non-Western cultures besides the subjection to passive spectacle that critics of orientalism argue.... What does it mean for

non-Western intellectuals to live as "subjects" and "agents" in the age of "the world as exhibition?"

(13)[26]

In regards to Chow's claim that the East is *not* just a spectacle, but also involved in the "dialectic of seeing" (13), we are of course reminded of passages in *Orientalism*. In one such passage, as he discusses Arab literature, Edward Said says of a literary text:

> Its force is not that it is Arab, or French, or English; its force is in the power and vitality of words that, to mix in Flaubert's metaphor from *La Tentation de Saint Antoine*, tip the idols out of the Orientalists' arms and make them drop those great paralytic children—which are their ideas of the Orient—that attempt to pass for the Orient.
>
> (291)[27]

Although Said here speaks of a literary text (rather than a film), the thrust of his argument is that the East has its own agency; its own "dialectic of seeing."

In *Primitive Passions*, Chow extends this notion of subjectivity and dynamism further by stating:

> How are the "subjective origins" of the previously ethnographized communicated in *visual* terms? They are, I think, communicated not so much through the act of looking as through what may be called "to-be-looked-at-ness"—the visuality that once defined the "object" status of the ethnographized culture and that now becomes a predominant aspect of that culture's self-representation.
>
> (180)[28]

What Chow means here is that non-Western film directors must somehow work in this idea of reduction to "objecthood" as they use visuality to construct subjectivities. Thus, Chow's "to-be-looked-at-ness" would be a condition used deliberately and strategically by cinema directors to underscore past objectification of non-Western cultural subjects. The specter of such objectification is always present in *Chokher Bali*, particularly with its parallel narrative of lives of other widows and the possibility of what Binodini would become in the absence of her dynamism. Yet, Ghosh also unhesitatingly provides a new or alternative representation of the Bengali widow, one that foregrounds her desire for pleasure rather than her submissiveness to social forces that work towards the effacing of that pleasure. Furthermore, in his attempts to work against such possible reduction to "objecthood," Ghosh brings us Binodini's "exploitation" of the *static* aspects of Hindu widowhood. As acting (and assertive) subject of a "technologized visuality" (Chow, *Primitive* 6),[29] Binodini opens up for question a single or dominant world perception of a Bengali widow. And as a "non-Western [intellectual]" directing films in "the age of 'the world as exhibition'" (Chow

120 *Narratives of waste, rupturing the prohibitive*

13), Ghosh, in my view at least, provides us with an exciting version of Bengali "culture's self-representation" (Chow 180).[30] In his film, Binodini refuses to be an "immobile" object, positioned and restrained by Hindu orthodoxy, or the kind of widow who according to the Western ethnographic gaze needs some form of redemption. Instead, she is ready to reverse and re-write her own given predicament as well as to some extent that of others in a similar situation.

Effects of British Colonialism and women's solidarity

It is not surprising then that Binodini's last letter to Ashalata, delivered to the latter by Behari after her disappearance from *Kashi*,[31] urges Asha to conceptualize a world beyond the interiors of the second floor of Darjipara Street—those domestic spaces encompassing kitchen, half-eaten food, courtyard, and shutters in which the two had pledged friendship to each other. And because Mahendra was the one man both had known, they both tried to fulfill their desire through him. But of course, this ruptured their world, leaving their little "country," as Binod calls it,[32] in pieces. Binodini reminds Ashalata, however, that once she stood on the banks of the Ganges in *Kashi*, she understood that there was a world beyond the interiority of Darjipara Street.

In this last section of *Chokher Bali*, Ghosh foregrounds once again Binodini's awareness of India's (and in particular Bengal's) political predicament. For in the letter to Ashalata, Binod warns Asha of the British viceroy, Lord Curzon's plan for the Partition of Bengal. (This would separate the eastern part of Bengal, from the province itself, and add it to Assam.)[33] If put into effect, Binod and Asha would live in different "countries," because it is to be assumed, the former is no longer in the vicinity of Kolkata, located in the western section of Bengal.[34] To recapitulate, the relegation of the Hindu widow to prescribed social spaces, devoid of the possibility of passion, not only intensified Binodini's desire, but also caused the rift with her *sõi*, Ashalata. However, Ghosh shows how the position of the female subject in early twentieth-century Bengal is not just determined by a national patriarchal vision, but weakened further by the effects of British colonialism. For the rupture in the bond between Binod and Asha seems deeper and more ominous to Binodini because now, there also looms the possibility of a permanent geographical hiatus between them. The fragmentation of their "country," their female space as each other's *sõi* is mirrored externally in the potential fragmentation of Bengal by a foreign power.

Yet, just as Asha, by asking if Binod has left any address behind, remains open to the possibility of communication with her, so Binod, in this last letter to her *sõi*, suggests to Asha that they should move beyond their sense of insults, sadness, and deprivation that they both had felt, confined within the (prescribed) women's spaces of Darjipara Street. For, if situated in their potentially separate(d) "countries," they focused on these, then, they had already lost to Lord Curzon. If, however, they looked at the "country within" and stood by their pledge of eternal friendship to each other, it would be impossible for Lord Curzon to teach them a lesson.

At the close of *Chokher Bali*, then, Ghosh looks to the solidarity of women not only as a force against the stipulations and injustices of Hindu patriarchy, but as a shield against the divisive strategies of British colonialism in India. In the face of such fragmentation, the references in Binod's letter to Abhimanyu and the Ganges, the first a young, undaunted warrior of the Indian epic The Mahabharata[35] and the second the sacred river of India, solidify for the viewers the Bengali woman's faith in national symbols that provide strength.[36] It should be clarified here that Binod writes to Asha that it is noted in The Mahabharata that Abhimanyu grew to be a considerable warrior in his mother's womb, and the child Asha carries bathed every day in the Ganges with her (during Asha's stay in *Kashi*). The implication is clear that blest by the sacred waters of the Ganges, Asha's child could grow to be a warrior, a fighter undeterred.

Ghosh moves fluidly between concepts of threatened geo-political spaces and empowering women's spaces at the end of *Chokher Bali*, as Binod concludes her letter, pleading with Asha not to keep her child confined to the interiority of Darjipara Street, whether it is a boy or a girl. The last line of her letter translates, "You will see, s(he)[37] will teach you what 'country' is."

Perhaps the text of Binodini's letter conflates nationalist imperatives with issues of urgent importance for women. It is difficult to not hear in it a sub-text: about the Bengali anguish over partitioning of land; warnings against native (individual) schisms; calls for unity and a militant spirit; as also a marked patriotism, particularly in the repeated use of the word *desh*. However, despite its mammoth and devastating econo-political effects, colonialism, in this letter, is used as a springboard to move to issues that affect Bengali women's everyday lives in a more immediate sense. In prioritizing the female quotidian realm over the colonial predicament, Ghosh effects yet another reversal in *Chokher Bali*. Even though the national political conversation, especially as filtered through the character of Behari, remains a persistent strain in the film, it is situated as peripheral to Binodini and Ashalata's lives.[38] I am reminded of Adrienne Rich's observation at the end of her essay "When We Dead Awaken: Writing as Revision (1971)":

> "Political" poetry by men remains stranded amid the struggles for power among male groups; in condemning U.S. imperialism or the Chilean junta the poet can claim to speak for the oppressed while remaining, as male, part of a system of sexual oppression. The enemy is always outside the self, the struggle somewhere else.
>
> (49)[39]

As a committed feminist, Ghosh understands how, historically, such "political" conversations have taken precedence over discussion of the difficulties of women's daily lives. (This is not to minimize the importance of such "political" conversations or see the two issues as, necessarily, mutually exclusive.) Thus, in a final reversal at the end of the film, we see that Curzon's territorialism is subordinated to Binodini's vision of *desh*/country as suggested to Ashalata.

122 *Narratives of waste, rupturing the prohibitive*

This vision is also more inclusive than one that, to put it simplistically, would address the Indian nationalist effort but ignore or subsume the particular difficulties or impediments of certain groups within the sub-continent.[40] As mentioned earlier, Binodini is interested in the freedom struggle and very cognizant of how Bengal is threatened by Curzon's plans. However, at the end of her letter to Ashalata, she focuses on Bengali women's freedom from confining domestic spaces and the concept of a nation/*desh* that is both an independent India and a more liberating terrain for women. Her message to Asha that her child could grow to be a warrior, together with her closing thought—"You will see, s(he) will teach you what 'country' is"—illustrate the simultaneity of notions of a freedom fighter and a subject who will bring to her (his) mother a sense of a fuller world for women. It is no accident that Ghosh has Binodini attempt to frame nationalist concerns and women's issues within a maternal perspective, a perspective that she, in all likelihood, will never be able to have in reality. The director's use of the lens of motherhood at the end of *Chokher Bali* brings us back squarely to the spaces of the female quotidian, reminding us that for Ghosh, this is a vital area for exploration in cinema.

Cinema, culture, and the "continuous future"

Yet, the directorial strategy here is also clearly to complicate a traditional, one-dimensional conceptualization of motherhood in which nurture is the primary maternal objective. *Chokher Bali* ends with Binodini's hope of Ashalata as a future mother who will understand her country fully; and if Binod, in her letter, is in any way displacing her own unrealized wishes for motherhood onto Asha, the film has already revealed to us the extent of her erotic desire and the depth of her understanding of socio-political issues. As I address in my Introduction, a number of contemporary Bengali directors are invested in going beyond representing woman as an "idealized" mother only.

Binod is not a mother, and Asha is about to become one, but in Chapter 2, in my discussion of *Utsab*, I show how Parul, a mother, by considering the possibility of romantic/erotic pleasure with the momentary return of a past lover, faces a transformative point in her life. Similarly in Chapter 3, on *Dekha*, I address Goutam Ghose's depiction of another mother, Sarama, who does not hesitate to seek out and indulge in erotic pleasure after she, together with her son, has left her abusive husband. These representations connect to two specific foci of this study: first, an analysis of contemporary directors' presentation of examples of rupturing what is traditionally prohibited; and second, an analysis of their sustained effort to cinematize processes of unmaking and making in women.

In Bengali cinema of the last 15–20 years, selected directors' focus on such mothers, who consider going beyond or in actuality defy traditional expectations of the "nurturer only," also signifies a desire to see a conceptual shift within the culture itself. More generally, these representations foreground a cultural terrain in which women are ready to reject any overly-determined positioning and guard against their possible disposability. As I show in Chapter 4 on *Bariwali*, the narrativizing of a woman's capitulation to her "culturally" determined disposability can also work to mobilize audiences to think beyond such relegation and determinism. Overall then, these directors encourage us to conceptualize culture as a field that is open, shifting, and time-appropriate, a field whose dynamics clearly have us question an "idolatry of the past" and turn us towards a "continuous future" (Tagore 86, 87).[41]

Rituparno Ghosh's treatment of Binodini in *Chokher Bali*, with her unreserved interest in erotic pleasure, alerts us to her rupturing prohibitions against the widow in early twentieth-century Bengal. All through the film, Binod's movement is also away from traditionally determined (domestic) spaces in which she would largely be a disposable body. Further, within the parameters of the film, her ultimate rejection of marriage with Behari and openness to the possibility of friendship with Asha dramatize her personally determined processes of unmaking and making. What I should point out here then is Ghosh's divergence not only from Tagore's text in ways I address earlier in this chapter, but from the conclusion of his novel in his making of the film version.

Ghosh's *Chokher Bali* departs from Tagore's original in two significant ways. First, as addressed above, Ghosh unhesitatingly explores the dimension of passion in Binodini's life. To do this, he draws on the relationship between Binod and Mahendra, but imbues this relationship with a strong erotic charge. Next, even though he retains and presents Binodini's romantic interest in Behari, at the close of his *Chokher Bali*, Binod is spoken of as having left for an unspecified destination of her choosing. In representing her in this way, unlike in the Tagore text where she spares Bihari social rebuke and yet stays committed to him, Ghosh returns to his investment in women's rights and autonomy.

Not to be minimized here are some audience responses to Ghosh's film. In more than one instance, I have heard comments that, in sum, express a degree of disappointment that Ghosh has produced a "mish-mash" of Tagore's novel. It is understandable that a section of the Bengali audience wants to see in representation what would traditionally be a "pristine," unchanged rendering of Tagore's text. However, in presenting Binodini as one who aggressively ruptures traditional prohibitions and stipulations against the Hindu widow and as one who "makes" her own destiny, Ghosh himself also ruptures one particular kind of expectation of textual reproduction and engages in what could be read as an unmaking and making of expectations as texts are reproduced. Thus, in this case, my discussion of patterns of rupture and making in Bengali cinema must go beyond the representation of the filmic character herself and extend to the directorial endeavor as this also connects to shaping audience expectations. In my view, Ghosh's endeavor here was to reproduce Tagore's text as one more contextually appropriate for the early twenty-first century. In this regard, his work reminds us of Benjamin's notion of film being a "powerful agent" which facilitates "the liquidation of the value of tradition in the cultural heritage" (22), a notion discussed earlier in this chapter. However, I want to conclude here by reiterating that this notion applies beyond the depiction of one particular character and connects to Ghosh's attempt to make a text more time-appropriate in

124 *Narratives of waste, rupturing the prohibitive*

cinematic reproduction. Thus, even though a section of the audience might resist the changes that this necessarily involves, it speaks to Ghosh's courage and his unfailing effort to say to his audiences through cinema that culture is an evolving field.

Notes

1 In *"The Work of Art in the Age of Its Technological Reproducibility" and Other Writings on Media.* Eds. Michael W. Jennings, Brigid Doherty, and Thomas Y. Levin. Trans. Edmund Jephcott, Rodney Livingstone, Howard Eiland, and Others. Cambridge, MA: Belknap-Harvard UP, 2008. 19–55.
2 A more elaborate discussion of this notion may be found in John Berger. In *Ways of Seeing*, Berger speaks of cameras and television screens "reproducing" paintings. These reproductions then enter viewers' homes and are framed by their contexts (19–20). See *Ways of Seeing*. London: British Broadcasting Corporation and Penguin, 1972.
3 *Chokher Bali* was published serially in the Bengali magazine *Bangadarshan*.
4 I am also indebted here to Rey Chow's line of thought in a section of *Primitive Passions: Visuality, Sexuality, Ethnography and Contemporary Chinese Cinema.* New York: Columbia UP, 1995. Chow draws on Benjamin's essay "The Task of the Translator" to posit how just as translation releases an " 'intention' of standing-for-something-else" that is "imprisoned ... in the original" (187), so some contemporary Chinese cinema, such as films by Zhang Yimou, by focusing on so-called "primitive" subjects, exhibits/explores the cruelty of certain aspects of Chinese tradition (47, 202). In this reading, Chow of course sees cinema itself as a form of translation, an idea that applies to Ghosh's making of *Chokher Bali* in a similar but also different way.
5 The word *sōi*, a Bengali one, literally translatable as "friend" needs a bit of explanation. *Sōi patanō* refers to the practice among Bengali girls or women of very deliberately forming a friendship, with the friends often bestowing special names of affection, such as *Chōkher Bali*, on each other. There is a clear and mutual sense of commitment in these friendships, an understanding that the friends will stand by each other, no matter what the circumstances. In Tagore's novel and in Ghosh's film, Binodini and Ashalata become each other's *sōi* soon after the former's arrival into the household that is Ashalata's home after marriage.
6 In *The Nation and Its Fragments*, Partha Chatterjee gives us the impressions of a mid-nineteenth-century Bengali married woman, Kailasbasini Debi, who notes in her diary that "widows are traditionally restricted to a hard life devoid of luxury in order to make them unattractive to men, so they do not become objects of their lust" (146). Chatterjee does clarify for us that Kailasbasini's views, as in this case, were often "rationalist" ones used to justify "traditional beliefs and customs" (146). See *The Nation and Its Fragments: Colonial and Postcolonial Histories.* Princeton: Princeton UP, 1993.

   The deprivation in the life of a widow in a Bengali household is also addressed in the opening paragraphs of Tagore's renowned short story "The Living and the Dead." A recent film with striking scenes that highlight the contrasts in the life of a widow and other married women (and unmarried young girls), in the twentieth-century Indian colonial context, is, of course, Deepa Mehta's *Water*. Perhaps the most poignant of such scenes are ones that underscore these contrasts in the lives of very young girls, even children.
7 In the opening sequence of *Utsab*, for instance, we are told through a voiceover that the utensils that will be used for *Durga Puja* in the house whose courtyard the camera roams over were used by Ray in his film *Devi*. We are also told that Ray visited this

particular house. Whether these are facts or fiction remains unclear. Whereas *Devi* and Ray are merely mentioned in *Utsab*, *Devi* itself has obvious connections with another, more recent, Ghosh film—*Antarmahal*. In *Antarmahal*, the rustic sculptor, Brij Bhushan, reputed for his clay images and replicas and chosen to sculpt the image of Durga in the *zamindar*'s (landed gentry) house, falls in love with the *zamindar*'s beautiful second wife. On the designated day of worship, when the image is unveiled, the face of the goddess is seen to be a replica of that of the *zamindar*'s wife. The displacement of romantic or erotic attraction onto the divine in this Ghosh film is clearly reminiscent of themes in Ray's *Devi*. In the latter film, Doyamoyee, the younger daughter-in-law of Kalikinkar's household, is accorded the status of Ma/Devi/goddess after she is seen as a reincarnation of the Goddess Kali in a dream by Kalikinkar. As per the instructions of her father-in-law, she is regularly worshipped in the household, a practice that eventually destroys the romantic and erotic relationship between her and her husband, Umaprasad.

8 In order to convey the best possible meaning I am able to, I am not necessarily translating these or the following lines of the song in sequence.

9 See Bose, "The Political Aesthetic of Nation and Gender in Rituparna Ghosh's *Chokher Bali*." In *Indian Literature and Popular Cinema: Recasting Classics*. Ed. Heidi R.M. Pauwels. London: Routledge, 2007. 191–202. However, in a short reflective piece on *Chokher Bali* published in Kolkata shortly after its release, Amit Chaudhuri notes that these borrowings from Ray—the swing sequence and the binoculars (to be discussed shortly in this chapter)—do not fit into the texture of the film. He observes "these moments, like cockatoos or imported eunuchs, are neither at home and nor do they have anywhere else to go." See Amit Chaudhuri, "Madmen, Lovers, Artists." *Telegraph* (Kolkata, India) December 14, 2003. Online, available at www.103124/asp/opinion/story_2676546.asp.

10 In *Aranyer Din Ratri*, one of the female characters, Jaya, is a modern-day widow, who nonetheless still chooses to dress mostly in white sarees (white being the color traditionally worn by widows in India—actually, since Ray's film is in black and white, it is difficult to say whether these are, in fact, white sarees or simply light-colored ones). As an unspoken love interest begins to develop between her and one of the male characters, Sanjoy, in the film, Ray gives us a sequence in which she dons a dark-colored saree and elaborate jewelry and inquires of him how she looks and whether he is afraid. In general, widows wore no jewelry, to underscore the austerity of their existence. Her over-adorning of herself suggests the extent of desires she has repressed to conform to tradition. Her breaking down in tears at the end of the sequence and escaping alone to her room implies the temporary nature of this "transgression." In *Chokher Bali*, Ghosh also weaves in a sequence in which Binodini, at the insistence of Ashalata, puts on elaborate jewelry, another instance of an echo from Ray's canon.

In *Mahanagar*, Ray details the experiences of a Bengali housewife, Arati, from a conservative family, who decides to find a job because of the household's financial difficulties. Arati has the force of character to give up her job, at the end of the film, when a colleague is unfairly dismissed. She does this in spite of the fact that her husband has no job at this point. Ray's *Nayak*, although majorly focused on the character of film actor Arindam Mukherjee, has as its female lead Aditi Sengupta, an editor of a women's journal, who is traveling from Kolkata to New Delhi to attempt to get a grant for this journal. Similarly, although *Pratidwandi* is centered on the character of Siddhartha Chaudhuri, a sub-plot addresses the allegations against his sister, Sutapa, an attractive woman who has found a lucrative job that helps out her family financially after the father's death.

11 *Satidaha* was the practice in which a Hindu widow burnt to death on the funeral pyre of her husband in order to prove she was *sati* (the perfect, chaste wife). Some widows chose to do this voluntarily. In other cases, they were forced to become *sati*. Whether suicide or collective killing of women, *sati* showed the entrenched patriarchal power

126 *Narratives of waste, rupturing the prohibitive*

structure and ideology. In Bengal, the nineteenth-century social reformer Ram Mohan Roy worked vigorously to abolish *sati*. For a comprehensive discussion of debates surrounding recent occurrences of *sati* in India, as also artistic representations of and postcolonial feminist positions on *sati*, see Rajeswari Sunder Rajan, *Real and Imagined Women* (15–63).

12 It is perhaps relevant to note here that Tagore's depiction of the picnic scene in his novel includes no mention of such issues, although it is obvious that the novel itself captures Tagore's concerns about the position of the widow in Bengali culture. It is also necessary to mention that *sati* was outlawed in Bengal in 1829 by the British governor-general William Bentinck, and the Widow Remarriage Act was passed in 1856. In the picnic scenes of his film, Ghosh captures early twentieth-century responses to these issues, with a clear focus on Binodini's understanding of these much needed changes.

13 It is true that Charu later looks at Amal through the binoculars, but Ray focuses more on an incipient romantic interest rather than a markedly erotic one.

14 Towards the end of *Chokher Bali*, Binodini again uses binoculars in *Kashi* (Benaras) only to see through the lenses a very pregnant Ashalata, traumatizing evidence to her of Asha's relationship with Mahendra. Asha moves temporarily to *Kashi* with an aunt after she finds out about Mahendra and Binodini's betrayal. For a different comparative analysis of the significance of the binoculars in *Charulata* and *Chokher Bali*, see Sangita Gopal, *Conjugations: Marriage and Form in New Bollywood Cinema*. Chicago: U of Chicago P, 2011 (169–72). Further, in a recent article on *Chokher Bali*, Kaustav Bakshi argues that in contrast to "classical" cinema, which privileges the male gaze and renders women as spectacles, *Chokher Bali* by representing Binodini with the binoculars foregrounds the desiring female gaze and female agency. See "*Chokher Bāli*: Unleashing Forbidden Passions." *Silhouette* 9.3 (2011): 1–9. Online, available at: http://silhouette-mag.wikidot.com/vol.9–3-kaustuv.

15 All translations of dialogue from the film are mine.

16 *Kalighat* is a holy site in Kolkata where one of the toes of *Kali* (*Kali* is a manifestation of *Durga/Sati*) is reputed to have fallen during her husband, *Shiva*'s, enraged dance with her body, following their insult and *Sati*'s death at her father, *Daksha*'s religious ceremony, *Daksha Yajna*. (*Shiva* was not invited to the ceremony, and *Sati* was insulted when she attended.)

  After one offers prayers at *Kalighat*, one is given a little basket of *proshad* (flowers and sweets first offered to and believed to be blessed by the goddess). This basket also contains some *sindoor*, which has been applied to the goddess by the priest during worship on that day.

17 I am not thinking here of social reformers such as Ram Mohan Roy, who worked to abolish *satidaha*, Ishwar Chandra Vidyasagar, whose endeavors led to the Widow Remarriage Act of 1856, and others who strove to improve the conditions of widows overall. In *Real and Imagined Women*, Rajeswari Sunder Rajan also makes the following very interesting observations on nineteenth-century India:

> Among the indigenous reformers, a sentimental affiliation to indigenous "tradition," the early stirrings of nationalism, and an acute recognition of the resistance of social forces to change, created a complex inheritance which considerably complicated the ideological stance towards issues relating to women. Thus while sati could be condemned on both humanitarian and religious grounds, the prescribed alternative for widows, ascetic celibacy, was not so easily opposed. Therefore the remarriage of widows, long after it was made legally permissible, was a practically non-existent practice.
>
> (48)

Further, Rajan draws on Gayatri Chakravorty Spivak's "Can the Subaltern Speak? Speculations on Widow-Sacrifice" to note that "for Spivak, what is of 'greater

Chokher Bali   127

significance' than the debate on sati is that 'there was no debate upon this exceptional fate of widows [i.e., celibacy]—either among Hindus or between Hindus and British'" (55).

18 It should be mentioned here that Behari is educated, a radical thinker, and also actively involved in meetings of nationalist protest against the British.

19 In my 2009 interview with him, Ghosh mentioned that in one (released) version of *Chokher Bali*, Binodini is shown as having bought and wearing the red shawl that she wanted. According to Ghosh, when Tagore wrote the novel in the early twentieth century, red was very likely a color associated with passion. However, 100 years later, when Ghosh's film was released, red had also become a "symbol of rebellion" (Ghosh 2009 interview) as evident, if I may add, in different world political contexts. Binodini's giving of the red shawl to the dying widow thus associates her with red in a different way and suggests, according to Ghosh, her renunciation of passion, her statement that passion is not everything for her any longer. She wants to live in her own way, free of such ties.

20 Shohat and Stam, *Unthinking Eurocentrism.*

21 Ibid.

22 Shohat and Stam, *Unthinking Eurocentrism.* Another point on cinematic representation made by Shohat and Stam in *Unthinking Eurocentrism* deserves mention here. They note:

> The analysis of a film like *My Beautiful Laundrette* (1985), sociologically flawed from a mimetic perspective—given its focus on wealthy Asians rather than more typically working-class Asians in London—alters considerably when regarded as a constellation of discursive strategies, as a provocative symbolic inversion of conventional expectations of a miserabilist account of Asian victimization.
>
> (181)

In presenting Binodini as agentive, and at times aggressively so, Ghosh is no doubt thinking of a global audience interested in women's voices and rights and simultaneously reversing "conventional expectations," both in the national and world contexts, of a downtrodden or ultimately defeated Hindu widow.

23 It would be normal for a widow to visit *Kalighat* and offer prayers on such an occasion. In reality, Binodini leaves the house to indulge in a passionate encounter with Mahendra.

24 Shohat and Stam, *Unthinking Eurocentrism.*

25 A point made by Rajeswari Sunder Rajan, in the Introduction to *Real and Imagined Women*, is worth mentioning here.

> but since [culture] is also heterogeneous, changing and open to interpretation, it can become a site of contestation and consequently of the reinscription of subjectivities. Therefore cultural analysis both calls forth the critique of ideology, and—given the crucial function of representation in the dialectic of social process—enables political intervention, scenarios of change, theoretical innovation and strategic reinterpretations.
>
> (10)

Ghosh seems to be involved in several of these projects mentioned by Rajan in his cinematic representations.

26 Chow, *Primitive Passions.*

27 See Edward W. Said, *Orientalism*. New York: Vintage, 1979.

28 Chow, *Primitive Passions.*

29 Ibid.

30 Ibid.

31 Binodini disappears on the day Behari comes to her house, ready to marry her, with all the necessary items for a Hindu wedding ceremony. She is gone when he arrives.

128 *Narratives of waste, rupturing the prohibitive*

In a separate letter to Behari, she says that she ran away so that there was no dearth in the wedding feast. In one of her last communications then, Binodini presents herself as one eager to eat, another sharp reversal of the traditional image of the Hindu widow who withholds physical desires.

32 The Bengali word used by Binod here is *desh*, a word that often has patriotic undertones.

33 The Partition of Bengal was put into effect on October 16, 1905. After considerable public protest, the Partition was revoked in 1911.

34 However, if Binodini is going to live in some part of a divided Bengal, it also implies that she has left *Kashi*, located outside of the province of Bengal, in northern India.

35 In the Mahabharata, Abhimanyu was the son of Arjuna by Subhadra and was tricked into single combat with the *Kauravas* inside of a *chakravyuha* (labyrinth) that he knew how to enter but not exit. Abhimanyu was killed in this encounter, in the *Kurukshetra* War, after fighting valiantly, and his death was avenged by his father, Arjuna.

36 For a much cited discussion of how the Indian nationalist movement saw women/the domestic realm as preserving the essence of the country's tradition and culture, see Partha Chatterjee's *The Nation and Its Fragments*, chapter 6. I do not find Chatterjee's reading totally unproblematic.

37 The third person singular pronoun *shey* is not gendered in Bengali.

38 For a different response to Ghosh's treatment of the nation in *Chokher Bali*, see Bose, "Political Aesthetic" (200–01). Bose comments on the ineffectiveness of the "woman-nation" metaphor in the film because "the nation is hardly visible and ... because the politics never progresses beyond personal power struggles in the family" (200).

39 In Adrienne Rich, *On Lies, Secrets, and Silence: Selected Prose 1966–1978*. New York: Norton, 1979. 33–49.

40 In the film, Ghosh *does* show Behari to be both involved in the nationalist issues and sensitive to the predicament of women.

41 Tagore, *Religion of Man.*

References

Antarmahal (Views of the Inner Chamber). Dir. Rituparno Ghosh. Jaya Bhaduri and Vashu Bhagnani. Shree Venkatesh Films, 2005. Film.

Aranyer Din Ratri (Days and Nights in the Forest). Dir. Satyajit Ray. Asim Dutta and Nepal Dutta. Priya Films, 1969. Film.

Bakshi, Kaustav. "*Chokher Bāli*: Unleashing Forbidden Passions." *Silhouette* 9.3 (2011): 1–9. Online, available at: http://silhouette-mag.wikidot.com/vol. 9–3-kaustuv. Accessed May 26, 2012. Web.

Bariwali (The Lady of the House). Dir. Rituparno Ghosh. Anupam Kher, 1999. Film.

Benjamin, Walter. "The Work of Art in the Age of Its Technological Reproducibility." *"The Work of Art in the Age of Its Technological Reproducibility" and Other Writings on Media.* Eds. Michael W. Jennings, Brigid Doherty, and Thomas Y. Levin. Trans. Edmund Jephcott, Rodney Livingstone, Howard Eiland, and Others. Cambridge, MA: Belknap-Harvard UP, 2008. 19–55. Print.

Berger, John. *Ways of Seeing*. London: British Broadcasting Corporation and Penguin, 1972. Print.

Bose, Mandakranta. "The Political Aesthetic of Nation and Gender in Rituparna Ghosh's *Chokher Bali.*" *Indian Literature and Popular Cinema: Recasting Classics.* Ed. Heidi R.M. Pauwels. London: Routledge, 2007. 191–202. Print.

Charulata (The Lonely Wife). Dir. Satyajit Ray. R.D. Bansal and Co., 1964. Film.

Chatterjee, Partha. *The Nation and Its Fragments: Colonial and Postcolonial Histories.* Princeton: Princeton UP, 1993. Print.

Chaudhuri, Amit. "Madmen, Lovers, Artists." *Telegraph* (Kolkata, India). December 14, 2003. 103124/asp/opinion/story_2676546.asp. Accessed May 26, 2012. Web.

Chokher Bali: A Passion Play. Dir. Rituparno Ghosh. Shrikant Mohta and Mahendra Soni. Shree Venkatesh Films, 2003. Film.

Chow, Rey. *Primitive Passions: Visuality, Sexuality, Ethnography, and Contemporary Chinese Cinema.* New York: Columbia UP, 1995. Print.

Dekha (Seeing). Dir. Goutam Ghose. Ramesh Gandhi, 2001. Film.

Devi (The Goddess). Dir. Satyajit Ray. Satyajit Ray Productions, 1960. Film.

Ghosh, Rituparno. Personal interview. September 28, 2009.

Gopal, Sangita. *Conjugations: Marriage and Form in New Bollywood Cinema.* Chicago: U of Chicago P, 2011. Print.

Mahanagar (The Big City). Dir. Satyajit Ray. R.D. Bansal, 1963. Film.

Nayak (The Hero). Dir. Satyajit Ray. R.D. Bansal, 1966. Film.

Rajan, Rajeswari Sunder. *Real and Imagined Women: Gender, Culture and Postcolonialism.* London: Routledge, 1993. Print.

Rich, Adrienne. "When We Dead Awaken: Writing as Revision (1971)." *On Lies, Secrets, and Silence: Selected Prose 1966–1978.* New York: Norton, 1979. 33–49. Print.

Said, Edward W. *Orientalism.* New York: Vintage, 1979. Print.

Shohat, Ella and Robert Stam. *Unthinking Eurocentrism: Multiculturalism and the Media.* London: Routledge, 1994. Print.

Tagore, Rabindranath. "The Living and the Dead." *Rabindranath Tagore: Selected Short Stories.* Trans. and introd. William Radice. New Delhi: Penguin, 2000. 31–41. Print.

Tagore, Rabindranath. *Chokher Bali. Uppōnyas-Sommogrō (Collected Novels).* Vol. I. Kolkata: Sahityam, 2003. 199–362. Print.

Tagore, Rabindranath. *Religion of Man. Rabindranath Tagore Omnibus II.* New Delhi: Rupa, 2003. 1–175. Print.

Utsab (Festival). Dir. Rituparno Ghosh. Tapan Biswas and Sutapa Ghosh. Cinemawallah, 2000. Film.

Water. Dir. Deepa Mehta. David Hamilton, 2005. Film.

Part III

From transactional commodities to subjects in meaningful exchange

6 *Mondo Meyer Upakhyan*

A reading of rebellion within broken social systems

This chapter, primarily on Buddhadeb Dasgupta's *Mondo Meyer Upakhyan* (*A Tale of a Naughty Girl*, 2002), engages the last focal theme of this study: the movement of women from being transactional commodities in a system largely controlled by men to points where they enact meaningful processes of exchange as subjects. In this regard, the chapter addresses the motif of the "journey" that Dasgupta believes informs the theme and texture of the film on many levels.[1] For instance, this motif marks the narrative of the very old couple in the film who initially seem on the brink of death; it is evident in the progress towards lesbianism of a group of much-used female prostitutes; it is what culminates in the escape of the film's young protagonist, Lati from the space of the brothel; and it appears in a broader global context in the film's references to the United States' mission to journey to the moon. Although very specific to the diegesis in this film, this motif of the journey also operates to critique social systems that are anachronistic and in need of revision. Further, I understand Dasgupta to use this motif in *Mondo Meyer* to comment more implicitly on global economic disparity and how this affects an individual's access to opportunity, particularly educational.

I must return briefly here to Gilles Deleuze's notion of the "time-image." One very interesting way in which Deleuze describes the "time-image" in *Cinema 2* is the following:

> The body is never in the present, it contains the before and the after, tiredness and waiting. Tiredness and waiting, even despair are the attitudes of the body.... This is a time-image, the series of time. The daily attitude is what puts the before and after into the body, time into the body, the body as a revealer of the deadline.
>
> (189)[2]

If we apply Deleuze's conceptualization of the body to social systems, then in *Mondo Meyer Upakhyan*, prostitution is represented as an outdated social system, devoid of any possibility of benefitting women and "waiting" to be demolished and replaced by things more meaningful. Dasgupta's cinematic discourse in this film conveys in various forms the imperative need for a

134 *From transactional commodities to subjects*

"deadline"—a deadline by which loveless social arrangements must be left behind for relationships and environments that revitalize.

"Time" in the body and atypical possibilities of rebellion

Although Dasgupta's primary aim in *Mondo Meyer* is to graphically dramatize and undercut the commodification of women, he complicates his objective through the form of the film, which moves away from an exclusive focus on prostitution. Of course in the above sentence, I use the word "complicates" positively. A poet himself, Dasgupta's comprehensive vision enables him to bring into dynamic interplay more than one social system that appears broken. That one system can also stand for another, and on occasion offer commentary on the other, gives the texture of the film a richness that a simple and unbroken addressing of prostitution may not have.

The narrative of the very old couple in the film, presented in fragments, although parallel to the story of the brothel and prostitution, no doubt intersects with it in its emphases on lovelessness and the need to find and verbalize a sense of belonging. Deleuze's notion of "the body as a revealer of the deadline" is concretized in the figures of the ailing old man and woman abandoned by their fellow villagers to the only man, Ganesh, shown to regularly drive a car in the film. The villagers warn Ganesh that the couple is critically ill and must be transported to a hospital (this is the "deadline"), and then they flee. The driver, however, never finds one.[3] He conceals the frail couple in the trunk of the car as he drives the solvent owner of the vehicle around; brings them food; and somewhat surprisingly, offers them a measure of love and companionship a son would. As they revive, he helps avert the consequence of not meeting the "deadline" for the couple, a consequence which in this case would have been death.

Of course, Dasgupta's intention in using this narrative or paradigm tangential to the central storyline is to indicate that illness, in this case, is not so much a bodily issue as springing from a neglect and abandonment of those members of society considered "useless" and disposable at a particular point in time. This abandonment is complicated by the tragic fact of the absence of hospitals in impoverished Bengal villages as portrayed by Dasgupta. Thus, the villagers who desert the old couple are culpable of abandonment at the same time that they are signifiers of a hope of deliverance for the couple. Such deliverance becomes almost impossible, suggests Dasgupta's film, in a social system where the infrastructure leaves much to be desired.[4] In such a scenario, the directorial linking of both the abandonment and the hope of "recovery" to the notion of mobility, via the apparatus of the car, is no doubt significant. This mobility is Dasgupta's cinematic index for the broader necessity for a journey, a journey from malfunctioning social structures to forms of recovery and freedom.

Thus, his excitement is understandable when he recounts how audiences of *Mondo Meyer* mentally and emotionally process the film as a "journey." When the film was a sell-out at the Toronto Film Festival in 2002, where it was screened in the "Masters of World Cinema" section, Dasgupta gave up his own and a few friends' tickets to a group of four girls who seemed disappointed that they would not be able to see it. At the conclusion of the screening, the girls asked Dasgupta, who was still at the location, "Why can't we take a journey like this?"[5]

Although these particular spectators may have identified more closely with the various "journeys" of young women in the film, the path of "revival" of the old couple is no less significant, both as it offers a commentary on public vulnerability and abandonment in severely depressed economic circumstances and as it helps us segue into what is beneficial in transcending the stark commodification that is prostitution. As I indicate earlier, the villagers' act of abandonment also bespeaks vulnerability in the face of socio-economic odds. Yet, the narrative of "revival" is interesting here, for Dasgupta situates it within the context of a mobility that never ends for the couple. While they are sick, when Ganesh asks them if they wish to return home, their answer is a categorical "no." When they recover and are unable to give Ganesh specific directions back to their village, he says he will take them as close to home as possible, and then they can ask directions and return the remainder of the way on foot. The old woman says they will never return home, and the sky over their heads is far more inviting. At one point in their journey, Dasgupta even goes so far as to introduce romantic ambiance as the old man sings feebly to his wife in the moving vehicle, "You are my moonlight in the darkness. Do not go away and make it dark."[6]

This progression from a condition of disposability and imminent death to the space of being able to verbalize love once again is framed very deliberately within the concept of mobility. The "romance" briefly depicted here is, obviously, much larger than itself. It is also the director's romance with the motif of the journey, the possibilities the journey offers within economically depressed social systems and as a way out of institutions in which love has lost its power and relevance.[7]

What I must address here is that as much as Dasgupta deploys material signifiers of mobility in this film, such as the car and the train, he never fails to complement these with the mental-emotional forces that determine and shape the journey as well. Two such forces predominate in his representation in *Mondo Meyer*, these being love and the impulse towards rebellion. In his *The History of Sexuality Volume I: An Introduction*, Michel Foucault speaks of myriad possibilities of resistance and rebellion that exist within networks of power:

> These points of resistance are present everywhere in the power network. Hence there is no single locus of great Refusal, no soul of revolt, source of all rebellions, or pure law of the revolutionary. Instead there is a plurality of resistances, each of them a special case: resistances that are possible, necessary, improbable; others that are spontaneous, savage, solitary, concerted, rampant, or violent; still others that are quick to compromise, interested, or sacrificial; by definition, they can only exist in the strategic field of power relations.

> (95–6)[8]

136   *From transactional commodities to subjects*

Within the narrative of the old couple, the impulse towards rebellion, in their refusal to return home, aligns them more with my reading of "culture" in this study than with "tradition." In the Foucauldian sense, their resistance is "possible, necessary, improbable." As they choose to remain on a continuing journey within the limits of Dasgupta's film, they also subvert audience expectations that are more traditional. Such expectations would re-situate them within the locus of their own community in their age and frailty, even if they are less "desirable" members of that community. Although earlier in this chapter, I link their abandonment partly to the vulnerability of their fellow villagers, it is also true that they are left to the mercy of a stranger, and no member of their community accompanies them on the search for a hospital. As he discusses Knud Løgstrup's notions of morality and the "ethical demand," Zygmunt Bauman devotes a section to "[i]mmediacy."

> "Immediacy" seems to play a role in Løgstrup's thinking similar to "proximity" in Levinas's writings. "Immediate expressions of life" are triggered by proximity, or by the immediate presence of the other human being— weak and vulnerable, suffering and needing help. We are challenged by what we see; and we are challenged to act—to help, to defend, to bring solace, to cure or save.
>
> (Bauman 94)[9]

Bauman clarifies Løgstrup's distinction between the "ethical demand" and such "immediate expressions." Whereas the "ethical demand" is best not articulated, lest it become associated with "a motive for conduct," " '[i]mmediacy of human contact is sustained by the immediate expressions of life' and it needs, or indeed tolerates, no other supports" (Bauman 93).[10]

In the same section of his work, Bauman continues as he discusses such "spontaneous" or "immediate" acts, that "blunders *and* right choices arise from the same condition—as do the craven impulses to run for cover that authoritative commands obligingly provide *and* the boldness to accept responsibility" (93).[11] He addresses a necessary preparedness for possible "wrong choices" in the quest for the "right choice." Bauman asserts that "*uncertainty*" is therefore "*the home ground of the moral person*" (93).[12]

Even if Dasgupta presents the absence of hospitals in economically depressed Bengal villages as a hard reality, the villagers fulfill perhaps only half of their responsibility as they leave the old couple with Ganesh. They embrace no "uncertainty," that is uncertainty for their selves, and show no openness towards "wrong choices" by accompanying the couple who had been an integral part of their community. They help connect the couple to the car, and hence to signifiers of mobility and a journey in the film, but tragically, remain out of the journey themselves. It is not just the journey in the car that they remain out of moreover. In opting out of "uncertainty" and showing only perhaps qualified "love" for members of their community, Dasgupta represents them as cowardly and unready for the journey(s) dramatized in his film.

Mondo Meyer Upakhyan   137

Economic odds, women's commodification, and queer desire as validation

More pertinent to my study, as regards the distinction between tradition and culture as represented by the directors under discussion, is how three young female prostitutes in *Mondo Meyer* undercut our "traditional" understanding of prostitution as a system that commoditizes women's bodies, often using women as conduits for social interaction between men.[13] As mentioned earlier, the tangential narrative of the old man and woman helps us move, as spectators, into the sequence in which Dasgupta dramatizes the shift from a heteronormative commodification within the system of prostitution to lesbian desire, love, and valuing. What is useful to mention here is other than the gendered commodification within prostitution, Dasgupta also weaves into his film the economic factors that often culminate in such commodification. In fact, it is safe to say that his film is about prostitutes from economically depressed backgrounds. *Mondo Meyer* depicts that sometimes these women are pushed into prostitution by men, and sometimes they choose or perpetuate it themselves to escape economic odds. Even when young, their encounters with adversity have hardened them, so that they go through the day-to-day transactional process without illusion. One sequence with the three women, for instance, conveys this through their dialogue, dialogue that also includes graphic language about the many men who objectify them.[14] However, what is surprisingly beautiful is the contrasting emergence of a lesbian love and validation of one another against the backdrop of a clear understanding of unattractive transactionality.

In his book *Dangerous Outcast: The Prostitute in Nineteenth Century Bengal*, Sumanta Banerjee notes:

> All through the 19th century, there was a continuous influx of poor women, mainly from the toiling cultivating and artisan communities of the depressed castes, into the red-light areas. As mentioned earlier, they were driven by famines to leave their village homes and move to places like Calcutta or nearby towns in search of a livelihood—only to end up in brothels. But, having been used to tough living and self-reliance for survival needs, these women in their new profession were quick to introduce unsqeamish norms in their dealings with their male customers. In driving a hard bargain with them, they carried out the transaction in terms which were quite often sexually explicit and down-to-earth—unlike the language of their submissive sisters who came from the sheltered upper caste *kulin* or middle-class homes.
>
> (106)[15]

Just as in Banerjee's comment, Dasgupta depicts how economic causes lead women to prostitution, but in the latter half of the twentieth century in rural Bengal. Of the three women who move towards lesbianism, one describes the steady decline of her parents' financial situation as they were hit by one flood and storm after another and remarks that this is what compelled her to return to

138 *From transactional commodities to subjects*

the brothel. She has determined to help her family by selling her body.[16]A second of these three women mentions how even in her past, when she was newly-married, her husband traded her body to another man. We can assume this was for money. In fact, it is her husband she charges with this when he comes to the brothel to collect money from her, something he does on a monthly basis. When she says she will cease giving him money from the following month, he says emphatically that it is her body (not she) that will provide him the money.

A strikingly different representation of such a "transaction" is seen in the Ritwik Ghatak classic *Subarnarekha* (*The Golden Thread*, 1965) when Ishwar is brought to listen to a "singing girl" who is also referred to as a "bhodrōlōker maiya" ("a gentleman's daughter") by the woman who helps conduct the transaction. The biting irony of Ghatak's film of course is that Ishwar is the brother who both raised Sita, the "singing girl" to whom he is brought, and from whom he has been estranged because she defied his wishes and married out of caste.

The word "singing" itself is heavily layered in *Subarnarekha*, Ghatak using it to suggest the idealistic Sita's naivete prior to her husband's death in an accident. Reference to an earlier sequence clarifies this. Because of the family's extreme poverty, Sita, instigated by the same "neighborly" woman who ultimately conducts the transaction, asks her husband, Abhiram, if she should make money by singing to clients. Abhiram responds forcefully in the negative, adding she did not know what she was saying and there was much she did not understand.

Unlike the hardened, illusionless bargain-makers of Dasgupta's film who are shown to come from economically depressed backgrounds, Ghatak's Sita, in *Subarnarekha*, is raised in a sheltered, relatively comfortable environment by her brother, Ishwar, even though they initially arrive in West Bengal as refugees from Bangladesh (then East Bengal) following the Partition of India in 1947. This middle-class background, also marked by a fraternal protection and love, differentiates Sita from the characters of Dasgupta's *Mondo Meyer Upakhyan*. And although her marital life is one of economic hardship, she remains in a romantic relationship with her husband and in the private realm as he continues to search for jobs or attempts to publish his writings.

Social class and being situated only in the private sphere keep Sita oblivious to the connotations of "singing" in *Subarnarekha*. When she is told late one night after her husband's death that a wealthy client awaits, she protests aghast, but the woman overseeing the transaction "consoles" her saying he will only listen to her "singing," pay, and leave. Ghatak, however, hints beautifully that even the idealistic Sita, sheltered in her upbringing and sheltered in her marriage, somehow understands the implications of the word "singing" in a moment of crisis. For seeing her brother Ishwar framed in her doorway, she unhesitatingly kills herself.

To return to my discussion of *Mondo Meyer Upakhyan*, the more privileged and fortunate members of any culture conceptualize the brothel as existing on the periphery. Often, as Dasgupta shows us, economic disparity marks off its members from the more affluent. Within this space are women who have struggled with natural, personal, and relational disasters. Their present is an unremitting tale of brutal commodification. Yet, "other" as it is viewed from a more normative or privileged perspective, it is a space *within* the culture. When Bengali directors such as Dasgupta make a brothel the focal space of a film, they are also putting at center the inhabitants of this "non-normative" or marginal cultural space. Not only are these inhabitants women, often accorded secondary status in a patriarchal culture, they are doubly dispossessed because traditionally they are marked as prostitutes whose entry into mainstream cultural circles is undesirable.[17]

Through the art form of cinema, directors such as Buddhadeb Dasgupta offer a more comprehensive and inclusive vision of culture. Dasgupta also illustrates how a "traditional" understanding of a prostitute as an entrapped and used commodity is a limited one. Thus, he deliberately links the car, the most obvious and persistent signifier of mobility in the film, to the three young prostitutes. As they are returning from a brief outing together, they see Ganesh, whose car, with the old couple inside, has stalled. At his request, they push it until it starts again. Their three figures, receding into the distance, are framed within the perspective of the old man as he looks out and begins the romantic song I mention earlier. A shot shows him singing to his wife in the car. Dasgupta keeps going the song of the old man as he cuts from the interior of the moving car, to the outdoors with the setting sun, a frame into which the car moves in from right to center of screen, and then cuts again to the interior of a room with the three young women. In the background, visible through a window is the moonlit night, which complements the old man's song ("you are my moonlight in the darkness") as it continues on the soundtrack—"behind, the thick clouds; ahead, the moonlight."[18]

One of the young women, Basanti,[19] stands with her back to the moonlight, holding up her arms, yet if Dasgupta is matching audio to visual, then the "moonlight" is "ahead" of her as well, both as regards the potent immediacy of a romantic bonding and as regards a possible future escape from a space of relentless commodification. For what we see as the scene unfolds is that "ahead" of or before Basanti is another of these three women, Bokul, reaching up from the floor and caressingly closing up her blouse. Basanti reaches down to stroke her face and hand. As we hear sighs of delight, the camera tracks slightly to the left to reveal the third young woman, and Bokul puts out her hand and strokes her cheek and lip with her finger. This third woman, on whose lap Bokul's foot rests, slowly and lovingly paints her toenails and fingers her anklet.

The scene has multiple close-up shots of the women's faces and bodies and very deliberately underscores their valuing of these. The romantic and erotic desire for each other is clear in this scene, and Dasgupta conveys that this is something that has developed over time between them. The slow pacing of actions within the scene itself hints at something beyond it—that this feeling is one that has matured progressively between the women and is in contradistinction to their furious and "valueless" transactions with different men every night.[20]

Dasgupta prepares us for this culmination through various preceding sequences, but none as beautifully evocative as the one discussed above. On

140 *From transactional commodities to subjects*

their outing together for instance, the three women discuss the possibility of leaving the brothel and going far away, and when one asks what they should do if they felt bodily desires again, Basanti responds that they will be each other's partners. Another sequence, although it captures a more light-hearted interaction between Basanti and another woman, also deserves mention. This sequence shifts from interior to exterior of the brothel. Inside, a music tutor teaches Lati, the film's young protagonist, a bawdy song that could be profitable to her in drawing a client.[21] As we hear this tutor singing "When your wax light (flame) comes on/I will be your partner,"[22] outside the dilapidated brothel, the two women laugh, suggestively swing their hips rhythmically with the song, knock against and slap each other. Through each of these sequences, Dasgupta traces the development of lesbian desire against the background of women's commodification, whether the background is explicitly the space of the brothel or an implicit understanding of this fact in these women's minds.

As I argue earlier in this chapter, in *Mondo Meyer*, Dasgupta presents a broader, more inclusive view of culture by making prostitutes and the space of a brothel important people and sites on which to focus. The charting of the development of erotic desire between the three women figures as one of the sub-plots in the film and helps foreground Dasgupta's objective. In relation to issues under discussion in my study, he moves away from a "traditional" inclination, which tends to situate and keep prostitutes on the periphery, often denying them public visibility, access to important public events, and possibilities of re-positioning themselves socially.[23] In more ways than one, Dasgupta, as he makes this film in the early twenty-first century, suggests that such otherization must end. In addition to focusing on the brothel and the predicament of prostitutes, he does this by dramatizing the brokenness and irrelevance of certain "traditional" social systems; by highlighting possibilities of escape from spaces of marginalization; and by strategically linking the moon and issues of broader public interest, such as the American moonlanding of 1969, to prostitution.

In *Mondo Meyer Upakhyan*, Dasgupta returns more than once to the themes of broken social systems and the urgent need to escape from these, no matter how unsupported such escapes may be. The sub-plots of the old man and woman and the three young female prostitutes are interwoven because they manifest such themes. The Deleuzian notion of "time" in the body, "the body as a revealer of the deadline" is evident in the figures of the old man and woman not only because of their age, but because of their "tiredness and waiting," "even despair" in the face of a community that no longer has the capability, energy, or inclination to care for them. As I address earlier, this particular embodiment also helps Dasgupta convey of course the tragic lack of resources in very impoverished Indian villages, rendering the villagers' abandonment an act that is fraught with contradictions. In this case then, "time" in the "body" as "waiting" helps expose not just the detachment of a particular community, but the stark disparity between parts of the "Third World" and the "First World," a contrast that becomes clearer as Dasgupta begins to focus on the American moonlanding.

The resistance or even rebellion seen in the old couple's refusal to return home can thus be read metaphorically as defiance against more than a local community that is indifferent. Through their unexpected gesture, Dasgupta presents his denunciation of malfunctioning social systems within a regional context, but also comments on global economic disparity. Even as he shows us how certain "traditional" social systems are broken and best abandoned, he invites us to ponder the vast inequality in resources in a world context.

The fact that Dasgupta chooses the most unlikely of actors, the most unexpected social agents to mobilize concepts of resistance brings me back to Foucault's observation that "[t]hese points of resistance are present everywhere in the power network" (95).[24] The power of abandonment lies in the hands of a compassionless community, but the most vulnerable members of such a community can show up its cracks by refusing to return to it. Dasgupta demonstrates here not just a rejection of "traditional" expectations, but culture as a field or terrain with many embedded possibilities of rebellion that can unfold at any time.

The mother as commodifier

In contrast to such potential sites of rebellion, Dasgupta presents Rajani, the mother of the young female protagonist, Lati, as one who understands her daughter as a pleasure-giving commodity for men. However, Rajani applauds herself for not having given her daughter over to the "blood-sucking"[25] string of clients whom the "auntie" of the house brings in for Lati. This "auntie" describes Rajani as selective, and Rajani herself observes that she is looking for a "badha babu," a permanent client who will take care of Lati and provide her, the mother, basic necessities as well. In my 2007 interview of him, Dasgupta noted that Rajani has grown up in the environment of the brothel herself and is used to a social system in which women are nothing but commodities. She has understood this "truth" through her own life.

The supreme irony here is that Rajani helps commodify her daughter in her belief that this will ultimately prevent Lati and herself from becoming disposable objects. Here, a mother is complicit in the masculinist gaze of commoditization of women, and in this sense, her daughter becomes a coveted form of wealth. The clearest dramatization of this by Dasgupta is a sequence in which a possible "badha babu," Notōbor Palōdhi, finally arrives at the brothel, and as per the procurer's instructions, Rajani displays parts of the daughter's body to him.

The sequence is set at night, and the camera cuts from shots of the mother holding the daughter in place to those of the much older Notōbor, with the pimp behind him, gazing fixedly at Lati. The pimp at first asks Rajani to "open up" Lati's hair which the mother does. She takes the initiative to turn the daughter around so Notōbor can witness the flow and thickness of Lati's gorgeous hair. The procurer next asks her to turn the daughter back around, so she faces the client. Rajani obliges as Lati resists. Then, the man instructs Rajani to display Lati's ankle. The mother lifts up the daughter's saree to do this, but Lati breaks away to run back inside the brothel.

142   *From transactional commodities to subjects*

In this particular sequence, Dasgupta's focus, of course, is not just commodification of woman, but how parts or "fragments" of her body are deliberately foregrounded to enhance her appeal for a certain kind of man. More of this focus on a woman's body as manipulable object is seen in a subsequent sequence in which a male music tutor tries to teach Lati a song that will entice a client. Rajani indicates that the client will be Notōbor, and not only is he the owner of a movie theater, but that of an oil-mill, a rice-mill, and a motor-car as well. This small industrialist, who will "secure" the mother and daughter's future, must be captivated through a song that is about the bloom of youth smeared all across a girl's body. The words of the song entreat him to come closer and clasp the singer to his heart, so that this "bloom" may "ripen" and come to fruition.[26] While Lati categorically refuses to learn this song whose words she calls "dirty,"[27] a previous shot in the sequence captures Rajani with an appreciative smile on her face as the tutor renders it. She is incensed when Lati leaves the room as a gesture of protest.

Rajani's complicitness in such objectification of women; in presenting and preparing her daughter as a commodity for "exchange" within a system manipulated by men links her with tradition as discussed in my study.[28] That is, even when she thinks she is saving her daughter from the daily humiliation of being sold to different men as a prostitute, she attempts to ensure her "security" by giving in to men who use women as a "conduit"[29] for their own gains and pleasure. In Dasgupta's *Mondo Meyer*, such men are the pimp and Notōbor himself. Dasgupta accentuates the horror of Notōbor's commoditization of women through two sequences in the film where he is shown to watch the same rape scenes of women over and over again. One assumes that the "privilege" of owning his own movie theater, Anjali Cinema, allows him to do this privately.

Yet, just as Goutam Ghose in *Antarjali Jatra* links a static, debilitating tradition with death and in *Dekha* with mental-emotional sterility,[30] so Buddhadeb Dasgupta in *Mondo Meyer Upakhyan* connects such "traditional" ways of conceptualizing women with signifiers of negativity. Three things are of note here. First, through introducing notions of tedium and monotony as the rape scenes of women are playing over and over again, Dasgupta suggests that such displays are "out-of-time." Both the man who operates the projector and Notōbor himself fall asleep more than once as these scenes are playing, suggesting they have had their fill of such things, but underlining their exhaustion as well. Dasgupta uses "traditional" men here to comment on the broader scenario of a tradition that is not only oppressive, but worn out, having nothing new or dynamic to offer. In two other sequences, Notōbor is also shown to take inordinate interest in rotting tree trunks with lines of insects crawling up or down. His fingering of disintegrating pieces of bark and close identification with the insects, wondering where they go and whether they talk, again link his limited vision and thinking to decay. Finally, the music tutor who attempts to teach Lati the song about youth smeared across a woman's body is contrastingly portrayed as aging and skeleton-like in appearance. Such use of visual image and music also helps Dasgupta convey his message that a "traditional" marketing of woman is part of a decrepit and dying system.

In *Mondo Meyer*, Rajani is clearly connected to such forms of tradition. Her crass display of her daughter's body parts for transactional purposes can be contrasted to how the three young female prostitutes finger and treasure parts of each other's body as Dasgupta portrays the beginnings of queer desire in them. While the former helps perpetuate the objectification of women, the latter represents solidarity between women and the possibilities of escape from male dominance. Yet, it would be reductive to say that Rajani is only aligned with a form of tradition that sees women as transactional commodities in Dasgupta's film. While she is very much a part of the system of prostitution that commodifies women, Dasgupta also uses her character to rupture stereotypical representations of the mother as solely benevolent nurturer in Bengali cinema. In Rajani, he brings us a mother economically disadvantaged and sexually exploited. This is a mother who because of her own ignorance firmly rejects the possibilities of education for her daughter[31] and aggressively pushes her to become a product to be used by a man. Because Lati will be used by one man rather than many, Rajani deems this "security."

Rajani is not associated with any progressive impulses within what I have called the shifting terrain of culture as represented by the directors discussed in this study. Yet, Dasgupta uses her to bring us the narrative of an alternative motherhood; to move from periphery to center this story of a single, commoditized, struggling but disillusioned mother,[32] who nonetheless stubbornly believes she is doing the best for her daughter. In the figure of Bhagabati in *Utsab*, Rituparno Ghosh, in my reading, presented a mother who temporarily moved beyond her role as nurturer only, to show an impassioned identification with India's freedom movement. In Sarama in *Dekha*, Goutam Ghose brought before audiences a mother who left her abusive husband and did not hesitate to seek out erotic pleasure with her lover.[33] In Rajani, Buddhadeb Dasgupta brings us another atypical mother who uses her daughter as commodity because this is the best means of survival she knows. As I mention earlier in this chapter, Dasgupta makes the marginal cultural space of the brothel the center of his film, exploring at length the vicissitudes of the lives of many of its inhabitants. In this gesture itself, he performs an act of rupture. However, his focus on Rajani as one of the primary characters of this film, a mother not averse to "heartless" commodification, also ruptures more conventional representations of the mother in Bengali cinema.

Mobility and agents of subversion

Yet, the themes of my study that Dasgupta's *Mondo Meyer Upakhyan* best dramatizes are unmaking and making and the movement of women from being transactional commodities to assertive subjects in processes of meaningful exchange. The last shot of the film shows the three lesbian women leaving the brothel, and I have already addressed how they prioritize queer desire over masculinist commodification. Other scenes of the film close to its end foreground more of their unqualified disgust with nights given to prostitution and exploitation.

144   *From transactional commodities to subjects*

It is Lati, Rajani's young daughter, however, through whom Dasgupta most beautifully mobilizes notions of unmaking and making and a fearless discarding of spaces of women's commodification for individual choice, mobility, and possible empowerment. From early in the film, Dasgupta suggests such possibilities by metonymically linking Lati to the moon and a globe.[34] A number of shots frame her with her back to the moon, or gazing at the moon, or discussing the imminent American moonlanding with her teacher or friend from school, Shibu. She is also shown more than once with a globe her teacher got for her from Kolkata to reward her excellent academic performance in the limited time she was allowed to attend school by her mother. Dasgupta shows Lati fingering the globe while staring intently at it or discussing excitedly countries depicted on it with Shibu. Because of such (represented) contiguity with the moon and globe, Dasgupta's associating of Lati with a spatial dimension beyond the prescriptive limits of the brothel, both personified and specified by her mother,[35] becomes clear.

At the beginning of this chapter, I mention how the motif of the journey operates in *Mondo Meyer* as directorial commentary on broken social systems that are out of date and need to be revised or discarded. I argue that through the film, Dasgupta also explores a dynamic cultural terrain with many possibilities of rebellion, even from those members of society from whom we least expect it. If the old man and woman in the film who refuse to return to their community are two such agents of rebellion, others in *Mondo Meyer* are the three prostitutes who embrace lesbianism and leave the brothel and Lati whose unveering love of education leads her to reject commodification without hesitation. I discuss earlier how she thwarts her mother and the music tutor's efforts to teach her a song to draw a client. In a later sequence, she attempts to convince her mother, although to no avail, that her education will help them move out of the brothel.

Dasgupta's cinematization of the sequence in which Lati does, in fact, leave the brothel is quite remarkable in a number of ways. First, just as he links the "traditional" Notōbor and the music tutor with negative signifiers indicating decay and approaching death, here he connects prostitution and the "benefits" men reap from it to a corpse. It is the murder of Basanti's husband that starts off the sequence.[36] In the film, he is the most graphic (and scathing) representation of a member of a masculinist system, as he commodifies the body of his wife and collects his monetary "gain" every month. As the sequence unfolds, we see half his mutilated corpse (head and torso) positioned on the ground at a slant and taking up most of the screen. Women's feet approach hastily and move away from it to the left of the frame. The camera cuts to a much wider shot with multiple women's figures continuing to run from the corpse, and their movements, as those of the women's feet in the previous shot, are deliberately choreographed as in a dance. The background music is that of drums and a melodious flute. The scene is shot within a courtyard surrounded by columns on three sides. The camerawork draws our gaze to the open spaces between the columns rather than to the structure of the brothel behind them. As we watch the figures of the women in a "dance" of flight from the corpse, Lati is shown to escape through one of these spaces. Soon after, Dasgupta cuts to Ganesh's car, and eventually, it is in this car that Ganesh takes Lati to the railway station. Lati asks him if he will do so, knowing her schoolteacher, Nagen, who encouraged her education, was leaving for Kolkata that day.

Just as women's movements and stirring music predominate in the scene of Lati's escape from the brothel, her escape is also linked to the signifiers of mobility in the film—the car and the train. Rajani has dressed Lati as the traditional Bengali bride for Notōbor's pleasure. Yet, her running swiftly to the train bedecked in her ornate saree and heavy jewelry captures how she easily ignores and repudiates such markers of a stifling tradition to choose her own "making" instead. Just as the old man and woman "exchange" a familiar community for their own space, and the three young women "exchange" daily commodification for the possibilities of a lesbian relationship, so Lati "exchanges" her mother's outdated vision for a journey to Kolkata with her schoolteacher in order to further her education.[37] Dasgupta cuts from the shot of the slowly moving train to a shot of Apollo 11 rising from the American Space Center and then to a brief shot of man walking on the moon, thus connecting Lati's escape and agency to various journeys and scenarios of exploration and discovery.

However, even as Dasgupta presents Lati as a rebellious subject in rural Bengal of the late 1960s, he also uses her journey and the maternal context she abandons to comment, through cinema, on the marked economic disparity between parts of the "Third World" and the "First." In an early scene of *Mondo Meyer*, when Lati's teacher, Nagen, speaks about man's imminent journey to the moon, Lati asks, "Which moon, Sir?"[38] While access to educational opportunities, as demographic studies show, varies for populations in all nations of the world, I am inclined to wonder about John F. Kennedy's audience as he gave the by now renowned "Moon Speech" in Houston in September, 1962. In reference to the city of Houston, Kennedy says:

> During the next 5 years the National Aeronautics and Space Administration expects to double the number of scientists and engineers in this area, to increase its outlays for salaries and expenses to $60 million a year; to invest some $200 million in plant and laboratory facilities; and to direct or contract for new space efforts over $1 billion from this Center in this City.[39]

Would there be anyone in America listening to Kennedy's speech in 1962 who would ask the question Lati asks in rural Bengal in 1969 even as invested as she is in education? Through her simple question, Dasgupta brings to the forefront what she does not yet know. But for audiences of the film in the early twenty-first century, this one question reminds us how the deployment of vast economic and other resources, such as media, in the "First World" facilitates the spread of knowledge to much greater segments of populations than is possible in parts of India in the 1960s.[40] Even as Dasgupta repeatedly connects Lati to images of the moon and stars, as spectators, we do not fail to note the deliberate presentation of these signifiers as artificial; as if they were parts of constructed sets. Just as

146   *From transactional commodities to subjects*

association with such images helps Dasgupta convey Lati's daring and ambition, their multiple depictions as constructed and "unreal" suggest the disjuncture between Lati's dreams and the possibility of them becoming reality. Her "making" is all the harder because there is almost nothing in her environment to encourage the "exchange" she undertakes: from non-status as a body to be transacted to a journey whose outcome she does not yet know. It is not just the fierce maternal opposition to education that she struggles with. Through her questions "Which moon, Sir?", and whether they will be able to view the moonlanding from their terrace, and her schoolteacher's sincere efforts to inform his students about this event with a scrap of soiled newspaper that lands near him, Dasgupta holds up the gap between Lati's educational ambitions and the resources available in the global context in which she is situated and from which she operates as fearless subject.

Conclusions

The penultimate sequence of *Mondo Meyer Upakhyan* shows Lati's mother Rajani, left behind, posing provocatively in front of a tree before the brothel. The camera gives us the same long shot and medium shot three times as she is brought forward from the vicinity of the tree and positioned to the right of the screen, winking crassly at an unknown spectator. A shot immediately preceding suggests the spectator could be Notōbor, and Rajani has been filmed for his viewing pleasure, currently replacing the scenes of rape. Behind Rajani, the same man accompanies the same woman into the brothel three times. In light of her daughter's recently undertaken journey, Rajani, as a commodity, appears trivial if not ridiculous here. Yet, it seems clear that Dasgupta does not intend for us to be humored by the image of this female body, which the camera easily moves forward to the side of the frame or pushes back at will. The voiceover in the sequence is male, journalistic, and Western, delivering precise and scientific information following the moonlanding: "... set up an ultra-violet camera to provide the first astronomical observations from the moon. He took pictures of the earth's upper atmosphere.... He also photographed ... the ultra-violet halos that appear around galaxies."

Dasgupta brings us a moment of ludicrous winking, this anachronistic, exaggerated exhibition of the commoditized female body juxtaposed with the information-giving voiceover to underscore not so much Rajani's ignorance as gaps in understanding because of enormous disparity in global resources. He deliberately leaves unclear who Rajani's spectator may be, blurring the lines between Notōbor and anyone who may watch this film. Seen this way, the viewer of Rajani's body in this sequence is not necessarily one who commodifies, but one who is encouraged by Dasgupta to ponder the inequality that keeps her in her predicament.

As I argue in this book, at the turn of the twenty-first century, selected directors of parallel Bengali cinema mobilize female characters reiteratively as resistant or rebellious cultural subjects against outworn and oppressive aspects of "tradition." This form of tradition is sometimes foregrounded as restrictive patriarchal spaces within the private sphere or the legal-juridical system as in Rituparno Ghosh's *Dahan*; sometimes as the opaque, sterile vision of a poet as in Goutam Ghose's *Dekha*; and sometimes as the unremitting commodification of women's bodies in prostitution as in Buddhadeb Dasgupta's *Mondo Meyer Upakhyan*.

These auteurs of contemporary Bengali cinema also bring us the dynamism of a shifting cultural terrain by aligning our vision with women such as Parul, in Ghosh's *Utsab*, or Sarama, in Ghose's *Dekha*, who move out imaginatively or in actuality from stifling and abusive marriages. Further, these directors cinematize female agency in various striking ways: whether by showing a widow rise up against the stipulations of orthodox Hinduism in early twentieth-century Bengal and eventually prioritize female friendship over a hetero-sexual relationship; or by depicting women rejecting the "comfort" of the familiar to proceed on journeys that they believe will best benefit them. Such journeys, when female subjects challenge double-standards within tradition, or rupture aspects of tradition, engaging in processes of unmaking and making and securing meaningful exchanges for themselves, are never easy these directors say to us. Yet, perhaps they are the most difficult when a young girl's right to education is denied and when the resources available to impart that education itself are indeed minimal because of global economic disparity.

Notes

1 Dasgupta's personal interview with me was conducted on August 19, 2007.
2 Deleuze, *Cinema 2*.
3 In a subsequent scene charged with both humor and pathos, Ganesh drives to another village and asks an inhabitant, a young boy, if there is a hospital there. When he replies in the negative, Ganesh inquires where they take the ailing. The boy responds, "to the burning *ghat*." Translation mine. This boy's friend, the girl who accompanies him in this scene, is Lati, the young female protagonist who eventually escapes from the brothel.
4 *Mondo Meyer Upakhyan* is a 2002 film, but ten years later in July 2012, Mahesh Thapa, a soccer player, died in the city of Jalpaiguri after colliding with a goalkeeper on the field. The news reports said Thapa was carried from hospital to hospital on a motorcycle as no ambulance was available. He died "after being refused admission to three hospitals because no beds were available." See Yahoo news article, online, available at: sports.yahoo.com/news/soccer-player-dies-colliding-goalkeeper.
5 Dasgupta narrated this incident to me in the 2007 interview.
6 Translation mine.
7 See the film *Lal Darja/The Red Door* (1997) for Dasgupta's treatment of mobility as he addresses stagnation in the life of a protagonist from a more privileged class.
8 See Foucault, *The History of Sexuality Vol. I: An Introduction*. Trans. Robert Hurley. New York: Vintage, 1990.
9 See Bauman, *Liquid Love: On the Frailty of Human Bonds*. Cambridge, UK: Polity, 2003.
10 Ibid.
11 Ibid.
12 Ibid.

148　*From transactional commodities to subjects*

13　This is originally an idea from Gayle Rubin's essay "The Traffic in Women" used more extensively in my discussion of arranged marriage in Chapter 2.

14　The women indicate their disgust with the process, referring to their customers/clients as "moles" and "lizards." Translation mine.

15　See Banerjee, *Dangerous Outcast: The Prostitute in Nineteenth Century Bengal*. Calcutta: Seagull, 1998. One of the definitions of *kulin* offered by Bengali dictionaries is "of well-known families or lineage."

16　The dialect this girl uses as also the veil that covers her head and face the first time we see her indicate that she is a Bengali Muslim from Bangladesh. Her reference to repeated flooding and typhoons also suggests that she comes from Bangladesh, Dasgupta, in this instance, showing the necessity of a border-crossing to make a living.

17　Sumanta Banerjee notes how even prostitutes who contributed significantly to Bengali theater as skilled actresses suffered discrimination and public humiliation. When Girish Chandra Ghosh, the renowned actor and playwright, died in 1912, his mentees, actresses such as Notee Binodini and Sukumari Dutta were not allowed to offer their respects to him at the public condolence meeting held in the Calcutta Town Hall. See Banerjee, *Dangerous Outcast* (122).

18　Translation mine.

19　This is the woman whose husband had traded her to another man and who now comes to collect money from her.

20　The pace in this scene is easily contrasted with one much earlier in the film when Bokul first comes to the brothel, and the two other women dress her up for male clients. As one does her make-up for her, the actions are captured at a quicker pace. When the three of them go to an older, more seasoned prostitute's room to seek her approval, Dasgupta depicts them moving quickly down a balcony surrounded by prostitutes ready to solicit and begin their transactions for the evening. The markedly faster pacing in this sequence when contrasted with the one in which Dasgupta represents the culmination of lesbian desire suggests less emotional investment when the women prepare one of their own for the processes of commodification and transaction.

21　I discuss this song at greater length later in this chapter.

22　Translation mine.

23　See Sumanta Banerjee's comprehensive study mentioned above, *Dangerous Outcast*, for a discussion of all of these issues in nineteenth-century Bengal. Banerjee also draws our attention to the fact that many prominent members of society visited these prostitutes.

24　Foucault, *History of Sexuality.*

25　The Bengali word she uses is "pishach."

26　I have tried to convey the best possible meaning of the song through translation.

27　The Bengali word she uses is "nŏngra."

28　In a following sequence, Notŏbor assures her that Lati is "shŏnar cheyŏ dami" ("more valuable than gold"), and he will put both daughter and mother up in a house he has built. They will have maids, a servant, and others to cook meals for them and tend to their needs. Notŏbor himself is married with children and grandchildren.

29　As mentioned in Note 13 of this chapter, I address this point, taken from Gayle Rubin, in my Introduction and Chapter 2.

30　See the discussions in my Introduction and Chapter 3.

31　Lati's schoolteacher pleads with Rajani to let her return to school, but Rajani refuses.

32　Rajani says in a scene that soon she must dress to light the "lamp of hell"—"norŏker pidim."

33　See my Introduction and Chapters 2 and 3.

34　Again, as in Chapter 4, I draw on Christian Metz and his notion of metonymy in cinema as regards association of images. See Metz, *The Imaginary Signifier*.

35 Right after she rejects the schoolteacher's request, Rajani asks Lati not to go anywhere from the brothel until Friday, when Notōbor would come to take them away.
36 The indication we get as spectators is that he is stabbed to death by a well-meaning man, who is shown drawing a knife at the entrance to the room with Basanti and her husband when the latter threatens her with a knife.
37 This entire sequence—Rajani dressing Lati, the murder of Basanti's husband, and Lati escaping from the brothel—is set at dawn. This is the morning on which Notōbor would take Lati and Rajani away from the brothel.
38 Translation mine.
39 See Kennedy, "Moon Speech." Rice University, Houston. September 12, 1962. Online, available at: er.jsc.nasa.gov/seh/ricetalk.htm.
40 A slightly different though related point is of interest here. *Mondo Meyer Upakhyan* was released in 2002. Just prior to this, in a 2000 publication, Arjun Appadurai comments on the uneven distribution of resources worldwide, so that little or no "global" perspective of globalization actually emerges.

> globalization as an uneven economic process creates a fragmented and uneven distribution of just those resources for learning, teaching, and cultural criticism that are most vital for the formation of democratic research communities that could produce a global view of globalization.
>
> (Appadurai 4)

See Appadurai, "Grassroots Globalization and the Research Imagination." *Public Culture* Special Issue on Globalization, ed. Arjun Appadurai. 12.1 (2000): 1–19.

References

Antarjali Jatra (The Voyage Beyond). Dir. Goutam Ghose. Ravi Malik. National Film Development Corporation, 1987. Film.

Appadurai, Arjun. "Grassroots Globalization and the Research Imagination." *Public Culture* Special Issue on Globalization, ed. Arjun Appadurai. 12.1 (2000): 1–19. Print.

Banerjee, Sumanta. *Dangerous Outcast: The Prostitute in Nineteenth Century Bengal*. Calcutta: Seagull, 1998. Print.

Bauman, Zygmunt. *Liquid Love: On the Frailty of Human Bonds*. Cambridge, UK: Polity, 2003. Print.

Dahan (Crossfire). Dir. Rituparno Ghosh. Vijay Agarwal and Kalpana Agarwal. Gee Pee Films Pvt. Ltd., 1997. Film.

Dekha (Seeing). Dir. Goutam Ghose. Ramesh Gandhi, 2001. Film.

Deleuze, Gilles. *Cinema 2: The Time-Image*. Trans. Hugh Tomlinson and Robert Galeta. Minneapolis: U of Minnesota P, 1989. Print.

Foucault, Michel. *The History of Sexuality Vol. I: An Introduction*. Trans. Robert Hurley. New York: Vintage, 1990. Print.

Kennedy, John F. "Moon Speech." Rice University, Houston. September 12, 1962. Speech. Online, available at: er.jsc.nasa.gov/seh/ricetalk.htm. Accessed March 15, 2015. Web.

Lal Darja (The Red Door). Dir. Buddhadeb Dasgupta. Chitrani Lahiri and Dulal Roy, 1997. Film.

Metz, Christian. *The Imaginary Signifier: Psychoanalysis and the Cinema*. Trans. Celia Britton, Annwyl Williams, Ben Brewster and Alfred Guzzetti. Bloomington: Indiana UP, 1982. Print.

Mondo Meyer Upakhyan (A Tale of a Naughty Girl). Dir. Buddhadeb Dasgupta. Arya Bhattacharya. Arjoe Entertainment (India), 2002. Film.

150 *From transactional commodities to subjects*

Rubin, Gayle. "The Traffic in Women: Notes on the 'Political Economy' of Sex." *Toward an Anthropology of Women*. Ed. Rayna R. Reiter. New York: Monthly Review P, 1975. 157–210. Print.

"Soccer Player Dies after Colliding with Goalkeeper." Online, available at: www.sports. yahoo.com/news/soccer-player-dies-colliding-goalkeeper. Accessed January 10, 2013. Web.

Subarnarekha (The Golden Thread). Dir. Ritwik Ghatak. Radhesyam Jhunjhunwala, 1965. Film.

Utsab (Festival). Dir. Rituparno Ghosh. Tapan Biswas and Sutapa Ghosh. Cinemawallah, 2000. Film.

Index

ABC's *World News Tonight* 44
Abohomaan (*The Eternal*, 2009) 22, 24–5, 66–8
Adorno, Theodor W. 37, 49–50
Amrita (journal) 102
Antarjali Jatra (*The Voyage Beyond*, 1987) 11, 142
Antarmahal (*Views of the Inner Chamber*, 2005) 125n7
Anuranan (*Resonance*, 2006) 23, 26–7
Appadurai, Arjun 45, 149n40
Aranyer Din Ratri (*Days and Nights in the Forest*, 1969) 115, 125n10
art film, shooting of 95
Autograph (2010) 21–2, 24, 25

Bandit Queen (1994) 43–4, 46, 49, 50
Banerjee, Sumanta 78–9, 137, 148n17
Bariwali (*The Lady of the House*, 1999) 20, 122; audience expectations 97; Banalata, representation of 91, 93, 97, 106; on Banalata's craving for marriage 95; Behula–Lakhindar legend 97; on Bengali wedding ceremony 93; birthday sequence in 99; cinematic illusion and the ideal spectator 102–6; on cultural reality 106; on cultural stigma 104; depleted remnants in 91–2; disposability in life and art 100–2; on dream as explosion of desire 95–6; female protagonist in 91; *hijra*, depiction of 94; on impact of the heroine, Sudeshna, on Banalata 96; "manifest content" of Banalata's dream 93; on metaphor of waste 92–5; property and the romantic circuit of exchange 97–100; on sexual intimacy and gratification 94; shooting of art film 95, 101–2; on theme of woman's body 91; theme song of 94;

three dream sequences of 94–5; visual appeal and mood 102
Bauman, Zygmunt 136
Beder Meye Jyotsna (*Jyotsna, the Snake Charmer's Daughter*, 1991) 25
Bengali cinema: empowering of the female figure in 3; history of 16; innovativeness in transferring poetry 43; representation of filmic characters 123; television sets, impact of 24; women's roles in 2
Bengali widow: deprivation in the life of 124n6; representation of 119
Bengali women, perceptions of 43
Benjamin, Walter 12, 110; notion of film 123
Bergson, Henri 76
bhalo meye (good girl), concept of 9
Bhaskaran, Gautaman 15
Bhattacharya, Suchitra 37
Binodini, Nõtee 22, 25, 66, 148n17
Blanchot, Maurice 83–4; conceptualization of poetic vision 84
Bollywood films: popularizing of 47; in United States 46–7
Bose, Mandakranta 114
British colonialism, effects of 120–2
Butler, Judith 57–8

Capital (book) 98
Charachar (*Shelter of the Wings*, 1994) 4–7
Charulata (*The Lonely Wife*, 1964) 112, 114–15; story of 112–13
Chatterjee, Arun 21
Chatterjee, Partha 124n6
Chen, Kaige 60
Chokher Bali: A Passion Play (2003) 11–12, 15, 17–18, 102; on aspects of Hindu widowhood 119; on Bengali anguish over partitioning of land 121;

152 *Index*

Chokher Bali continued
  on Binodini's vision of desh/country
  121; cinema, culture, and the
  "continuous future" 122–4; cinematic
  representation of Binodini's character
  111; cinematization of sequences 117;
  on corpse of the widow 116–20; on
  desire and specters of orthodoxy
  115–16; difference with Tagore's
  Chokher Bali 123; on econo-political
  effects of colonialism 121; on effects of
  British colonialism and women's
  solidarity 120–2; force of desire,
  depiction of 115; Ghosh's treatment of
  Binodini in 123; "historically situated"
  dialogue 116–20; masculinist culture,
  depiction of 116; picnic scenes in
  112–13, 115; representation of passion
  116; on rupturing "tradition" and
  reactivating the subject 111–12; shots of
  Behari's face 117; on space of widow in
  Bengali (Indian) culture 115; spectral
  presence of the dead husband 115; on
  stipulations and injustices of Hindu
  patriarchy 121; story of 110–24; swing
  sequence in 113; on transgressive
  desires 114; use of song written by
  Tagore 113–14
Chow, Rey 44, 61, 104, 118–19, 124n4
Chowdhury, Aniruddha Roy 6, 27;
  Anuranan (*Resonance*, 2006) 23, 26
Cinemas of India, The (2000) 2
*Cinematic Imagination: Indian Popular
  Films as Social History, The* (2003) 2
class-based oppression 8
commodification of women 22, 24,
  137–41, 143–4, 146; for prostitution 147
Communist Party of India Marxist-
  Leninist 78
Corliss, Richard 46–7

Dahan (*Crossfire*, 1997) 8, 147; audience
  reception of 42–3, 46; based on novel by
  Suchitra Bhattacharya 37;
  cinematization of 37; on
  commodification of Indian women 37;
  comparison with *Bandit Queen* film
  43–4; defense attorney's attempts to
  defame Srobona 41; on different kind of
  woman 47–51; domestic and economic
  structures of domination 38–40; on
  effects of hierarchized Indian class
  structure 39; feminist resilience 37; on
  gendered relationship 40; impact of

class and privilege 37; on media
  representations of the "Third World"
  42–7; molestation and rape, issue of 39;
  opening scenes of 38; on patriarchal
  Indian legal system 42; on perceptions
  of Bengali women 43; publicizing of
  private injuries 40–1; representation of
  Romi 38, 41; scenes of Srobona's
  vilification 41; screening of 46; on
  silence, "honor," and the patriarchal
  legal system 40–2; Srobona, depiction
  of 38–42, 45; story of 37–51; on
  woman's sense of self 42
Dakhal (*The Occupation*, 1982) 4–7, 14
*Dangerous Outcast: The Prostitute in
  Nineteenth Century Bengal* (book) 137
Dasgupta, Buddhadeb 3–7, 10, 14, 66, 86,
  134–5; *Charachar* (*Shelter of the Wings*,
  1994) 4–5; *Mondo Meyer Upakhyan*
  (*A Tale of a Naughty Girl*, 2002) 10, 18,
  23, 26–7, 66, 133–47
Debdas (Bengali classic) 67
Dekha (*Seeing*, 2001) 8, 10, 66, 143, 147;
  character portrayal of Sashi 73, 80, 83;
  on "continuous future" in Bengali
  culture 85–6; failed poet and the passing
  of his "present" 83–5; female characters
  73; Ghose's central character in 72;
  Ghose's cinematic technique in 72, 77;
  impermanence, notion of 75–8;
  intersections of the maternal and the
  erotic 73–5; on protagonist's
  psychological aberrations 74; on
  response to resistance in the public and
  private spheres 78–83; reverie sequence
  74; Sashibhushan, story of 72–3; story
  of 72–86; strategic points in 72–3
Deleuze, Gilles 18, 72, 75;
  conceptualization of body to social
  systems 133; time-image, notion of
  76–7, 133
Devdas (1935) 10
Devi, Kanaklata 102
Devi, Mahasweta 9
Dosar (*Emotional Companion*, 2006) 20–1
Dubai International Film Festival (2012) 15

Ebong Alap group 50
emotional expression, depiction of 22, 24
ethical demand: difference with immediate
  expressions 136; notion of 136

female body, hyper-visibility of 2
female prostitutes 133, 135, 137, 139, 143

Index   153

Fernandes, Leela 43–4, 50
film-making, process of 105
"First World–Third World" hierarchy, in cinematic representation 46
Foucault, Michel 135, 141
Freud, Sigmund 93, 101, 103; *Mourning and Melancholia* 100

Gandhi, Mahatma 7
gender education 41–2
German film industry 49
Ghatak, Ritwik 3, 14; *Jukti, Takko aar Gappo* (*Reason, Debate and a Story*, 1974) 82; *Subarnarekha* (*The Golden Thread*, 1965) 138
Ghose, Goutam 3–7, 66, 122; *Antarjali Jatra* (*The Voyage Beyond*, 1987) 11, 142; cinematic technique 77; *Dakhal* (*The Occupation*, 1982) 4, 6; *Dekha* (*Seeing*, 2001) 8, 10, 66, 72–86; sense of impermanence 72; "time-images" 76–7
Ghosh, Girish Chandra 22
Ghosh, Rituparno 3–7, 13, 86, 106; *Abohomaan* (*The Eternal*, 2009) 22, 24, 66; *Antarmahal* (*Views of the Inner Chamber*, 2005) 125n7; *Bariwali* (*The Lady of the House*, 1999) 20, 91–106, 122; *Chokher Bali: A Passion Play* (2003) 11–12, 15, 17–18, 110–24; *Dahan* (*Crossfire*, 1997) 8, 37–51; *Dosar* (*Emotional Companion*, 2006) 20–1; filmic language 62; representation of the central character 20; *Shubho Muharat* (*The First Shoot*, 2003) 6–7, 15; *Titli* (*The First Monsoon Day*, 2002) 64–6; trajectory as director 68; treatment of idea of "waste" 91; *Utsab* (*Festival*, 2000) 8, 17–18, 55–68, 122
Gooptu, Sharmistha 3, 16–17, 24–5
Gumrah (*Deception*, 1963) 10

Habermas, Jürgen 7
hijra 94, 107n15
Hindi films, representation of women in 2
Hindu widowhood, aspects of 119
History of Sexuality Volume I: An Introduction, The 135
Hyde, Lewis 99

immediate expressions, notion of 136
impermanence, notion of 75–8
incestuous relationship, depiction of 55–8, 61, 64; *see also Utsab* (*Festival*, 2000)

Indian cinema 1; disposability and substitutability of woman 19–21; impact of the 1947 Partition on 3, 16; portrayal of women in 2; unmaking and making in women 12–19
Indian Cinema in the Time of Celluloid: From Bollywood to the Emergency (2009) 2
Indian institution of marriage 39
Indian legal system 42
Indian widow, global perceptions of 118
India's Simmering Revolution: The Naxalite Uprising (book) 78

Jackson, Michael 14
Jana, Sushil 14
Jukti, Takko aar Gappo (*Reason, Debate and a Story*, 1974) 82

Kalighat 126n16
Kumar, Uttam 17
Kurian, Alka 2

lesbians 137, 143
Lévi-Strauss, Claude 58
Løgstrup, Knud 136

Mahanagar (*The Big City*, 1963) 16, 115, 125n10
Manashamangal (Bengali epic) 94–5
marketing of woman 142
Marx, Karl 98, 106n5
Mazumdar, Charu 79
media representations, of the "Third World" 42–7
melodramas 16, 24–6, 47
Menon, Nivedita 40–1
mobility, concept of 135
Mon Amour: Shesher Kobita Revisited (2008) 25
Mondo Meyer Upakhyan (*A Tale of a Naughty Girl*, 2002) 10, 18, 23–4, 26–7, 66; audience expectations 134–5; characters of 138; cinematization of the sequence in 144; on economic odds, women's commodification, and queer desire 137–41; female prostitutes in 137, 143; "journeys" of young women in 135; lesbian women, depiction of 143; on marketing of woman 142–3; mobility and agents of subversion 143–6; on mother as commodifier 141–3; motif in 133; narrative of "revival" 135; on objectification of women 142–3;

154 *Index*

Mondo Meyer Upakhyan continued
  penultimate sequence of 146; sexual
  exploitation, depiction of 143; story of
  133–47; on "time" in the body and
  possibilities of rebellion 134–6; women
  as transactional commodities in 143
morality, notion of 136
*Mourning the Nation: Indian Cinema in
  the Wake of Partition* (2009) 2
Mukherjee, Srijit 6; *Autograph* (2010)
  21–2, 24, 25

Nandy, Ashis 2
Naxalbari peasant uprising (1967) 78
NBC's *Dateline* 45
Nietzsche, Friedrich 13
Nishi Padma (Bengali classic) 67, 71n37
non-Western film directors 119

objectification of women 119, 142–3
Osteen, Mark 99, 107n22
Outline of Psycho-Analysis, An (book) 93

Paroma (*The Ultimate Woman*, 1984) 47,
  49; story of 47–8
Paromitar Ek Din (*House of Memories*,
  2000) 48–9
"political" poetry 121
Prasad, M. Madhava 25
Pratidwandi (*The Adversary*, 1970) 80–2,
  115
Primitive Passions (1995) 118–19
primitive reciprocity, theory of 58
prostitution: commodification of women's
  bodies in 147; economic causes leading
  to 137; *see also* female prostitutes
Public Culture (journal) 45

Rajadhyaksha, Ashish 2
Rajan, Rajeswari Sunder 29n29, 126n17,
  127n25
Ray, Satyajit 3, 15, 112; *Aranyer Din
  Ratri* (*Days and Nights in the Forest*,
  1969) 115, 125n10; *Charulata* (*The
  Lonely Wife*, 1964) 112–15; *Mahanagar*
  (*The Big City*, 1963) 16, 125n10;
  Pratidwandi (*The Adversary*, 1970)
  80–2; *Sonar Kella* (*The Golden
  Fortress*, 1974) 6, 15
Religion of Man (1931) 1, 84
representations of women, in the films
  2–3; as transactional commodities 21–7
Rich, Adrienne 121
Rilke, Rainer Maria 83

River, The (film) 104
Roy, Ram Mohan 115, 126n17
Rubin, Gayle 22–3, 58–9

Sahib Bibi aur Ghulam (*The Lord, His
  Wife, and Slave*, 1962) 10
Said, Edward 119
Sangam (*Confluence*, 1964) 10
Sarkar, Bhaskar 2–3, 16
satidaha, practice of 115, 125n11
*Secret Politics of Our Desires: Innocence,
  Culpability and Indian Popular Cinema,
  The* (1998) 2
self-representation, of Bengali culture 120
Sen, Aparna 3, 43; *Paroma* (*The Ultimate
  Woman*, 1984) 47–8; *Paromitar Ek Din*
  (*House of Memories*, 2000) 48
Sen, Ramprosad 85
Sen, Suchitra 3, 17
Sengupta, Dipankar 92, 95
sexual identity 13–14
sexual violence 40–1, 50
Shohat, Ella 118
Shubho Muharat (*The First Shoot*, 2003)
  6–7, 15
Silverman, Kaja 77
Sonar Kella (*The Golden Fortress*, 1974)
  6, 15
Spivak, Gayatri Chakravorty 10, 22,
  59–60, 126n17
Stam, Robert 118
subaltern insurgency in India 59
Subarnarekha (*The Golden Thread*, 1965)
  138

Tagore, Rabindranath 20, 26, 61, 63;
  Chokher Bali (novel) 15, 110; depiction
  of picnic scene in his novel 126n12;
  Religion of Man (1931) 1, 84
Temptress Moon (film) 60–1
Thoraval, Yves 2–3, 10; *Devdas* (1935)
  10
time-image, notion of 76–7, 133
Titli (*The First Monsoon Day*, 2002)
  64–6
Toronto Film Festival (2002) 134
transaction of women, notion of 23
Tsai, Ming-liang 104; cinematic
  discursivity 104

unmaking and making, notion of 144
*Unthinking Eurocentrism:
  Multiculturalism and the Media* (1994)
  52n10, 118, 127n22

Utsab (*Festival*, 2000) 8, 17–18, 122, 147; on "aberrations" within the family 55; absence, concept of 60; cinematic strategies 59; "construction, deconstruction," notion of 56; on controlled expression of frustration 62; domain of home and struggles for liberation 60–1; Ghosh's cinematic message in 64; incestuous desire, depiction of 55–6, 61, 64; love scene between a couple 55; on masculinist systems of the society 59; on notion of incomplete freedom 64–8; Parul's arranged marriage 58; Parul's character in 59; Parul's verbal outburst 59; on potential of incestuous romance 64; prohibition on incest 58; on reconstruction of different kind of desire 56; representation of Parul's sense of pleasure 63; representations of the mother's stillness 57; on rights to freedom and love 58; on Shishir's rejection of Parul's plea for secrecy and silence 62; story of 55–68; on "tradition" and the circulation of woman 57–60; "tradition" and the "instrument" of transformation 61–4; unmaking and making in maternal figure 55–7; use of Spivak's ideas in analysis of 59–60

Vidyasagar, Ishwar Chandra 126n17
Virdi, Jyotika 2, 10, 53n13

waste, idea of 91, 92–5
Western ethnography 120
Widow Remarriage Act (1856) 126n17
woman as redundant object, notion of 91
woman's body, theme of 91
women's rights in Bengal 51, 111, 115, 123

Taylor & Francis eBooks

Helping you to choose the right eBooks for your Library

Add Routledge titles to your library's digital collection today. Taylor and Francis ebooks contains over 50,000 titles in the Humanities, Social Sciences, Behavioural Sciences, Built Environment and Law.

Choose from a range of subject packages or create your own!

Benefits for you
- Free MARC records
- COUNTER-compliant usage statistics
- Flexible purchase and pricing options
- All titles DRM-free.

REQUEST YOUR FREE INSTITUTIONAL TRIAL TODAY

Free Trials Available
We offer free trials to qualifying academic, corporate and government customers.

Benefits for your user
- Off-site, anytime access via Athens or referring URL
- Print or copy pages or chapters
- Full content search
- Bookmark, highlight and annotate text
- Access to thousands of pages of quality research at the click of a button.

eCollections – Choose from over 30 subject eCollections, including:

Archaeology	Language Learning
Architecture	Law
Asian Studies	Literature
Business & Management	Media & Communication
Classical Studies	Middle East Studies
Construction	Music
Creative & Media Arts	Philosophy
Criminology & Criminal Justice	Planning
Economics	Politics
Education	Psychology & Mental Health
Energy	Religion
Engineering	Security
English Language & Linguistics	Social Work
Environment & Sustainability	Sociology
Geography	Sport
Health Studies	Theatre & Performance
History	Tourism, Hospitality & Events

For more information, pricing enquiries or to order a free trial, please contact your local sales team:
www.tandfebooks.com/page/sales

The home of Routledge books

www.tandfebooks.com